THE SEVENPENNY GATE
A LIFELONG LOVE AFFAIR WITH CELTIC FC

JOHN CAIRNEY

MAINSTREAM
PUBLISHING

EDINBURGH AND LONDON

To the memory of
TOMMY BURNS
1956–2008

He lived his life the Celtic way
Through all its twists and turns,
Supporter, player, manager,
Immortal Tommy Burns.

'It's the good memories keep you warm on a cold night.'
Tommy Burns

First published in Great Britain in 2011 by
MAINSTREAM PUBLISHING COMPANY
(EDINBURGH) LTD
7 Albany Street
Edinburgh EH1 3UG

ISBN 9781845967772

A catalogue record for this book is available
from the British Library

Printed in Great Britain by
Clays Ltd, St Ives plc

1 3 5 7 9 10 8 6 4 2

Contents

Acknowledgements

Thank you to Bill Campbell of Mainstream Publishing for the idea for this volume and to Mainstream partner Peter MacKenzie for agreeing with him. Graeme Blaikie, editorial coordinator, has been a great help from the start and thanks are also due to Claire Rose, senior editor, for her rigorous attention to the text and to Kate McLelland for her imaginative cover.

Any book about Celtic can only benefit by being submitted for their comments on accuracy and content to those twin pillars of Celtic research and scholarship Pat Woods and Tom Campbell. I have done so, and I thank these fine gentlemen profusely, especially for the help I've had from their seminal book *The Glory and the Dream*. In the same vein, I am especially indebted to my old friend Archie Macpherson for his wonderful biography of Jock Stein. I must also thank my fellow Celtic author Gerard McDade for his helpful comments, David Potter for his various Celtic books, the late Bob Crampsey for all his excellent football writing and Graham McColl for *Celtic: The Official Illustrated History 1888–1995*.

Acknowledgement must be made of valuable quotations given by Russell Leadbetter of *The Herald* and by my actor friend Bill Paterson from *Tales from the Back Green*. Thanks as well to Janette McGinn for allowing me to reprint the lyrics to the song 'The Ibrox Disaster', taken from *McGinn of the Calton: The Life and Works of Matt McGinn, 1928–77*, published by Glasgow City Libraries in 1987.

Gratitude is also due to other good friends, such as Richard McBrearty of the Scottish Football Museum, Lisbon Lions Jim Craig and Billy McNeill for their words of wisdom from the inside, and their teammates John Fallon and Charlie Gallagher for their valuable asides. I have also to thank Dr Bill Murray for his erudite comment, school-

7

friends Frank McGuire and Dr Gerald McGrath, my cousins Philip Cairney and Liz Donaldson for the cover photo, my hairdresser Tommy Fleming for his reminiscences, Bob Adams for his wit, Irene McDade for her calm good sense, Jim Brown for his hospitality, Danny Dickson for his memories, writer Dean Parker for his Celtic passion, IT guru Ray Neale for his brain, Angus Morton for his football enthusiasm (even though he supports Chelsea), Jordan Cleary for supporting my team, James McGrory for the photo of his father and last but by no means least young Thomas Doherty for his liking for Jimmy McGrory and his foreword to the following pages. He obviously has a future as a sports journalist as well as as a footballer.

I also wish to acknowledge the help I have had with this book from the anonymous army of Celtic friends who have stood beside me, behind me and before me on the terracings of so many football grounds around Scotland and from those who have sat beside me in the stands. They have contributed their humour, good sense and wit to my enjoyment of every football occasion I have known, even when the result did not go our way. I only hope that something of what I have learned from these admirable and stoic companions on my march will find its way into these pages.

Finally, all my love and thanks to my wife, Alannah, for her patience and forbearance while I lived with Celticia, for her timely computer rescues that saved the day, for her comments on the first draft and, most of all, for being Alannah.

By the way, the various Celtic players mentioned in my little verses at the head of each chapter are, in my personal opinion, the pick of the footballers I have seen play during my own active supporting years, when I lived my life according to Celtic.

John Cairney
August 2011

Foreword

by Thomas Doherty (aged 13)

I prefer to read stories that are factual rather than made up. I'm a huge Celtic fan and I read John Cairney's book about Jimmy McGrory when I was 11. I found it hard to put down sometimes when I should have been asleep.

I would love to play for Celtic when I'm older. I want to be a footballer as my job. It's every boy's dream to be a football player. The odds are one in a million, but I'm prepared to take those odds.

For me, football isn't a game, it's a way of life. It connects every nation whatever their language or culture. Celtic is not just the club, it's the players and the history. It's magic.

Preface

It was a bleak, cold, miserable afternoon in foggy Glasgow in December 2010 and, like so many of my fellow citizens on that particular day, I was snowbound at home. Had the doors been bolted and the windows barred, I couldn't have been more effectively imprisoned; icy pavements and snow-blocked roads rendered the outside world a definite no-go area. My wife, Alannah, on the other hand, was quite captivated in another sense. Looking out of the window, and being from New Zealand, she positively raved over the constantly falling snow, which brocaded the trees and laid a white carpet over everything.

'Isn't it beautiful?' breathed Alannah.

'Is it hell!' I grunted. 'It'll mean no game tomorrow if this keeps up.'

All I could do then was stand and watch with her in absolute silence. There wasn't a sound to be heard. With no traffic on the roads except those poor souls unlucky enough to be caught in the blizzard, there was no noise from the streets. It was eerie. Glasgow had lost its voice in this untypical, hazy, Arctic world. It was a whole other country.

I slumped over to the couch and picked up the TV remote to bring up Sky Sports. A large close-up of David Beckham appeared; he was looking glum and fashionably unshaven next to a downcast Lord Coe and a tight-lipped Prime Minister. Was that Prince William in the back of the shot? What was going on? Had we declared war or something? It was almost as grave – it seemed that the Fédération Internationale de Football Association (FIFA) had denied England in its bid to host the 2018 World Cup. The presenters had on the kind of faces they use only for state funerals. Every well-practised voice was in mourning. Now FIFA, in the assured person of its president, Sepp Blatter, was awarding the prized plum to Russia, in spite of the controversy preceding the vote: England had complained that Russia had contravened FIFA's rules by talking about a rival bidder. Russia had apologised for the comments made, but the damage had been done. And now, stepping into the picture to receive the official confirmation, was no less than the Prime Minister of Russia, Vladimir Putin.

In keeping with the meteorological frost and chill, another Cold War broke out, this time on the football front. There were immediate cries of 'Fix! Cheat! We was robbed!' All that day in the media, the yelps of pain went up. Twitter users tweeted frantically. The whole of England was hurting. Conspiracy theories rose and rolled across the airwaves. Many serious writers blamed discussion by the British media, prior to the decision, of FIFA's alleged corruption and lack of moral fibre arising from its many decisions taken behind closed doors. The organisation's secret voting procedures were called into question. Who did FIFA think it was? Did it live entirely in its own world? Was it even above being challenged?

Watching it all, I never felt a thing. I couldn't even feel British about it. From my point of view on my Glasgow couch, this was strictly an English affair. It was a back-page matter blown up into a front-page sensation and the media were making an opera of it. What was it all about, this song-and-dance about a football competition? This wasn't just another soccer event, this was a top political priority at world level and no one was messing about. It was about prestige, it was about power, it was about status, but most of all it was about *money* – and lots of it.

This was all the more evident when FIFA, in its wisdom, on the very same day, 2 December 2010, decided to offer the 2022 tournament to Qatar, a tiny peninsular emirate that didn't even boast an appropriate football stadium. However, what it did have was money. It was one of the wealthiest Arab states. In common with Russia, it had the oil and gas revenues to build and renovate several stadia in time for their respective competitions. This was the nub, this was at the root of the English resentment: money. The English view, volubly expressed in the letters pages of every newspaper the next day, was that the winners had effectively bought their privileges instead of earning them and so England, football's founding nation, had lost out on the big prize once again.

FIFA's defence, especially in the incredible choice of Qatar, was that the decisions had been made in the interest of spreading the game beyond its Western European strongholds, but had they forgotten that the 'Scotch Professors', like Celtic's Johnny Madden, had done that more than 100 years ago? Johnny had retired from football in 1898 and resumed work as a boilermaker in the shipyards. He was a great pal of the then Rangers captain Jackie Robertson, who had been invited to coach the Czech side SK Slavia Prague. Mrs Robertson, however, didn't want to leave Greenock. Jackie suggested that 'the Rooter', as Madden was known, should try for it. Madden jumped at the chance. He had himself photographed in his friend's jersey and got the job. The Czech language was no problem. As he said afterwards, 'I never could speak English anyway, but I learnt enough Czech to swear in.' What he did know all about, however, was how to play football, and by sheer personality, skill in coaching and tactical innovation, he became a brilliant success in his adopted country and remained there for the rest of his life. His funeral in 1948, given by SK Slavia, was a public affair and huge crowds turned out to bid him farewell.

In 1904, FIFA itself had come into being in Paris only because the then secretary of the English Football Association (FA), Sir Frederick Wall, being of the opinion that 'wogs begin at Calais', would not recommend the admission of the various Continental football associations that had applied to join the original FA in London; so the French, Germans, Dutch and the rest naturally went their own way, with the results we all know. By its xenophobic arrogance, London lost the chance to rule world football. Had they taken that initial opportunity, who knows how many World Cups England might have hosted by now.

And all this fuss was about a game, a leisure pursuit, a pastime. Was it not a little overhyped? After all, although it might seem so to the most fanatical of fanatics, England's losing bid wasn't the end of the world. Wouldn't all this indignation and outrage be better directed against global warming or worldwide famine? This was only about a simple choice of football venue.

It is a fact, however, that the people's game has long attracted its share of pretension to great significance. Everybody interested in the sport knows that Bill Shankly said, 'Some people believe football is a matter of life and death . . . I can assure you it is much, much more important than that.' However, few know the dictum of goalkeeper-philosopher Albert Camus, who said, 'All that I know most surely about morality and the obligations of men, I owe to football.' I never heard that on the terracing, although when I lived in London, I once sat in the stand at White Hart Lane beside Professor A.J. Ayer, a learned philosopher who was also a Spurs fan. Nabokov was a football enthusiast, as were Gramsci and Wittgenstein, not to mention Sir Elton John, that emeritus of the pop keyboard, who was chairman of Watford FC. I know for a fact that Sir Arthur Conan Doyle was also a goalkeeper (for Portsmouth AFC) and that Sir Edward Elgar supported Wolverhampton Wanderers. Since the latter was a Roman Catholic, he might have supported Celtic had he been born in Glasgow. Sir Arthur, coming from Edinburgh but also born a Catholic, would have been a Hibs man. Pondering these unlikelihoods, I rose from the couch and moved back to the window.

Alannah and I then went out to watch the South Side Glaswegians turn Queen's Park's slopes into home-made ski runs and toboggan chutes as their 'dear green place' of a city was transformed into a Muscovite replica. The tennis courts wore a thick white mantle of snow and the recreation grounds sported an outsize duffel coat of the same. I couldn't help thinking of the original Queen's Park football team, which had been formed on those same acres. There, some YMCA lads, experimenting with the newfangled Association Football rules they had learned from the newspapers of the day, collided with a group of caber-tossing Highlanders from Mount Florida. After some heated discussion, the Highlanders were persuaded to join the footballers in a rudimentary form of the new game. Thus, in 1867, began Queen's Park Football Club, and indeed football in Scotland. It all started when that level field of sheer white I was looking at, marked only by dogs' paws and their owners' footprints, was grassy green and adorned with goalposts without nets.

I found it hard to understand how, from these simple, parish-pump origins, the game had developed into the devouring modern monster, enticing princes and presidents to its inner sanctum, spreading its tentacles to the furthest ends of the earth, pitting nation against nation, and all in the name of sport. Can that term still apply to football when clubs have the status of small nation states and considerably more wealth than many countries, when corporate commercial considerations take precedence over football decisions, when television moguls determine the starting times of games, when players are paid more per game than the aggregate annual income of several streets of their club's supporters, when the price of a season ticket requires the taking out of a small mortgage and when the ordinary supporter is virtually priced out of the game he created by his paying presence over the past 150 years? Ultimately, it all comes down to one person's feeling about a particular club, and in my case the club in question is Celtic.

One last thought. I have a somewhat tenuous thread of connection with the controversy arising out of the selection of countries for the 2018 and 2022 World Cups. Much was made of the millions flowing from the vast gas reserves of Russia and Qatar. In my early childhood in a tenement in the East End of Glasgow, I had similar good fortune from my own family's gas resources. A lot of house and street lighting was still fuelled by gas in those days. It was the practice of the local gas authority to send a man around to make a regular check of the meter. I tried to be at home when he came, because as he counted out all the coppers on the kitchen table, he pushed aside a small amount that was the householder's bonus, depending on the total amount inserted since the last collection.

I always tried to beat my mother to this little windfall. I remember scooping seven copper pennies across the table into the palm of my hand. She saw me but let me keep them for the next Saturday, which sometimes I thought would never come. Admission to the boys' gate had been sixpence when I first began attending, at the start of the war in 1939, but in October 1940 they added a penny to make it sevenpence. That extra penny was often hard to get hold of, but somehow it was always found.

So, at precisely half-past-two on the day, and clutching in my hand the hankie that contained the pennies – new King George VI coins, the more common King George V ones and even at times a discoloured Queen Victoria – I ran down the two flights of stone stairs from our room and kitchen, turned left out of the close, ran up Williamson Street, then left again across London Road to the Springfield Road traffic lights, where, even if they were green and the number 9 tram was bearing down on me, I sprinted across the road at Tait's pub and on to turn right at Kinloch Street, where, puffing a bit, I joined the queue of other wee boys lining up at the boys' gate to place their pennies on the brass plate above the iron turnstile, push hard against it then climb up onto the dirt terracing and into Paradise. The rest of the world called it Celtic Park.

Looking back now over 60 years of following football, I honestly don't know if Celtic was just something that threaded its way through the events of my life or if it was my life that threaded its way through Celtic.

What I do know, however, is that this particular football story begins for me at the sevenpenny gate.

CHAPTER ONE

Getting in Line

Willie Miller, Goalkeeper
Bandaged head, flying leap,
These are images I'll keep.
So even before this book's begun,
Willie Miller's my number one.

Growing up a boy in Glasgow was a matter of knowing your parameters. Mine were bounded by stone tenements to the right and left of me and the front and rear of me, but these were by no means confining. I knew where I was at all times. To the north was Alexandra Parade, which, to my young eyes, was high society. One step down was Duke Street, which was middle class. Come down one further, there was the Gallowgate, which was better working class, and below that was London Road, which was my level and lower working class. Finally, there was Dalmarnock Road, which was for the leftovers. Anything that cost half-a-crown in Alexandra Parade cost two bob in Duke Street, one and six in the Gallowgate and a shilling in London Road but only a tanner in Dalmarnock Road.

It was at this lower end of things that Celtic began. This basis cannot be forgotten. Abercromby Street, where the club was formally established, runs vertically through the above horizontals; so does Springfield Road. Between these two, at London Road, is where Celtic Park stands, in the very heart of the East End. It belongs there, among the streets and beside the graveyard looking up to Paradise.

The presence of this stadium loomed over my part of Parkhead, and indeed over my entire boyhood. It was only minutes away from our tenement close, and Saturdays were always marked by the number of

17

cars that parked in our street. Nobody owned a car in Williamson Street, so all these Austins, Rileys, Vauxhalls and Morris Eights at the edge of the pavement were a novel and welcome sight for us wee boys on match days. These were the successors of the horse-drawn hansom cabs that had once stood the whole length of Janefield Street waiting to carry their fares back into the city after the match. Their cry was 'Cab, sir?' Ours, as street urchins, was 'Watch yer car, mister?' as the driver got out. We got a penny a time if we were lucky. If the driver didn't pay up, he was in danger of having his tyres let down or his windscreen wipers wrenched off. Sometimes we had to bargain.

'Watch yer car, mister?'

'It's a'right. I've goat the dug.'

Pause.

'Dis yer dug know how tae blaw up tyres?'

The man would laugh, his hand would go to his pocket and he'd give my pal and me a penny each. But there was no great money in car-watching, so instead we began to follow the crowds to Celtic Park.

At first, we relied on being lifted over the turnstile by an accompanying father or uncle, but this depended a lot on the discretion of the gatekeeper. 'On ye go' was the expression you wanted to hear. Once you were in, you could transfer to the enclosure, which was an extra shilling. The grandstand, at two and six, was way beyond even our gas meter.

So much of following football belongs to the senses: the sweet smell of freshly mown grass, the not-so-sweet smell of male urine, the comfortable press of the crowd on cold winter days and, above all, the first sight of your team coming out of the tunnel. It was then that you felt not one of many but part of a huge whole, one that had its own voice, its own way of telling you that you belonged for the next ninety minutes to everything that happened around you. It's rare to be so focused, so centred, so free of all unnecessary mental clutter. It was so simple – you only wanted your team to win.

The day war broke out, we were playing Clyde at Celtic Park and we won 1–0. The Celtic team contained eight members of the Exhibition Trophy-winning side of fifteen months earlier. 'Clutha' of the *Evening Times*, reporting on the game against Clyde, wrote, '[John] Divers, with graceful ease, evaded several opponents and with a slanting shot opened the scoring for Celtic.' This glimpse of skill was at odds with the general standard of Celtic's play at the time. Next day during Gran

18

Cairney's weekly Sunday lunch, the disparity prompted much discussion among my uncles, which grew heated as it went on. Suddenly, Gran's voice shut them up, telling them to listen to the wireless because the Prime Minister, Mr Chamberlain, was making an announcement. That sounded boring, so I signalled to Jim, my young brother, and we skipped out. We were playing 'wee heidies' under the outside stairs, and that was where we were when war was declared – with a tennis ball, heading it hard from one to the other.

The Tom Cairneys left about four o'clock to have tea and home baking with our other gran, Coyle, in Shettleston. All everybody could talk about now was the war. I didn't see how it could affect me, so I ate up the nice warm scones and listened to my uncle Hughie's jazz records.

On Monday, 4 September, football was abandoned and I thought my whole world had fallen in. Never mind Poland – this, for me, was a really serious matter. Only a week later, the RAF took over the Strathclyde Juniors pavilion, which was less than 100 yards from our close. Climbing over the wall at our side and lying down at the top of the terracing, we watched them rig up a barrage balloon in the centre of the pitch. It didn't look very warlike to me. Barrage balloons were going up everywhere. A national state of emergency was declared and we braced ourselves for something terrible to happen, for bombs to rain from the sky or Germans to come off the next London train. Everybody dutifully sat in their shelters at night and waited, but nothing happened – at first – and people went back to their beds. During the day, we wandered about the streets, which were now looking very odd with all their windows taped up and blackout curtains in place. It was all unreal somehow – that was why they called it 'the Phoney War' – but to us it was a funny war.

We didn't really know what to do with ourselves. It was soon decided for us. We were evacuated. That is, like children from every big city in Britain, we were taken from our urban homes and our urban parents and removed to distant rural parts 'for our own safety'. Nobody anticipated the danger all these terrible wee townies might pose to the country folk.

All at once, my mother had ready for Jim and me new Burberry overcoats with caps, new shirts and socks, zip-up jackets and freshly ironed pyjamas you could hardly bend in. Where did she get the money? Dad must have been putting in plenty of overtime on the furnaces at the Parkhead Forge. Then everything was packed into two little brown suitcases. At school, we were given a cardboard box with a long string attached and told to sling it over our shoulders. In it was our gas mask. Everybody had one. Then we were told to report the next morning to Parkhead railway station in Whitby Street.

Holding our cases in one hand and a brown-paper bag, which held our wellington boots and slippers, in the other, we found ourselves standing in another line, with the rest of St Michael's Primary, including our teacher, Miss Susan Callaghan, my favourite. It was just like a school trip. We were all very excited, but some of the mothers who had come to wave us off were crying. I noticed my mother in her red coat. She was biting her lip. 'Behave yourselves, youse two' was all she said.

It was crowded in our compartment. I remember during the journey one boy peed out of the window. He was always a bit of a show-off. Wee Alec, sitting in the window seat, got most of it and started crying. Chic Liddell punched the show-off and a fight started. I paid no attention; I was too engrossed in my *Hotspur*. Jim pretended he was just as involved in his *Adventure*. We got these comics every week. We never bothered with *The Beano* or *The Dandy*; they were for weans, and the 'Oor Wullie' cartoon in the *Sunday Post* was for people who couldn't read. Chic and the show-off were still at it when we arrived at another station platform. We piled out and were lined up again. We had no idea where we were, but it was somewhere in the country. The only sign said 'Gentlemen'. One wee girl thought it read 'Bethlehem'. Miss Callaghan was holding one of the younger girls in her arms. Her big sister, who was in my class, suddenly asked, 'Whit's that funny smell, miss?'

Miss Callaghan answered briskly, 'Fresh air, Jean.'

Then the toffs turned up. They arrived in cars and inspected us as if we were for sale. True, we had labels round our necks with our names on them, but it didn't dispel the uncomfortable feeling that we were a bargain lot to be disposed of to the highest bidder. Well-dressed strangers walked up and down that little platform looking at us with obvious distaste. The less well dressed looked on from the other side of the railings. They would have the leavings, no doubt. Eventually, a tall lady wearing gloves pointed at Jim and me. I think it was the Burberry raincoats that did it. Miss Callaghan gave us a cheerful smile. 'That's you and Jim settled, John. Off you go.'

We went, and that's how we found ourselves sitting in the back of a big black car being driven away before the popping eyes of our classmates. We didn't know it then, but Jim and I had just been temporarily adopted by Sir Malcolm and Lady Campbell. He was a world-famous racing driver who had broken the world land and water speed records with various vehicles called *Blue Bird*, but how were we to know that? Motor racing was a sport for toffs and way beyond our ken.

It was an experience, I'll say that. From the upstairs life of a Glasgow tenement to the above stairs of a mansion in the south-west of Scotland, near the village of Westerkirk, was quite a jump. Sometimes it was very trying. It might have been a long way from Parkhead, but what hurt me more was that it was just as far from Celtic Park. I could find no one who could talk Celtic. Living in the big house, we never saw much of Sir Malcolm – he was in his own world most of the time – but we saw a little too much of Lady Campbell, a formidable woman indeed. If she'd never seen anyone like us before, we'd never met anyone like her, either. She came from a long line of upper crusts. Our line of ancestry was just as long as hers in its unheralded way, but she seemed to think we were spontaneous.

Their son, Donald, was a few years older than us but very friendly. We thought he was English, but it was only because he attended public school. I had only read about public schoolboys in books and here I was actually talking to one. I tried to tell him that football had started in the English public schools. He said it might have done, but it had been taken over by the roughnecks. That was us, I suppose. I didn't agree with what he said, but I liked the way he said it. Jim wasn't into conversations. He was only interested in kicking a ball around on the beautiful lawns.

I had my scrapbook, which held my collection of Player's cigarette cards, lovingly amassed, carefully exchanged and assiduously built up. We had made a practice of searching Celtic Park for empty cigarette packets, hoping the cards would still be in them. Occasionally, we found a cigarette, which we threw away. There was a parody of 'You Are My Sunshine', a popular song of the time, which we all sang:

You are my Woodbine,
My Senior Service,
My full-strength Capstan,

21

My Craven A,
My old Swan Vestas,
My cigarette cards,
Please don't take my Player's away.

There were few Celtic players among those featured on the cards, but my hero Jimmy Delaney was one of them, and there were some old-timers like Jimmy McGrory. Jerry Dawson of Rangers and Tommy Walker of Hearts appeared, but the players on the cards were mostly English – like Stanley Matthews and Tom Finney, Bryn Jones of Arsenal and Sam Weaver of Newcastle, known for his long throw-in. These were great players, but they weren't Celts. Still, they were football.

Neither the butler nor the gardener was interested in the game, and I saw no pleasure in darts in the garage, although I did enjoy meeting Donald's girlfriend. Dorothy Carless later became a singer with Geraldo's dance band. I heard her on the wireless. I met her again in New Zealand 40 years later. She and I commiserated over Donald Campbell's death on Lake Coniston in 1967, attempting to beat his own world water speed record. He was his father's son. I gather Sir Malcolm lived to die in bed in 1948.

The Phoney War didn't last very long, but all hell wasn't let loose as the adults had expected. The only casualty for a while was a rabbit, supposedly killed in a solitary raid by a German plane over the Forth Bridge. It was thought the danger was over, so the authorities decided to send us all back home again.

We were soon back in the big car, back on the train, back in dear old dirty Glasgow, back in Parkhead and, best of all, back getting in line in Kinloch Street. Football had started again. It was the same unkempt crocodile of assorted keelies between nine and fourteen who paid their seven pennies.

We were now required to carry our gas masks everywhere, so the ARP (Air Raid Precautions) wardens told us. Some boys carried sandwiches in their gas mask boxes, others pet mice. I preferred to take mine to the football empty and bring it back with half a dozen empty beer bottles in it, collected from around the terracing after the match. They were worth money at the off-licence. One boy brought his mother's message bag with him, and on a good day he needed it. There was usually quite a haul of empties scattered on the terracing and we took as many as we could to the local pubs. At a penny a time at Flynn's or Tait's 'family department', as the carry-out window was called, it was enough to buy you a packet of PK chewing gum and, for the more daring, bigger boys, five Woodbine, the common man's smoke. Everybody smoked in wartime. A non-smoker was considered to be as odd as a vegan. None of us younger boys smoked, but I must confess I loved the sight of so many cigarettes being lit up on the terracing, especially on misty days. It was like a thousand little fires on a hill. A slight pall of smoke was always present. It spread a lovely veil over everything. I liked to think then we were in a foreign country. You needed a bit of imagination to survive in the East End. You also needed initiative.

I delivered newspapers twice a day for pocket money – the *Glasgow Herald*, *The Bulletin*, the *Daily Express* and the *Daily Record* in the morning for the Misses Brown at the corner and the *Evening Times*, *Evening News* and *Evening Citizen* at teatime for Mr Thompson at the traffic lights. Jim and I used to take turns and shared the five-bob-a-week wages between us. I was slower than Jim because I read the papers as I walked up the stairs before running all the way down. I read the front page (one headline I remember was 'Air Forces Wage Battle of Britain') and skimmed through the back pages with the sport, especially the football column by 'Waverley' in the *Daily Record*. I had to curb this habit when I went in No. 3, as Mr Robertson on the ground floor caught me reading one morning and threw the *Daily Record* back at me shouting, 'Ah don't pey fur secon'-haun' papers, son!'

He gave me back the rumpled paper and I kept it to hand in at the end of the round to the waste-paper collection point. There was one at every school. There was no money in it, but every day after school a gang of us would go round the shops asking for any kind of cardboard box or waste packaging – there were no plastic bags then – and hand them all in at the school. I think it was pulped down, 'for the war effort', they said. Phrases like 'civil duty' and 'in the national interest' were bandied about, but we took little notice, especially when they asked us to 'dig for victory'. Governments can go too far.

They even had brick walls built across the front of our close. A 'baffle wall', they called it. It was something to do with bomb blast. They built brick air-raid shelters on the patch of open ground that was our football pitch. Some supporters in Govan were still able to watch their favourite players at work – mixing cement. Crowds gathered at Govan Cross to watch the shelters go up because Celtic's Johnny Crum and Rangers' Jimmy Smith were employed as brickie's labourers. Footballers during wartime had to have day jobs doing some kind of war work, and no doubt they were glad of the extra money, but not many enjoyed the company of a non-paying audience while they worked.

Johnny Crum wouldn't have minded, though; he was an amenable little man. Dr Gerald McGrath, who was a school-friend of mine at St Mungo's Academy, tells the story of being at a Celtic match at Parkhead, watching from 'the Jungle', the famous (or infamous) covered enclosure, when the ball went out of play for a shy. Gerald was standing trackside and the ball rolled right in front of him. A Celtic player ran to collect it. It was wee Johnny Crum. 'Hello, Gerald,' he said. My friend's pals stared at my friend in wonder and Gerald's status in 1B Latin went up exponentially. They didn't know that Johnny lived up the same close as the McGraths in Maryhill.

Footballers were not a removed social species then. Sometimes, going to an away match at, say, Airdrie or Partick Thistle's Firhill, you'd find yourself sitting in a tram beside a Celtic player going to play in the same game. Most players made their own way to the ground on match day. The only difference was that they didn't pay to get in. Out of the football gear, footballers looked much the same as any other young men in the street. It was hard to tell they were footballers. My uncle Phil used to say you could always tell an ex-footballer by the way he limped. I once recognised the Celtic goalkeeper Willie Miller standing on the platform at Motherwell railway station. He'd failed to find a seat on the supporters' train back to Glasgow. I remember feeling very guilty, staring out at one of my great heroes standing among the crowd while I had a seat on the train steaming out of the station.

My Glasgow upbringing was pre-Technicolor. My world was black and white with tan and grey additions, so that the splash of green and white that I now knew on a regular basis was very welcome. It was a relief from the wartime drabness. Colour was life and action, and football offered both to the boy supporter with artistic pretensions. What is more, the other teams provided good contrast – the light blue of Rangers, the dark blue of Falkirk, the claret and amber of Motherwell, the red and yellow of Partick Thistle, the clerical black and white of St Mirren, the vibrant maroon of Hearts and the military scarlet of Third Lanark. It all went into the palette that was available on a Saturday to give us a different canvas every match day. It brightened up a dreary week and no matter the result you were always the better for your 90-minute experience in following a ball.

By the beginning of season 1940–41, I was ten and a regular at the boys' gate in Kinloch Street, with the rest of the toerags from Miss Callaghan's. We were a motley lot. All we had in common was our working-class background and a passion for a football team. There were no class divisions at the boys' gate, but there were boys there better dressed than I was, mostly Italian boys whose fathers had cafés. You could tell them by the quality of their shirts and by the fact they wore warm woollen scarves. None of the rest of us had scarves.

The opposite of these boys were the ones whose fathers were on low wages or bone idle. They were dressed courtesy of the Glasgow Corporation Education Department, and recognisable by their dark pullovers, Harris tweed jackets and big boots. Not always having the seven pennies required, they weren't as regular as we were at the boys' gate. They often waited instead with the unemployed men for the last ten minutes of the game, when the big doors opened to let the crowds spill out. Everyone then took the chance to see the end of the game. However, for the boys, it was also an opportunity to collect a few bottles and any cigarette cards that hadn't been cleaned up by us at half-time. Celtic had always made allowances for the poorer spectator. In the Great Depression, they had cut the price of admission for the unemployed, until the Scottish Football Association (SFA) made them reinstate full prices because Cowdenbeath FC objected to having a decreased share of the gate.

Now, in lumber jackets and baseball boots, we waited in line between the new Glasgow Corporation houses on our right and the railings of London Road Primary on our left. With their indoor toilets and baths, these new houses were our mothers' dream. What luxury that seemed to them – but not to Jim and me. A bath wasn't a boy's priority.

Jim had little interest in queuing up at the boys' gate with me because he was always playing – on Saturday morning for the St Michael's Boys' Guild and in the afternoon for Clydesdale Juveniles. Anyway, for some unknown reason, he supported Clyde. When Jim stepped up to play for Strathclyde Juniors, he was spotted by Celtic and agreed to go to Parkhead on the recommendation of Jimmy Gribben, their scout, who lived in Baillieston, where my father's family came from. Jim attracted a lot of attention as a boy centre-half. He was that good that soon.

He had first shown his football talent in our street team, which was called the Springfield Rangers. Jim and I and Felix McKenna were the only Catholics, so we were outvoted when we had to pick a name. It didn't go down too well around Parkhead. When we played other street teams, I was rarely picked. Jim had used up the family store of playing talent. Very occasionally, I got a game on the right wing. I could always run, so I was put on the wing out of harm's way. I would give my impersonation of Jimmy Delaney, who was Celtic's only star player during wartime, but my acting skills were not quite up to it. Sometimes I would play at right-half, when I would pretend, but with no greater success, to be Malcolm MacDonald, the most cultured Celtic player I ever saw. On one desperate occasion, I was put in goal, but Willie Miller I was not, and my short-lived football career safely petered out before it could even be said to have begun. As a sop, they made me the manager because they thought I could talk a good game. I tried to get them to play in Celtic colours at least, but that was carrying the *entente cordiale* too far in their eyes. We had plenty of *entente*, but we were a bit short on the *cordiale*. I didn't think I could manage a team in blue, however, so, using my new managerial authority, I somehow wangled a set of Aston Villa jerseys for us – no clothing coupons were required at the Barras, a street market in the Calton where you could get what you wanted when everything else failed.

My real priority, however, was the next Celtic game. I could hardly suppress my Saturday excitement as I inched my way up to a narrow wooden gate ahead of us. This was identified by a large number seven with a small letter 'D' beside it, both painted white on a blistered square board nailed to the brick wall. I think the 'D' was from 'denarius', meaning a Roman penny in Biblical times. That was the kind of thing a spectacled wee swot like me, who couldn't play football, knew. I only wore the glasses to read, but I hated them.

My mother thought I read too much, my father not enough, at least not the right stuff. He was into Burns and socialism. I didn't want to know about that sort of thing then. I devoured the *Celtic Football Guide*. We called it 'the handbook' because the wee green paperback fitted exactly into the palm of your hand. My copy for 1942 showed the manager as James McStay and his review of the previous season was one long apology. We were always being reminded about how great the club was before the war and how great we'd be again when things returned to normal, but meantime we'd have to make do. Didn't we know there was a war on?

What I know now is that my seven bronze pennies, already sweating in my hankie, would have been worth seven-hundredths of a pound today. Not a great sum. What a very small price it was to pay for the priceless drug that the weekly football game was to us. What a derisory amount to purchase so much passion in 90 minutes. Not to mention the half-time hot pie and Bovril, if you could afford it, or the Wrigley's chewing gum we bought from the man with the big tray round his neck – 'PK, penny a packet!' The men brought their own beer, McEwan's Pale Ale, the bottles clinking happily in their coat pockets. Such were the delights of the football occasion. As Jimmy Gordon (now Lord Gordon of Strathblane) put it in his *Celtic Story* documentary, it was the working man's revenge for the rest of the week. For us boys, it was a blissful escape from the daily classroom grind.

We always had to have the lights on in St Michael's Primary because it lay under the shadow of the towering Parkhead Forge in Salamanca Street. The Forge was William Beardmore & Co.'s engineering factory, where most of our fathers, uncles and big brothers worked. It's a shopping complex now, but just as vast. Parkhead fathers, uncles and big brothers are still to be seen there – pushing their wives' shopping trolleys. Beardmore's made motor cars, but with the outbreak of the Second World War it switched to tanks and shells. It was as if they were ready and waiting for war work. Our school was near the white gates on Duke Street, which closed to the tramcars while the brand-new tanks were shunted along on the factory's own railway line. We used to rush to watch them trundle past. The next time we saw them would be on the Movietone News, in some foreign field. We would cheer when we saw them in the cinema. After all, they were ours.

The pictures were a must on Saturday nights, a vital part of growing up in working-class Glasgow. It was known as 'Cinema City' because we were film crazy and expert in all things Hollywood. Our big brothers and sisters were also 'dancin' mad' and virtually every male was 'fitba' daft'. This last malaise you could hardly avoid. Watching Celtic Football Club kick-started my emotional life. It was my premier heart experience; indeed it was my earliest unashamed love. It introduced me to passion, drama, excitement, the heat of the blood, the over-riding importance of a football result in the great scheme of things, the priority the match had over everything, except eating and sleeping. There was also the mythical, heroic status we all gave to the players, even to the pretty indifferent performers Celtic had at that time. The club was not entirely to blame; young men were then in pretty short supply. Every one of us in the queue would have given our lives to play for Celtic, even for the capped wage of two pounds per week. We would have been glad to play for nothing. No, we would have paid to play for the club.

There were occasions at the ground when we made the odd unexpected copper. This was when ladies came round the running track holding the ends of a huge white sheet and the men in the crowd were asked to chip pennies, or silver coins if they could afford it, in to the collection the ladies made for local charities. We pushed our way to the front so that we were in the way of the coins that rained down from these generous men. The poor are often the best providers for their fellow poor. We weren't so charitable, however, and kept what we could catch.

If you made at least ninepence from these 'throw-ins', it meant you could afford the pictures that night. We had three cinemas at our disposal: the skimpy Black Cat at Springfield Road, the better-upholstered 'Three Ps' (Parkhead Picture Palace) on Tollcross Road and the luxurious Granada, complete with fitted carpets and central heating, in Duke Street at Parkhead Cross. It's odd to think now that in my adult acting years I would play the Earl of Bothwell to Sarah Churchill's Mary Stuart in the grubby Black Cat when it became a BBC television studio in the 1960s. My fellow actors didn't believe me when I told them I used to get into the children's matinee there on a Wednesday at four o'clock with two beer bottles left over from Saturday at Celtic Park. One boy in our class even offered his free Corporation boots one afternoon, but the man behind the till said they were too small for him – he let him in for nothing as a reward for his enterprise.

At the Granada, there was no such trading. It was a bit upmarket. Here we could see highlights of international matches on the Pathé or Movietone newsreels in plush and padded comfort. Here, too, was the proxy playing out on the big screen of a similar dramatic excitement but with a latent sexual undertow that I missed at the time. Kissing scenes were howled down by us, or just laughed at. It was only later I began to understand, but that's another story. Females, apart from mothers, sisters and some aunties, were not a great part of my life then. You never thought of your granny as a woman. She was a granny.

There were no girls in the sevenpenny queue. There were no girls on the terracing, either, simply because there was no toilet provision for them. It never occurred to the management to provide women's toilets, except maybe for the directors' wives in the grandstands. The men and boys appeared to be satisfied with the primitive facilities available. If not, they used their own initiative at the surrounding walls. You soon learned to avert your eyes.

During the late '30s and early '40s, another haven for the aspiring boy was the local public library, or 'lie-burry' to the Glaswegian. I actually broke into the Parkhead Library once when I found it closed during the day. I was so annoyed I climbed up the wall and got in through a window. The lady librarian nearly had a fit when she found me in the children's section, squatting on the floor and reading my favourite author at the time, Percy F. Westerman. I thought the library was a veritable treasure house. It was the working man's university. There was one man we heard about who spent all his out-of-work years in the library reading his way through the entire *Encyclopaedia Britannica*. He must have been the most educated man on 'the broo' (or bureau), as we called the Labour Exchange.

A lot of my library hours were spent catching up on all the football writers, especially on the histories of the great clubs at the beginning of the game. Before Celtic in Scotland, in addition to Hibernian, still with us, there had been Abercorn, Cowlairs, Renton (the first 'world champions' – having won the Scottish Cup in 1888 and beaten FA Cup holders West Brom, they properly considered themselves champions of the world, but only a few years later they folded), Third Lanark and Vale of Leven, now all gone. Not forgetting Glasgow Rangers, of course, and that prince of clubs, the still amateur gentlemen of Queen's Park. I loved to read about all these great teams and my head was crammed full of football facts.

I would bore my pals with my newly acquired football lore. Did they know, for instance, that the word 'soccer' belongs to the beginnings of Association Rules in 1848? No? So I told them. Semantically, it may have evolved from a contraction of 'Association', but it's more likely to have derived from the upmarket 'varsity' slang of the day. Cambridge students first played the game on Parker's Piece and formulated what became known as the Cambridge Rules. As rugby became rugger, so football became soccer. It was first attributed to one Charles Wreford-Brown, a famous Corinthian footballer who, when asked if he was going off to play rugger, is said to have replied, as he rolled his sock up over his trouser leg, 'No, old chap. Actually, I'm off to play soccer.' This was also the term later picked up by the USA, and later again by the television stations, so it has become a worldwide title for the sport, except in Scotland, especially Glasgow – well, working-class Glasgow.

My boys' gate comrades were not impressed by my tales of university life in Cambridge. 'Soccer' wasn't new to them. They had watched their own big brothers pull their socks up over their 'longies' for shilling-a-head games in the street with lamp posts for goalposts. Sometimes these absorbing inter-street games were cut short when the ball went through an open ground-floor window and the irate householder refused to give it back or by the arrival of the local bobby when a broken window had been reported. The solitary polis would rather have watched the game than tell anybody off for playing in the street.

These tanner-ba' games were often very skilful and honed dribbling techniques later put to good use in juvenile, junior and senior football. Several of our Springfield Rangers boys became professionals, like my own brother, Jim, who was a centre-half with Portsmouth and York City, or Felix McKenna, a tricky little forward who played junior with Shettleston, as did Tom Gibson with Bridgeton Waverley. The general standard of professional play in Scotland was much higher then. Football today is a passing and running game for super-fit athletes. Then it was a dribbling game for pint-size performers who had a puff of a fag before the start. Our best players may have been small in build, but they were big in status. They realised in the street that you couldn't have a game unless you had the ball, so they kept it at their feet as long as possible, thus honing their close-control skills. Even Jim, as a defender, could trap a ball in his own penalty area, beat a man and pass the ball forward. The street was his football academy and many working-class boys like him graduated *cum laude*.

If you weren't a great player, you compensated in the best way you could. Our great rivals in next-door Silverdale Street were a social cut above us; their tenements overlooked a bowling green, and still do. But in the war years, the street produced a top-class referee in Tom Wharton. Big Tom was large as a boy; that's why we called him 'Tiny'. He was too cumbersome to be nimble on the ball, but he was a smart fellow and quickly learned the rules. We made him our street referee and he went on to become a top-flight referee in Scottish football. He always called the players 'Mr'. Many years later, at Celtic Park, he awarded a free kick to Celtic. Charlie Gallagher went to take it. He placed the ball and noticed that Tiny Wharton was in the way. Charlie motioned him to move, but Wharton said to him, 'You do your job, Mr Gallagher, and I'll do mine. Please go ahead.' Charlie then hit the ball along the ground towards Bobby Murdoch, right in Tiny's path. Tiny jumped over it and Murdoch connected to score. Charlie said to him, 'Thank you, Mr Wharton,' and Tiny replied, 'Don't mention it, Mr Gallagher.'

Another Tiny Wharton anecdote concerned Jimmy 'Jinky' Johnstone. The wee man had committed his second foul and was due to be ordered off. Tiny rose to his full 6 ft 2 in. and summoned Jinky to him. 'You know now what I've got to do.'

Johnstone bowed his head. 'Aye.'

Tiny then produced his notebook with a flourish. 'Name, please.'

Jinky never even looked up. 'Roy Rogers,' he muttered.

Tiny showed no reaction and pointed imperiously to the tunnel. 'Very well, Mr Rogers. You'll find Trigger waiting in the dressing-room.'

Tiny Wharton made much use of humour in his refereeing. It was something he may have learned in Williamson Street, dealing with the rough street footballers. The professional version was no trouble to him after that. Tiny eventually became an international referee and a highly respected football legislator and member of FIFA's Referees' Committee.

The East End bristled with home-grown footballers who could really play, even if the game had started in the South Side of the city. Queen's Park of Hampden fame may have imported Association Rules to Glasgow, but the sport was taken up almost entirely by the less salubrious areas of the city, which soaked up this new football fashion in the latter part of the nineteenth century. Football clubs seemed to be springing up at every street corner. One of these was at Forbes Street in the Calton district, where, at St Mary's Hall, a group of Catholic youths congregated around Brother Walfrid, the headmaster of the Sacred Heart School. He was anxious to form a football team to play charity matches in aid of hungry children in the parishes of St Mary's, Sacred Heart in Bridgeton and St Michael's in Parkhead. It was as good a reason as any to found a football club and in due course one was started. It was nearly called Glasgow Hibernian in honour of the success achieved by the Edinburgh team, but at the last moment Brother Walfrid insisted on Celtic as a title, and on Sunday, 6 November 1887 the Glasgow Celtic Football and Athletic Club was born. Everything that this name means, everything it has done since then in that name, started from this date.

Brother Walfrid is justly celebrated as the founder of Celtic FC, but really, to be exact, he was more the catalyst, the agent, the originating impulse that got Celtic rolling. He was, in short, an enabler. Without this mainspring the people machine that was the first manifestation of this Celtic movement would never have got going in the first place. Without doubt, the groundswell started at root level among the Irish poor.

Walfrid's intentions were twofold: first, to get idle young men off the street and doing something, even if it was only playing football; second, to use this pool of energy to form a football team that could play in charity matches. For an unworldly man, his methods were extremely practical. A committee of very able men was set up, drawn largely from the very progressive St Mary's, boasting those who had made good in the Catholic diaspora. Joiner John Glass, tailor Pat Walsh and others set about acquiring a pitch and raising funds to set the new club in motion. Even the Archbishop of Glasgow chipped in with a contribution. But the main drive came from the people they served.

A great labouring brigade of Irish East Enders, armed with shovels, spades, rakes and barrows, and even their bare hands, cleared and levelled a vacant six-acre space among the tenements to make the first Celtic Park. It was an extraordinary project by any standards. Starting from scratch, this hardy coalition of outsiders, many implanted against their will among the smokestacks and workshops by the banks of the Clyde at Dalmarnock, undertook to build a football stadium.

Primitive it may have been, but it was there in due course – a perimeter wall enclosing an open-air stand over a pavilion containing all the necessary offices, including the luxury of a bath and showers for the players. There were nine admission gates, with the price set at sixpence. Mothers, wives and sisters were admitted free. In Walfrid's honour, all Catholic religious, including nuns, also got into Celtic Park for nothing. A simple track in front of a basic mound of earth served as terracing, although a better view could be got from standing on the wall of Janefield Cemetery, which bordered one side. Many were convinced that even the stone statues on the graves strained to get a view. It was the first step on the stairway to Paradise.

Prompted by a fierce Irish pride and aided by their communal energy, the three parishes asserted their common identity in this single stroke. By an act of the community will, a focus was given to an underprivileged section of citizenry that urgently needed a voice. They raised it now as they looked around at the result of their labours. The settlers had settled. By laying down their own piece of turf (110 yards long and 66 wide – with the centre spot from Donegal), they had made a claim to the land, and they called it Celtic Park. It would be a great compliment to these early pioneers if the present Celtic regime removed the '1888' from the front of their palatial pavilion and replaced it with '1887', although it must be accepted that the first match undertaken by the club was in 1888.

That first game was a friendly played on Saturday, 28 May, when the new Celtic begged, borrowed and stole 11 footballers, clustered them around James Kelly of Renton and called them Celtic. No call seems to have been made on any of Brother Walfrid's local boys. The names of these players deserve to be recorded and remembered, for they were the very first Celtic team. Wearing brand new uniforms, bought from Penman Bros of Bridgeton Cross (white with green collars and with a Celtic cross in green and red on their chests), this assorted XI beat Rangers Swifts 5–2.

Dolan (Drumpellier) was in goal; Pearson (Carfin Shamrock) and McLaughlin (Govan Whitefield) were full-backs; the half-back line was W. Maley (Cathcart), Kelly (Renton) and Murray (Cambuslang Hibernian); and the forward line was made up of McCallum (Renton), T. Maley (Cathcart), Madden (Dumbarton), Dunbar (Edinburgh Hibernian) and Gorevin (Govan Whitefield). Every Celtic boy grew up knowing these names, even if it was only for the legend about 'The McCallum'. This was a favourite ice-cream dish, so called in memory of Neilly McCallum, nicknamed 'The Shadow', the right-winger who scored the first-ever Celtic goal, a header from a corner after ten minutes. The dish was ice cream with raspberry sauce poured over it, as if to represent the first blood taken by Celtic.

On what was described in the press of the time as 'a cold dry evening', the event drew a healthy crowd of 2,000 to the new ground, which means they must have drained every local Catholic enclave. The baby's head had been well and truly wetted, and players and the gentlemen of the committee repaired to St Mary's Hall in the Calton, the very place where the club had been founded seven months before, for the then fashionable soirée and smoker concert to celebrate a day Celtic supporters have been celebrating – more or less – ever since.

It is not generally known that Brother Walfrid's original name for the club was pronounced 'Keltic' not 'Seltic'. As an educated man, he would have known the term in its ethnic sense, but the story goes that, with the advent of Renton's James Kelly to the club, it was thought by the first board that 'Kelly of the Keltic' was perhaps a little too alliterative. The truth is that it was called 'Seltic' because that's how Glaswegians pronounced it, and that was that.

In the unreal atmosphere of the 1940–41 season, I was only too glad to waken up on a Saturday morning knowing I was going to see 'the Bhoys' again. We never called them 'the Hoops' then. As far as we were concerned, that nickname belonged to Queens Park Rangers, the English team that played at Loftus Road, London.

Generally, matches were only played on a Saturday afternoon and the kick-off time was fixed for 3 p.m. to allow workers to finish their 6 a.m. until 2 p.m. shift and get to the game. It was not unusual for men to come straight to the match in their dungarees and overalls. They blended in easily with the grey flat caps and dun-coloured raincoats of the rest of the crowd. The terracing then was hardly a riot of colour. Clothes rationing ruled out any flamboyance and even scarves were rare. At most, a paper rosette was seen, but even paper was rationed.

The commercial value of merchandising was unknown to clubs then, and anyway the thought of standing in a public place wearing a full Celtic strip would have been anathema to the average supporter. It was an age of uniforms, but somehow the green-and-white jersey was more than sporting garb, it was a sacred vestment. One had to earn the right to wear it by playing for it on the park, not by shouting from the terracing. A Celtic jersey couldn't be bought over the Co-op counter like a semmit or a pair of long johns. Besides, there was a war on. Everything was scarce except opinions, although the nation was warned against the dangers of careless talk.

I lived for the weekly Christmas that was the Celtic match. It was the big treat for everyone, not only for wee boys but also for the relatives who brought them and initiated them into the Celtic experience. The simplest of football grounds was a gladiatorial arena where heart-stopping excitement could be felt between gasps of wonder at the skills shown on the park by sporting versions of the men all around you.

That was why Saturdays were special. It was hard to sleep on the Friday night. The next day, you woke up to no school and the thought of the match only hours away. As soon as the game was over, it was home to lentil soup and the Saturday night celebrations or rites of mourning: the reading of the *Evening Times* with the latest football results. The Sunday was given over to heated discussion of the game, which started at your granny's house over the Sunday lunch after last Mass. Your uncles didn't need a replay. They carried every move in their heads and any goal would be etched on the membrane of their eyes. Salt cellars and sauce bottles were moved around recklessly as tactics were illustrated and errors explained. Tempers flared as disagreements arose even among these sons and brothers who were all enjoined in one, all-embracing cause. I listened, rapt.

These ordinary working men, by no means stupid any of them, could articulate their memory of a game so colourfully and dramatically that you could see it all again in cosy, rosy remembrance, especially if it had been a victory. Defeats were skilfully glossed over to make them just palatable enough to swallow. Even great games of the past, like the 1931 and 1937 Scottish Cup finals, were analysed from armchairs or around the table so engrossingly that I felt I was there. It was memory as action replay. Wonderful.

The womenfolk would have long since left the table and be trying to clear up, grabbing the condiments and the sauce bottles from the gesturing hands when they could. The only thing they did not touch was the pint beer glass before every adult male. They would not dare, and old Granny would quietly fill any glass needing replenishing when the aunties weren't looking. One uncle, the youngest, would just as surreptitiously slip a thimbleful into my tumbler. I've never liked beer since, but I never missed a word. Sometimes I even earned myself a threepenny bit or a sixpence by naming a team from Celtic's history. It was my regular party piece and it proved that all my football reading had paid off.

On the Monday, a more objective view of the game would be taken and it might even be allowed that the opposing team wasn't too bad. This was praise indeed. Our bias was not something we tried to hide. Far from it. It was a badge to be worn proudly. That didn't stop us, however, from appreciating the finer points of the beautiful game and understanding that the more simply it was played the better it looked.

Tuesday was forgettable; very little ever happened on a Tuesday. Like its sister, Thursday, it was one of the dowdy twins of the week family. Saturday was the star, with Friday in close attendance. Sunday was the dowager of the week and deserving of every respect. Wednesday was the rebel; she could go either way. But who cared when the week was already turning towards Saturday? Only the next encounter on the pitch mattered by then.

This happy routine was interrupted by the Clydebank Blitz of March 1941. We could see the flames from our kitchen window in Parkhead. I loved the huge red sky it made. I didn't know then that it would rob a future Celtic player, Pat Crerand, of his father, who was killed while on fire-watching duty with the ARP. We children couldn't really take in the terrible tragedy of it all. War was a game that adults played. However, we lived in hope. Optimism is the prime essential in the true supporter's armoury. Anyway, the Blitz meant that we children had to face a second evacuation.

This time, it was to the Highlands and the holiday estate owned by Mr Chamberlain, the former prime minister. I went to the village school at Kinloch Rannoch and not long afterwards I was transferred to the home of the Earl of Cluny in order to attend secondary school. I was having a very aristocratic war. It allowed me the experience of attending Breadalbane Academy, a Protestant school, which did me no harm at all. When my mother came up to visit, she said I hoped I mentioned it in confession. I didn't tell her that they didn't do confessions in Aberfeldy. She told me that Dad had been transferred to London to the Ministry of Works. His job was to decide which bombed buildings were to be shored up and which pulled down. How he got to that level of responsibility, I don't know. He worked in the furnace in Parkhead Forge, but he was always plausible, was Dad, and he must have talked to 'somebody'. In wartime, there was work for everybody, somehow. Men and women were run off their feet with overtime. Ordinary people knew for the first time what something like prosperity was.

The same couldn't be said of the team I supported. Celtic had maybe the worst team they'd ever had. As boys, Jim and I had been brought up on tales of the great Celtic teams of the past, but not since the Exhibition Trophy of 1938 had we actually won anything and the early wartime sides did not promise much. It was hard to believe that this gaggle of well-meaning workhorses, with the exception of two or three survivors from pre-war, would ever make a Celtic team. I was glad to be out of it for a bit. Instead, I went to the pictures in Pitlochry and saw Robert Taylor in *A Yank at Oxford*.

Jim and I came back to Glasgow just in time for me to enrol at St Mungo's Academy at Townhead and get a glimpse of big John McPhail in the playground before he went off to sign for Celtic, leaving his young brother, Billy, at the school before he chose to sign for Queen's Park. However, Billy's Celtic destiny was not to be denied, as we shall learn.

It was at St Mungo's that I played my first and last game of rugby. I was a fast runner, which was the only reason I was chosen, but being brought to ground on a cinder pitch by great lumping lads from Allan Glen's put an end to my rugby career. Similarly, cricket was out. In a park game near Belvedere Hospital off the London Road, I played wicket-keeper and received the bat across my left eye. As the phrase has it, I 'retired hurt'. I couldn't swim and tennis was for West Enders, so football was all I had left.

I particularly remember one typical Celtic game around that time. I think it was against Third Lanark and our team of triers and trialists was doing its best. It was so dreary at one point that a great silence suddenly descended on the ground. Now, complete silence is not a thing you get often at a football match, but this was a total absence of sound. It was eerie. All we could hear was the thud of football boots on the turf; we could see the puffs of steam coming from the players' mouths as they ran about on the frozen pitch. It was an icily cold day and I huddled into my father on the terracing. Suddenly, a voice called out loud and clear from the other side of the ground, 'This is fucking boring!' The whole stadium burst out laughing.

We spent a lot of time laughing on the terracing. The crack was good among the flat caps, and humour abounded even on a bad day – especially on a bad day. Humour was the breastplate of our suit of armour. I felt safe, enclosed, hemmed in on all sides by my own kind of people. Although many had travelled in from far-off places like Croy, rural places beyond the city boundary, they were *us* in country clothes. I was happy in my tribe, secure in *belonging*.

It wasn't until I'd been evacuated that I realised there was a whole other world out there and that they didn't have to go to confession, either. It was a wiser wee boy who came back to our room and kitchen in Williamson Street. However, in all of this, one thing didn't change. That was my love of the Celtic. I had been baptised too thoroughly in the club for that belief to abate and my early trips to the sevenpenny gate only confirmed this devotion.

CHAPTER TWO

Players, Please

Danny McGrain, Right-Back
Hirsute matador, bastion at the back,
Resolute defender, dynamo in attack,
Danny boy was happy playing football either way,
A credit to Celtic and to Scotland to this day.

During the Second World War, football didn't officially exist in the record books, so from 1939 until 1946 it didn't officially happen with Celtic and me, but it did and I was there to prove it. It certainly existed in my own record books. I remember that the calendar year for the football boy began with the start of the League season in August and ended with the last game in May. 'Ne'er cast a clout till May is oot' was the slogan for me. It didn't apply to my winter overcoat, however, but to my zip-up lumber jacket, which was my wardrobe for match days. At twelve years of age, the two-month close season in between was interminable and the annual family Glasgow Fair two-week summer holiday in Ayr tedious. The ongoing conflicts in the war were getting more serious. Bombs had been dropped next door in Dalmarnock and we boys had trooped down Springfield Road to see real live dead bodies among the rubble in Allan Street near the power station. It was all hard to take in; this was the sort of thing we only saw at the pictures.

We were glad we could divert ourselves somehow, and sport was our favourite distraction. Boxers were heroes to most Glaswegians and champions like Benny Lynch were worshipped. So was the later Jackie Paterson. We saw boxing matches for free from the balconies of the new Corporation housing scheme then being built overlooking the ring in Carntyne Greyhound Track. I didn't like boxing; I preferred athletics. There were meetings at the Glasgow Corporation Transport track in Helenvale Street, where I saw Sydney Wooderson run. He was wearing glasses, which made me feel better about my own. He was a distance runner and he often came agonisingly close to the four-minute mile. That was why he drew the crowds. However, most of all, we chased the five-a-sides. This was football in miniature, as seen at all the big meets that were the main feature of a Glasgow summer. We especially enjoyed the Ibrox Sports, where the final of the five-a-side football tournament was the closing event of the meet. All the senior teams competed over the years and a Celtic Five appeared regularly. That was why most of the Parkhead boys' gate queue was there. We were starved of the sight of a football jersey. We needed the taste of green and white the five-a-sides provided. This was also the reason that the trial game at Parkhead was so anticipated.

It came with the first hint of autumn – the annual encounter between the first team and the reserves, Greens versus Whites. For once, there was no need to line up at Kinloch Street. Admission was by donation and that meant free for us. We made a real occasion of it, trooping into the enclosure and getting as near to the tunnel as we could. That way we could almost touch the players as they ran out, although we never would have done – that would have almost amounted to a sin. For boys like us, and for most of the ordinary support, it was a once-a-year chance to see the whole Celtic family on display. There were players you were seeing for the first time and players you were seeing for the last time. The game was always full of tensions and surprises, but the most important element by far was that you didn't care who won, for you were on both sides. You could enjoy the football purely for its own sake.

It was like a family wedding at which you were introduced to cousins you had never heard of and saw old uncles you had heard too much about. It was all part of the mix. You could get a lump in your throat seeing how the big names had come through the summer unscathed and a jump in your heart witnessing for the first time the skills of the new boys, some of whom would become big names before long. It was always exhilarating and unbearably exciting, because it meant that your world would soon be back to normal.

Professional football in wartime had been organised on regional lines so as to limit travel and save on fuel. 'Is Your Journey Really Necessary?' was the slogan on all the posters. Scottish football was divided into East and West at first, so that for us Edinburgh, Perth, Dundee, Aberdeen and Fife were out, and Greenock and Motherwell were borderline. Later, though, the League was divided into North and South, so we got Hibs and Hearts back. We were encouraged to walk everywhere, but not to Edinburgh, although some hardier supporters used to jump on the back of any lorry going east. Fortunately for us boys, the trams still went to Airdrie and Paisley, blue buses to Ayr, and if you had to go to Greenock, you got a train.

There was also a restriction on attendances; no more than 15,000 were allowed through any gate. This was hard to take initially, as, according to my uncle Phil, the Celtic home game against Rangers in 1938 had attracted an attendance of 83,500 – still a record for the ground. During wartime, players in the services were permitted to play for clubs near their place of duty. This was to offset the loss of young players through the introduction of national conscription. Wages all round were cut to £2 a week, but football was really a social currency for both players and spectators. Nobody was in it for the money.

I'm not sure if it was a form of air-raid protection in a time of national emergency, but the Celtic board of directors appeared to stick their collective head in the sand throughout the war years. At a time when fit young men in their 20s were at a premium, they seemed to put their trust in Exhibition Trophy survivors and Boys' Guild hopefuls, along with the occasional stray import who happened to be passing. Yet there was a vast pool of temporary talent they might have tapped into. This was the great number of professional players from all over Britain stationed around the west of Scotland on military service. Soldiers and airmen with peerless football credentials were begging to play on a Saturday, if only to keep fit and no doubt escape some barrack-room drudgery.

Matt Busby even trained at Celtic Park, but manager Jimmy McStay could not persuade the board to sign him on a temporary basis, even though he was known to be 'Celtic daft'. Instead, the future Manchester United legend went to Hibernian and helped them to have a great war. Who knows, had he gone to Celtic, he might have become manager in due course, and then what? The O'Donnell brothers, Frank and Hugh, of proven Celtic calibre, wrote offering their services but were turned down. Classy former Celtic players like Willie Buchan and Charlie Napier were stationed in Scotland but were ignored. The club persisted in fielding a side of mere journeymen and raw apprentices.

Meantime, Greenock Morton hired Tommy Lawton and Stanley Matthews, Aberdeen got Stan Mortensen, Hamilton Accies got goalkeeper Frank Swift and Partick Thistle Bill Shankly. Just imagine what Celtic might have done had they used the services of any one of these available servicemen (albeit Bill Shankly was, by his own admission, 'Rangers daft'). Think of the good influence that type of player might have had on the Parkhead youngsters. But it was not to be and the football soldiers marched past.

All members of the armed services were admitted free at the boys' gate. It was a great thrill to be standing beside or behind someone in uniform. There were lots of soldiers in khaki battledress, sometimes a sailor but not many airmen. I would have loved to have seen a pilot. When the Home Guard got their uniforms, a few old guys tried to join in, but their grey hair gave them away. It definitely cheered me up to stand beside my uncle Phil when he was home on leave from the Black Watch. He looked bigger in his uniform somehow.

Celtic were now playing some teams unfamiliar to us, and not playing very well. It was a good job we recognised our own. We knew them by their mannerisms – how Jimmy Delaney always hitched up his shorts before he took a corner, how wee Johnny Crum danced a jig after scoring a goal, how Jackie Gallacher would run his fingers through his hair in exasperation. It was all part of the signalling system to us watching that players, too, had their worries during the game and needed their individual foibles as a comfort. Football players observed their little rituals. We would see the goalkeepers spitting on their gloves, and some players would kneel down to tie their bootlaces at crucial moments. These were habits, totems, something to ward off the bad luck. On our part, it was the scrutiny of the passionate; there was nothing that we missed.

Strangely enough, I considered myself an expert judge of football skills even from an early age, even though I could hardly play the game myself. Perhaps it was because I soaked up so much from my fellow spectators. From the comments I heard from the men all around me, I realised that they knew their football well and were well qualified to judge a player. Some of them had been players – and good ones, too – or had watched a lifetime of professional games and had absorbed every nuance of it. They could tell what they called 'a real player' from his first touch of the ball and they were rarely wrong.

What I liked particularly was that their comments weren't confined to Celtic players. If the opposition included a real player, he would be recognised and acknowledged. In that way, I came to know and respect Johnny Mackenzie of Partick Thistle, Peter Galletly of Clyde, Johnny Kelly of Morton (an ex-Celt to boot) and Jimmy Duncanson of Rangers, all of whom were players of my early spectating years who didn't reach immortal heights in the game but did it so much credit by their sportsmanship, skill and general likeability.

I would have loved to have had even a tithe of the football flair shown by my young brother, but it seems it was as strictly rationed as sugar. In my later acting days, I played for a Show Business XI at one Edinburgh Festival, but I was sent off for kissing the goalkeeper. She was a blonde singer. I was never invited to play for them again. The only time in my career I was asked to don a Celtic jersey was for a publicity photo taken at Shawfield Stadium, where I was pictured taking a penalty against my cousin, Philip Cairney, then a fine goalkeeper for Clyde. (This is the picture that's on the cover of this book.) I turned up on the day, changed in the dressing-room, ran onto the park, put the ball on the spot, ran back, took the kick, scored and retired immediately. I had long since realised that spectatorship was my field, and I embraced it wholly, concentrating on my Celtic heroes.

Since my 'Bhoy's Own' days of football, beginning with my first sevenpenny gate adventures in wartime, I have seen the gradual decline of larger-than-life heroes. It may seem an over-generous term for football players, but we saw them as such because they only appeared once a week, running out from the tunnel like gladiators. We didn't know them from television interviews or newspaper coverage. We read nothing of their private lives. We never bought a programme, skimpy as they were, so we only knew who was in the team when we saw them on the pitch. Whoever they were, we welcomed them all lustily.

These figures in green and white were hardly household names, but they were like big brothers to us as we boys congregated in our own children's corner on the edge of the Jungle and muttered a quiet Hail Mary for a victory – just this once. Our prayers were rarely answered. A whole rosary would have been pointless, for at the time Celtic had a forward line the supporters called 'The Five Sorrowful Mysteries'. The only mystery was why some of them had been signed for Celtic in the first place.

We were brought up on stories of great Celtic games. Names like Sandy McMahon, Jimmy Quinn, Jimmy McMenemy, Alec McNair and Patsy Gallacher were as familiar to us as family; their deeds were still real and their presence palpable because they lived in our imaginations and were timeless. I can still see 'the Duke', as McMahon was called, running at more than 6 ft tall, like an eagle, arms high outstretched, through the opposing defence as if they weren't there. I never saw this, of course, but I read about it as I might have read *Treasure Island*. Because it has entered via the imagination, the picture will never dim, however historically distanced. Heart-snaps never fade.

I still remember snatches of men's talk I overheard on the terracing on match days. This is how all young boys should learn their football, from the roots. It's the only way, if the passion is to last and the enthusiasm grow. The social history of Celtic is its most vital component; it's the human thread that links the Celtic generations. Heroic exploits are the necessary fodder, like young Jimmy Quinn's hat-trick to win the Scottish Cup final of 1904, in which Rangers were leading 2–0 at the end of the first quarter of an hour. This was immediately registered as never to be forgotten, as was Patsy Gallacher's wonder goal against Dundee in another Scottish Cup final, this time in 1925. The story goes that he received the ball in the Dundee half and immediately began meandering his way past one man after another until he fell in the penalty area near the goal line with the ball at his feet. Gripping it firmly between his ankles, he somersaulted over the line to score. It was a feat, if you'll forgive the pun, that completely demoralised Dundee and won Celtic the cup.

It was reported far and wide and talked about on all sides, but I heard it first from an uncle, who heard it from a workmate whose brother was at the game, and I'm sure the remarkable goal improved with each telling, so that it now stands high in the history books and in my recollection to this day. Real legends are made of stern stuff and will outlast passing fashion and the mores of any given day, but, more importantly, they survive because we need our heroes.

Great Celtic teams survive in the same way because they are the heroic in a collective version. We remember the names in their order much as we remember a mantra, an invocation to gods now gone who occupy a semi-spiritual recess in our subconscious where even the recital of the past names sounds like prayer, summoning the picture memories up and bringing them into the light of day in their traditional 2-3-5 formation:

1905: *Adams; Watson and Orr; McNair, Loney and Hay; Bennett, McMenemy, Quinn, Somers and Hamilton; 12th man – Young.*
This was the side that introduced that one-club man Jimmy Quinn, knight errant exemplar and one-man forward line. Alec McNair had also set out on a long career with the club; his time with Celtic was to last 21 years.

1914: *Shaw; McNair and Dodds; Young, Johnstone and McMaster; McAtee, Gallacher, McColl, McMenemy and Browning; 12th man – Cassidy.*
The genius of Gallacher emerged in the years of the trenches and 'Napoleon' McMenemy began the strategic retreat that led him to the towel and the sponge as Celtic's trainer.

1931: *J. Thomson; Cook and McGonagle; Wilson, McStay and Geatons; R. Thomson, A. Thomson, McGrory, Scarff and Napier; 12th man – Hogg.*
The ghost of the prince of goalkeepers hovers over this fine side and John Thomson remains immortal, but McGrory, the goal poacher, may be the greatest Celtic servant ever.

1938: *Kennaway; Hogg and Morrison; Geatons, Lyon and Paterson; Delaney, Buchan, Crum, Divers and Murphy; 12th man – MacDonald.*
This was Willie Maley's final creation before he left amid acrimony over an income tax payment not long after the team's Exhibition Trophy triumph in 1938. He had been with the club since its beginning. Leaving it in the way he did was not his own choice, but it cannot be denied that he made all these great sides and he will be long remembered for that.

I loved reading about the club, learning by heart the names of all the great teams. You didn't have to support Celtic at St Mungo's, but it helped. The path from Townhead to Parkhead was well trodden and just ahead of me among the big boys was Billy McPhail, who would shortly leave for Queen's Park but eventually follow big brother John to Celtic. The playground produced a lot of good football players and a lot of priests. Tommy McInally was one – football player, I mean. He might not have made your conventional priest. Benny Connell did have a vocation and was also a very good footballer indeed. I could never quite understand why he chose to serve an Unknown God when he could have played alongside one at Celtic Park. I'm talking about Jimmy Delaney. He was my all-time star then, and still is.

Football success was something never to be taken for granted, even by the playground Delaneys who performed wonders with a tennis ball or the solitary boy who battered a tanner ba' endlessly against unresisting air-raid shelter walls or back-court dykes to the consternation of neighbouring women who were mindful of their vulnerable windows. At night, I would pore over my scrapbook of cigarette cards and pine for players like Stan Cullis of Wolves or Wilf Mannion of Middlesbrough or Denis Compton of Arsenal – he of the Brylcreemed hair and neat side parting who would later prove a gallant Test batsman for England. I can still see the shine of that hair on my Player's card.

As I've mentioned, most of the cigarette-card players were English, and the only Celtic player to attain the honour of a nationally distributed cigarette card was Delaney. Jimmy had been severely injured in a game against Arbroath at Celtic Park just before the war. His left arm was fractured so badly that he was out of the game for two years and it was feared he would never play again. Fortunately for Celtic and Scotland, he recovered fully.

He made a totally unexpected appearance at the Ibrox Sports in the five-a-sides in August 1941 and the gasp of delight from the Celtic support present could be heard all round the ground. A taxi was waiting to take him to Celtic Park, and when he made his appearance for the Greens in the Celtic trial that same night, the rapturous roar that greeted him could have been heard at Ibrox. It was no more than he deserved. Standing almost alone in that Celtic side, he was the one player who carried the torch from greater days, and he held it high until it was ungraciously snatched from him by those who ought to have known better.

On the evening of Sunday, 15 November 2009, I was invited by the Scottish Football Museum to attend a dinner at the Hilton Hotel in Glasgow honouring the new inductees to their Football Hall of Fame. My job was to speak for the nomination of Jimmy Delaney. Appropriately, I was seated at the Celtic table, along with Bertie Auld, Bobby Lennox, Tom Boyd and the manager of Norwich City, the ex-Celt Paul Lambert.

They were great company, particularly Bertie and Bobby, who might have made a good music-hall double act. Tom, on my left, was an easy and charming dinner companion, but the manager of Norwich City, on my right, said very little, as he was to be inducted himself later in the evening. The speeches by the famous and near-famous went on, with the laughter and the applause alternating while the black-tied audience steadily demolished the generous refreshments provided. Every kind of football person was there: those who had played, those who still played, those who wished they had and, last of all, those who were down to speak, of which I was one. I didn't know I could be so nervous. This was something I couldn't rehearse as for a normal play. This was football. This was real.

I was introduced to the audience by the BBC presenter Dougie Donnelly, who hosted the evening, and my first concern was whether their polite applause would last until I reached the podium, which was a long walk through the tables and a steep climb up several steps – it didn't. As far as I remember, this is what I said:

Thank you, Dougie. I wish you'd warned me about the steps. [Laughter.] Ladies and gentlemen, we are here to honour football and I am here to honour a footballer, Jimmy Delaney. It's a name known to most of you because you have a football connection. Some a very distinguished connection and some, like myself, a very tenuous one, but none of you here, whatever your connection, however acknowledged and proved by honours, can exceed me in my love of our game in all its aspects. As some of you will know, I am a Celtic supporter [reaction from the Celtic table, led by Bertie Auld], but I must quickly add that I have been a guest of the Rangers board on several occasions. [Reaction.] I've been a guest of the Celtic board only once. [Reaction] I was never asked back. Was it something I said?

What I will say now is that I am proud and flattered to be here in such company and I will begin by asking you this. Can any of you still name the players of the team you supported in the first game you ever saw? I can't because I was too young. It was Celtic, of course. [Cheers and groans.] But I do remember the team I got to know well in the early years of my support.

Miller; Hogg and Dornan; Lynch, Corbett and McAuley; Delaney, McPhail, Rae, McGinley and Long. [Cheers.] I don't know what the opposition was, but all I know was that we probably lost. [Laughter.] We always did then. It was that kind of Celtic. It was not that they had bad players, it was just that they were not a good team. You'll know what I mean. They didn't have that powerful, almost indefinable sense of the collective that the great teams had in the past and that the future Lisbon Lions would have. [Cheers from Bertie Auld and Bobby Lennox.] Willie Miller in goal was still to reach the courageous heights he attained later. Bobby Hogg was at the end of a good career. Pat McAuley and John McPhail were two naturals, but they were just boys, and Hughie Long had to wait to go to Clyde before he could show his full potential. There was only one quality footballer on show that Saturday, and every Saturday until he was obliged to leave the team he loved, and that was Jimmy Delaney on the right wing. [Cheers.]

It is appropriate, perhaps, that an actor should speak for him tonight, for, like any great athlete in the public eye, he was a performer of the highest class. Off the park, he was quiet, diffident about his status and modest to the point of indistinction, but let him don that famous strip and he was fearless, determined and unstoppable on the right wing. His speed off the mark was astonishing and his elusive, will-o'-the-wisp style on the ball was a delight to spectators and a terror to defenders. Whenever the ball came to him, there was an immediate growl of anticipation from the terracing, which quickly developed into a large sigh and then a mighty roar as he rocketed down the wing, heading for the byline, and yet another wonderful cross came over.

Of course, it was missed by dear old 'Doh' Rae at centre, but that wasn't unusual, and we had to wait until Jimmy got the ball again and went to centre-forward himself before we could get excited. It takes a very special gift to inflame a crowd, but to do it without oratory, without a word, just by a graceful or daring act on a field with a ball at your feet, is rare indeed. There were others with this God-given talent: Patsy Gallacher, Alan Morton, Stanley Matthews, Pelé, Bobby Charlton, George Best, Jim Baxter, Henrik Larsson – Delaney belonged in this company. And who knows, the next giant name may be sitting among you now. [Pause.]

As a 14-year-old boy, I was among the crowd that gathered outside the old SFA headquarters in Carlton Place in April 1944 to chant for the inclusion of Delaney in the Scottish international team after his return from injury, but the selectors were worried about the effect of that fractured arm. A Glasgow businessman offered to pay the medical insurance at Lloyd's. That may have won the day. Delaney was picked and scored the winning goal against Frank Swift of England in the Victory International at Hampden in April 1946 in front of 134,000 spectators. I was there; I saw it.

The only regret I have is that by that time Delaney was no longer a Celt. Matt Busby had signed him for Manchester United just before. It was his first signing for them and he always said it was his most important. But then, Sir Matt was a lifelong Celtic fan. Just like me. [Cheers and groans.]

Which is why it gives me extra pleasure to be here tonight to assist in honouring this very ordinary Scotsman from Lanarkshire who was an extraordinary footballer and was, from the beginning, destined for his deserved place in Scottish Football's Hall of Fame, not only – [applause] – not only for his prowess on the park but for his demeanour off it, for his sense of commitment and rightness, for his honesty and special integrity, which were there for all to see, but especially for his ability to pass on to thousands in a moment his love and enthusiasm for the game of football. He played on until they had to wrench the boots from his feet and it is with the same reluctance that I conclude this panegyric to a master footballer, proud Celt and wonderful, good man – Jimmy Delaney. [Applause.]

Delaney's son Pat accepted the Certificate of Induction on behalf of his father. We had our photograph taken and that was that. I'm glad to say that afterwards the applause lasted until I got back to my seat.

My only regret that night was that I hadn't time to speak of the post-Celtic Delaney or of how, for the sake of a couple of pounds, he was allowed to leave Celtic while still in his prime. He didn't want to leave the club but, as a family man, he felt he was due a rise, however modest, after more than 20 years' loyal service. When Celtic refused to up his wages, he was forced to agree to be transferred. It might have been a good financial tactic on Celtic's part, but it was short-sighted football strategy.

When Celtic first signed Delaney in 1933 from Stoneyburn Juniors, he was a general labourer in the local coalmine at less than a pound a week, but at the time of his provisional contract he was idle and on a single man's dole money of 17 shillings a week. Two pounds was a bonus, not to mention the signing-on fee, which, modest enough, would have seemed like a windfall.

Throughout his career, he made very little more than the average man and only made any real money when he was transferred: first for £4,000 to Manchester United in 1946 (the negotiations taking place in the waiting room of Motherwell station), next to Aberdeen for £3,000 pounds in 1950 and after that, for ever-decreasing but still substantial amounts, to Falkirk (1951), Derry City (1954), Cork Athletic as player-manager (1955) and finally, in 1956, to Elgin City. Not unnaturally, there was a spiralling down in class of club at the end, but there was no let-up in effort or effectiveness on his part. He is the only player to have won cup-final medals with four clubs: Celtic in 1937, Manchester United in 1948, Derry City in 1954 and as a runner-up with Cork Athletic in 1956.

He eventually retired, very reluctantly, in 1957 at the age of 43. He died in 1989, aged 70, in Cleland, having spent nearly a quarter of a century chasing a leather ball. He was still a Celt at heart and this was shown by his wish to be buried with a Celtic jersey thrown over the coffin. The request was granted.

They say that you don't have to be mad to be a goalkeeper, but it helps. Willie Miller, from that same wartime team, was obviously sane, but that only makes his exploits in the Celtic goal all the more remarkable. If ever I were asked again to nominate a player to the Scottish Football Hall of Fame, it would be him, because if one word could sum up his Celtic career it would be 'heroic'. Like Delaney, he was often single-handedly responsible for holding out against a continual bombardment from the opposition and salvaging a precious point for a draw. I often saw him play behind a halting and hesitant defence as a result of the chopping and changing being made during that time. The team played with no recognised stopper and this fact may indeed have made Miller the brilliant goalkeeper he became. He was extraordinary because he had to be.

He was frequently left cruelly exposed and too often had to improvise defensive measures that relied entirely on his lightning reflexes and sheer bravery. No wonder he was so often treated for head and shoulder injuries. I have yet a vivid mental picture of this remarkable custodian's body making a perfect 'C' figure against the goal net at the Mount Florida end of Hampden Park. I was standing at the Aikenhead Road end and had a perfect long-shot view of an arching save to tip a thunderbolt over the bar. I can still see the bloodstained bandage round his head, which was thrown back between those stretching arms. The save caused a gasp; it was so beautiful as well as brave. I can't remember who Celtic were playing, but if Willie won a medal for it, they should have added a Victoria Cross – and bar.

The thing is, he didn't just pull out all the stops for the big occasions, he did it week after week in routine fixtures, as if such dedication to the highest standard of play were normal. This is what marks out the great player and there is no doubt that Willie Miller, from Glasgow's Woodside Secondary, was an all-time Celtic great. His unexpected departure to Clyde sent the whole Celtic support into mourning. In my estimation, he is Celtic's greatest-ever goalkeeper. It is said that he died with 200 stitches in his skull. The surgeons ought to have fashioned them into a halo.

I now come to the last of my triad of Celtic heroes: Malky, or Calum as he was called at home. The MacDonald home was in the Garngad, a district to the north-east of Glasgow. It has now gone up in the world under the name of Royston, but when it existed as a virtual extra Free State of Ireland in the '20s and early '30s it produced a stream of footballers in addition to a flood of petty criminals and what we called 'fly men'. These did no real harm, but they did no work either. They hung about the corners waiting for this and that, here or there, now and then. It was safer to be vague about most things. They were afraid of no one except the parish priest, who would sometimes turn up with his shillelagh and lay about them mightily, scattering the young men to the nearby close-mouths.

From this unlikely environment came Jimmy McGrory, a world name in football for his scoring feats and another Celtic great, perhaps the greatest in terms of lifetime loyalty. However, Malky MacDonald was arguably Celtic's most complete footballer. He could tackle, beat a man, pass a ball and shoot a goal, all with style.

Malky was born in 1913. His Highland father worked in the local gasworks. Malky came to football via St Roch's school team and St Anthony's Juniors. He signed for Celtic in 1932, a year before Delaney, and quickly emerged as a valuable utility player. This is not always good for a player's advancement at a club: because he is good wherever

51

he plays, management becomes uncertain where to play him. As a result, his career will often hang in limbo while 'upstairs' decide what to do with him.

Malky had this problem; such were his natural skills, they had no idea where to play him to best advantage. He started off as a footballing centre-half, which was quite in keeping with Willie Maley's preference for a pivotal centre-half who controlled the game from the middle of the park. For this, Malky needed all the skills: dribbling, short and long passing, trapping the ball on chest or at feet, heading at any angle and a sense of where everyone on his team was at any given moment. He had all of these in abundance, and in addition a poise and calm that gave his play an assured, aristocratic elegance entirely at odds with his start in life. He had this quality all through his career. It gave him a reassuring quiet.

Unfortunately, the vogue at the time was for the third back, or stopper centre-half, made fashionable by Arsenal. Most clubs in Britain followed suit and even Celtic changed their ways by bringing in Willie Lyon from Queen's Park in 1935. This coincided with chronic cartilage trouble for Malky and he was on the bench again. He came back to take inside-forward, Willie Buchan's place, when that player was allowed to leave, and Delaney and MacDonald became a dream right-wing pair. The winger thrived on the service provided for him by the silky inside-right, who was also scoring freely. It was a pleasure for a young lad like me to watch. It looked as if Malky was in with the bricks at Celtic Park. Instead, he was soon struck down by appendicitis and out of action again.

When the war began, he was working night shifts, which limited his training. Nevertheless, his subtle and versatile style of play had not gone unnoticed by the Scottish selectors and he was capped three times during the war, first at right-half, then at left-half and finally, in the 1944 Delaney comeback international, at right-back. Between times, he played in every possible position for Celtic, even in goal in one emergency situation, and was excellent in all. Celtic still couldn't make up their minds what his best position was. Malky didn't care; he just enjoyed playing.

The trouble with some players is that all their brains are in their feet, but Calum MacDonald had brains in both head and feet. That was what made him very special. Celtic sold him after 13 quality years to Kilmarnock in 1945. He then went on to Brentford in the following year and became their player-coach two years later. He returned to Scotland as manager of Kilmarnock in 1950 and see-sawed between them and Brentford until he was appointed interim, part-time manager of Scotland in 1966. He left Kilmarnock in 1968 and became a scout for Tottenham Hotspur.

On 19 January 1947, the Celtic Supporters Association decided to honour MacDonald officially and summoned the faithful to a rally in his honour in Glasgow's St Andrew's Halls. They presented him with a testimonial of their admiration and affection, and in reply Malky said, through a brace (he had suffered a broken jaw), 'This might be the last link between me and Celtic [the occasion, not the brace], but I ask you not to think of me as MacDonald of Kilmarnock or MacDonald of Brentford but as MacDonald of Celtic.'

I certainly do. I met him once after a game at East End Park, Dunfermline, when the Pars were playing Kilmarnock. I was walking alone by the side of the stand on my way to my car when he suddenly appeared out of one the doors and almost collided with me. I was startled, but recognised him at once. He stared at me for a moment. 'You're that man Burns,' he said. He was, after all, manager of Kilmarnock at the time.

'No, I'm not. I'm the John Cairney who once queued up at the boys' gate to see you play for Celtic,' I replied.

'Oh, aye? You don't look old enough,' he said politely.

'Thank you for all those boyhood memories,' I said and held out my hand. He took it.

'Sure,' he replied and quickly walked away. I watched him go with a big lump in my throat. I had just shaken hands with a childhood hero.

When I was a boy, I didn't give much thought to Winston Churchill or General Montgomery or whoever was on the front pages of the papers. Between the dash and brio of Delaney, the sturdy defiance of Miller and the sheer artistry of MacDonald, I found all the surety I needed that God was still in his heaven and all could be well again at Celtic Park. What more could any boy want of a football club – except more? It didn't happen for Celtic for decades to come, but the flashes of gold given off from time to time by the trio above did something to weigh against the lacklustre metal of their playing companions.

The war years were tough going for Celtic supporters. Much of Celtic's woes in that sad valley between the heights of the pre-war Exhibition Trophy and the resurrection sparked by the winning of the post-war Coronation Cup were the immediate results of weak management and foolish, autocratic intransigence at director level. The idiotic dismantling of good teams by the loss of essential players in the end-of-season sales was only one area of incompetence. Such incidents badly affected the team's performance and the morale of the club generally, but, more importantly, they had a devastating effect on the support, especially the shabby treatment shown to Delaney. It took the club years to recover its self-esteem, in which time several new brooms were taken to the boardroom. Balancing the books can be counterproductive in football. Skimping on players only starves the spectator of witnessing success on the field and he stays away. The only way for Celtic to woo back their huge following was to win.

On New Year's Day 1943, Rangers beat Celtic 8–1 and I thought the whole world had fallen in on me. I couldn't even look myself in the face when I combed my hair in the mirror. It was such an unnatural result. Motherwell had beaten the great pre-war side 8–0 at Fir Park in 1937, but I had been too young then to take it in. The Rangers result numbed me. In a boy's way, I pretended it didn't matter, but inside I was bleeding. Somehow I felt I had failed with the failure of the team. That's how much results matter to the support. The euphoria that comes with a win is life-giving and happily informs everything you do. A defeat, especially one as shaming as the above, is almost fatal. Our grief lasted a whole week – until the next game.

It seems preposterous that a football match should so impinge on ordinary day-to-day life, but it does, and for more than 13-year-old boys. Grown men deep into their maturity can still behave like boys when their team gets a bad result, because, as far as football is concerned, they are still 13-year-olds. This is the Peter Pan principle. There is a part of a supporter of any club that never really grows up. He is nearly reasonable and almost objective before and after the day of the game, but on the actual day of the match, he is a boy again.

As the war was ended in August 1945, Celtic suddenly sacked Jimmy McStay, even though he had steered the club to wins in the Glasgow Cup in 1941, the Charity Cup in 1943 and was still in charge for the Victory-in-Europe Cup 1945, which was won by a goal from a corner against Queen's Park on VE Day plus one. Three cups might not have been a winning streak, but it was nothing to be scoffed at, either. It did not prevent the good-natured and likeable manager being dispensed with without ceremony in the peremptory manner that was the hallmark of the Celtic board. Poor Jimmy got off a tram at Parkhead Cross on his way to the ground to read on a newspaper placard, 'Jimmy McGrory, New Manager of Celtic'. McStay was astonished but, being Celtic to the core, offered his services to McGrory as scout and was accepted.

On Saturday, 18 August 1945, Celtic played their first home game of the new peacetime. By an extraordinary coincidence, it was against Clyde, the same team they had played in the last peacetime game in September 1939. Clutha was still writing for the *Evening Times*. It was as if nothing had changed. The world had been turned on its head, but Parkhead remained as unreliable as ever. Johnny Paton and John McPhail looked to have set Celtic up for a victory parade, but then, unaccountably, the team seemed to relax on the hour mark and allowed Clyde to equalise through Leslie Johnston, who later became a Celtic player, with the goal of the match. It ended 2–2 and it was a very disappointed support that left the ground that day. Time and again, we threw away winning positions like old socks. As a supporter, I felt as if I were in a football chasm. Looking up, on one side was the implacable face of Maley surrounded by his pre-war Invincibles and on the other side was the diffident image of the gentler McGrory in the middle of his post-war Imponderables. The comparison spoke for itself. They were represented that day by: Miller; Hogg and P. McDonald; Lynch, Mallan and Paterson; Delaney, Kiernan, McLaughlin, McPhail and Paton. I once saw Joe McLaughlin hit a ferocious shot from outside the penalty area that was so hard that it burst the net. It was a shame he didn't do it more often. Everyone, except us boys, knew that McGrory, popular as he was with everyone at the ground, was manager in name only. The real power lay with the directors. It is in this fact, and this alone, that we can look for the reasons for Celtic's patently obvious deterioration.

Now that peace had come, a whole new age had begun and nothing would ever be quite the same again. The bonfires were lit and everyone who had survived the war supporting Celtic hoped the bad times would all disappear with the smoke.

Season 1945–46 was a transitional one in order to 'rebuild' football, which resumed officially on Saturday, 10 August 1946. The putting-on of long trousers marked the official end of my long honeymoon with the sevenpenny gate. By the time I began to shave, I thought it better to shuffle left towards the adult one-and-sixpence gate.

Manhood was thus marked and I was on my way.

Celtic started off the first post-war League season against Morton at Cappielow, so my first adult admission was paid at Greenock. Celtic fielded the following line-up: Miller; Hogg and Milne; W. Gallacher, Corbett and McAuley; Sirrell, Kiernan, Rae, Bogan and Shields. It wasn't an inspiring assembly, but it was the best we could do in those utility times. I was a novice art student at this time and I had the feeling that many of the team had that beginner's look, too. Except, of course, for Willie Miller, who typically saved a penalty.

No matter how badly a team is playing, there is always a quite unreasonable confidence in the supporter that this game will be different. I can remember well the excitement of that sunny day in Greenock when Celtic supporters arriving at the station jumped out of the carriages before the train had stopped on the Cartsdyke platform, such was their eagerness to get to the ground and see their team play.

Oddly enough, it was at Cappielow during the war that I had got Stanley Matthews' autograph. It's funny, I never, ever asked for any Celtic player's autograph. Matthews was in Air Force uniform then. Little did I know that I would soon be in uniform myself. He was the best-known footballer in the world, and I needed heroes at that time. With my father in London, my uncles in the war in the Middle and Far East and both grandfathers dead, I lacked a male presence in my life. The only male influence I had came from 11 assorted footballers playing with a ball on a green space. They were not surrogate parents, not even near relations, but they were something I held on to at that time as a reassurance that things would somehow be normal again. The whole thing about a war, any war, is its abnormality. The goings-on of great nations had been unreal, artificial and false to me, but I had understood totally what was happening between two teams on the football pitch.

CHAPTER THREE

Home and Away

Tommy Gemmell, Left-Back
The best in the world, according to Stein,
Certainly the best that I have ever seen,
With a shot that might have come out of a gun,
A penalty to him was just a bit of fun.

Football is often described as more than a game, a match as more than a sporting occasion. It is an entertainment, a social outing, a political platform, a profit-making enterprise or a money-draining outlet. It is any or all of these, but most of all, to the ordinary supporter, it is a diversion, an escape. This is its true identity and its real value. It offers a lot of people a chance to come together in the moment – and enjoy.

Like the play in the theatre, the poem on the page or the picture on the canvas, it is its own world. It does not come to you, you have to go to it. You have to allow it to embrace you totally for the time span it claims – in this case, 90 minutes of action with extra time if need be. We have to live in its world according to its rules. It provides catharsis, something every theatregoer knows. It is a kind of cleansing, a sort of reliving made available to the individual by the experience of his being one of a mass at a specific event. This is the escape I mean. It is a necessary part of any artistic happening and is the reason, basically, why we have art in the first place; and, believe me, football is an art. It is an athletic ballet with one aim: to score a goal utilising fleetness of foot, quickness of brain, sharpness of eye and a wholehearted courage. Football is an unashamed physical spectacle that can raise the spirits by anaesthetising the problems of the outside world as it affects the ordinary man. It is his best medicine and should be taken as prescribed at least once a week if a good, healthy balance of mind and body is to be maintained.

This was not so easy to do in Glasgow. Like St Paul, I was a citizen of 'no mean city', but I also belonged to a rowdy one. The noise made, though, was only frightening to outsiders; on the inside, we knew all the gesturing and posturing was really harmless. Yes, there were gangs and violence, but they kept it to themselves and we thought it was none of our business anyway.

It was no accident that there was nearly a Red rising in Glasgow in 1917, following the example of Russia, and I know if they'd banned football during the Second World War, as the Government nearly did, the whole male population of Glasgow would have risen in indignation and protest. They needed their football as an outlet, a safety valve, and had they been denied it, they would have taken to the streets with banners. Why did so many Glasgow men join the Republicans in Spain and die in the battles against General Franco in 1937? The answer is that no one has a better sense of what the common man needs than the common man himself.

The game was an integral part of Glasgow's social code. Many would not have known what to do without it. Glasgow has no need of psychiatrists as long as a football match is available. The citizens can get rid of all tensions, aggressions, uncertainties in a day. They can be soothed, refreshed and uplifted if the scoreline is right. No need of pills, potions or remedies; it's all there in the game played out before them. Many people go through life without even shouting out loud – I mean loud – or knowing the leap at the heart that a good goal gives. It's all there in the match. All of life is in it, writ small but felt big. It's a tiny capsule, but it's got everything in it and all it costs is the price of a ticket. For what it offers the mind and body, it's a bargain.

Sometimes the weather took a hand in our football arrangements and, in the winter and early spring, games would be called off for snow, ice or fog. In the big freeze of 1947, a lot of games were 'snowed off'. Because of the fuel crisis, electricity was frequently cut off and we had to resort to candles. I missed my football games, but I loved the nights when the bulbs flickered and we sat in candlelight at home. With no wireless either, when it was really bad, we just had to sit and talk. Dad told us stories of his wartime in London, which he never usually had time to do. My mother would tell us later it was all a pack of lies. She used to refer jokingly to 'the day your daddy won the war'.

Around this time, I made my debut as a professional actor at the Park Theatre, just up from the fountain at Charing Cross in Glasgow. My new career was short-lived because in February 1948 I was called up for National Service in the RAF. The two spells of wartime evacuation had been brief false exiles; in comparison, my two years in the RAF was a serious absence.

I missed some just as serious matters at Celtic Park. In 1947, chairman Tom White died and the hand on the tiller was passed into the gloved leather fist of director Robert Kelly. It was a case of Paradise revisited as Robert was the son of James Kelly, the famous first Celtic centre-half. The son never played because the glove hid a steel hook instead of a hand, and how that iron fist was to show itself in the seasons to come. He sought to make a working partnership with McGrory, but gradually it became clear that the amiable McGrory was more and more the junior, and latterly merely the office boy. It was insensitive to say the least to treat a great servant of the club so cheaply, but McGrory, as ever, kept quiet, hoping the club would turn the corner soon.

There was no doubting Bob Kelly's love of all things Celtic, but there was considerable doubt about his ability to manage the daily running of a football club. This included initiating training methods, deciding team selection, negotiating transfer details and dealing with the thousand and one decisions to be made in the course of a season. Not to mention the diplomatic handling of the crunch of egos, gaggle of temperaments and battery of testosterone-driven talents that make up your average football team. All these matters need the combined attention of coach, trainer and tracksuit manager, but these three persons were now one in the self-appointed godhead, Chairman K.

I was glad I missed most of it. Apart from a short leave after recruit training in the north of England, I never came home until I was demobbed. I grabbed the chance to see the world, from Warrington to Hamburg via London, and soaked up all the foreignness I could. Anywhere other than holiday places like Ayr and Rothesay or Warrenpoint, County Down, and Letterkenny, Donegal, was new territory to me and I was eager to explore. I was a deeply impressionable teenager and took every advantage of the subsidised travel now available by courtesy of His Majesty.

It was an exciting time. The war was not long over and there was a lingering hysteria in the air. Rationing was still in force, but I never noticed. Being part of the occupying forces in a derelict Germany, I could strut with the best of them, even though I was no more than a humble 'erk' in accounts, seconded to NAAFI entertainments. Any Allied uniform was a passport to instant gratification and I soon realised there was much more to Germany than rubble. The first thing that hit me was that I was singularly lacking in culture.

I heard Beethoven's 'Emperor Concerto' played live for the first time, I saw my first opera, *Tristan und Isolde*, and I was smoothly introduced to sex by the widow of a U-boat commander. She was around 30, which I thought very old, but she was cosmopolitan, poised and a lookalike for Ingrid Bergman. It would have been hard for a 19-year-old to find her type around Parkhead. In my eventful German year, I also learned the basics of skiing and riding a horse and was, to a certain degree, sorry to come home again. The only thing that leavened it was that I could get to the football again and that grand old team called Celtic.

In a sense, I had never left, because every week my mother sent me a copy of Glasgow's *Sunday Mail* and I continued my other coming of age, with Celtic, via R.E. Kingsley ('Rex') and his sly, knowing football comments on the sports pages. In this, I was only doing what many Scotsmen were doing while servicing the Berlin Airlift. Where two or more Glaswegians are gathered together, the talk is football, and I soon got it round to Celtic and the latest result.

It could be said that I left my brother, Jim, with the club as a deposit until my return. As a 16-year-old he was training with Celtic and it was expected he would sign in due course. Meantime, he continued playing centre-half with Strathclyde Juniors, whose ground we could see from our window in Williamson Street. On Tuesdays and Thursdays, he was training with the likes of Bobby Collins and Charlie Tully and was reunited with a fellow Boys' Guild footballer from Shettleston Hill, one Tommy Docherty.

Jimmy Hogan, a famous coach, was brought from Hungary to help give the team a new approach, which involved creating playing areas in the pitch and assigning specific duties to particular players, illustrating all of it on a blackboard. He had a very mixed response. The older players remembered Tommy McInally's response when manager Maley tinkered for a time with blackboard tactics. 'Fair enough,' said Tommy, 'but whit's the other team daein' a' this time?'

Celtic were doing not badly, but, by their own high standards, not great. They still had only three players of any class. The Keeper of the

Gate, Willie Miller, was still there and he had been joined by Charlie Tully from Belfast Celtic and Bobby Evans, a Thornliebank Methodist who played junior for St Anthony's. During the war, I had seen his first game for Celtic at Coatbridge against Albion Rovers when Jock Stein was their centre-half. Bobby Evans was at outside-left that day. All I can remember is his bright red hair and tireless energy.

I gather that much of this was used up in squabbles during training with teammate Tully, which on one occasion at least led to a stand-up fight in the dressing-room. Not that it mattered, really; such explosions of temperament are nearly inevitable when tensions run high. The puritan Evans deplored Tully's lack of work ethic. Evans was all go and Tully would never go unless he had to, but both men (in their different ways) produced results on the field, the latter to the highest level. So their venial sins must be forgiven.

I felt something of a change in myself returning to the Celtic scene after two years away. I had gone away a boy and come back a man, but to my surprise nothing had changed. The team played with a volatility akin to Partick Thistle at the best, brilliant one week and dreadful the next and every shade of ineffectiveness in between. However, what was most surprising was that my own reaction was still that of a boy.

For all my determination to build on my German aesthetic and other discoveries, I had retained the Celtic addiction at its full power. I had my daily dose via the *Daily Record* and my weekly fix in the *Sunday Mail*, plus general gossip with my pals. I had an insatiable need to scale the heights and plumb the depths according to how the game went on the day. My first thought on waking on a Saturday was 'Where's the game today?' and my second was 'How do I get there?'

Nonetheless, I knew I had to build on my Hanover inspiration. I must get an education. I had worked in the theatre before joining up, but I had been no more than a paid amateur. I needed to learn the trade. So I enrolled at the new College of Drama within the old Athenaeum and matriculated at Glasgow University to take a BA in drama. I attended orchestral concerts at St Andrew's Halls and plays at the Citizens Theatre, determined to do everything that would feed the culture buds developing in me.

One thing I didn't do was look for a U-boat commander's widow. Instead, I became engaged to a very nice Glasgow girl I met at St Michael's Youth Club in Parkhead. We planned to marry when I graduated. Terry was a very good hockey player and wasn't interested in football, never mind Celtic, but I was sure I could win her round. I was wrong. We never married, but that was not because she didn't support Celtic. However, I was then free to return to my first love.

Because it is without doubt a love, this Celtic thing, a vast group hug standing on the terracing with the extended family that is that mass they call the support. Certainly, you might have to tolerate an occasional roughness, but at heart you know that the mix comes right out of the ingredients you share with everyone standing around you. You're comfortable there, you're easy and all you need to make it perfect is a good result.

We got that occasionally, like when John McPhail won the 1951 Scottish Cup for us against Motherwell with a beautifully chipped goal in the first quarter of an hour. Big John, or 'Hooky' as we called him, was captain that day. What better way to lead than by example? It was our first national silverware since 1937. It had been a long time between cups. The team could only go on to better things with talents like McPhail, Tully, Collins and young George 'Sonny' Hunter, a goalkeeper who promised to become another Willie Miller. Sadly, after a sensational start as a game-saver in the Miller tradition, he contracted TB and his form was never quite the same again. He was transferred to Derby County in 1954 and played out a limp career, descending to Matlock Town by 1966. George was very unlucky. He ought to have been a world-beater, but whom the gods love, their career dies early. Especially goalkeepers.

It can be a rough old game, the fitba'. A typical supporter's reaction may be that of an exasperated Celtic adherent at one match at Celtic Park when Jackie Gallacher played his heavy-footed, gangling centre-forward style in a team that promised much but rarely delivered. Gallacher was capable of going through a whole defence on his own in scoring, as I saw him do one Saturday against Queen's Park at Parkhead. He kicked off, took the return and dribbled his way through the whole QP team before scoring an amazing goal. However, on this particular day, he was not at his best. 'Come oan, Gallacher, fur God's sake, ye're playin' fur Celtic,' yelled the disgruntled supporter.

'Play fur us? He disnae even support us!' replied another voice wearily. Actually, the second man was quite right. Jackie supported Rangers – and still does.

I was now a first-year drama student and just getting used to the rigours of peacetime Glasgow again after the serviceman's luxury of war-ravaged Germany. Little did I know that in 1951 the stage was already set for unexpected triumph, and not only in the Scottish Cup.

Celtic have made a habit of winning invitational competitions. These special cup victories are a very proud record and a mark of a collective determination. In 1902, the Cup to be played for was the 1901 Glasgow Exhibition Cup won by Rangers when they beat Celtic in the final. The victors then decided to put the trophy up for competition to raise money for the 1902 Ibrox Disaster Fund – 25 people had been killed and hundreds more injured when part of the stand collapsed during a Scotland–England match. The teams invited to compete were Rangers, Celtic, Sunderland and Everton, the winners and runners-up of their respective leagues. The Scottish teams won through to make it an Old Firm final, which Celtic won thanks to a Jimmy Quinn hat-trick. The victory crowned Celtic as unofficial champions of Britain and they carried the cup back to Parkhead with proper pride.

The 1938 Exhibition Trophy was a clear-cut win against the other seven leading clubs of the day, again at Ibrox. Celtic were surprise winners, beating Everton in extra time by a 15-yard volley from the diminutive Johnny Crum, who danced a jig behind the goal to the delight of the Celtic supporters.

The 1951 Festival of Britain was a nationwide centenary celebration initiated to echo the Prince Albert Festival of 1851 and at the same time to intimate to the world that Britain had finally recovered from the Second World War. Glasgow's contribution to this event was the Glasgow Corporation's St Mungo Cup, open to all Scottish Division A clubs, with a quaich awarded to B Division teams (won, incidentally, by Dumbarton). Celtic eventually won through to the final of their competition, despite a replay required against Clyde after a wonderful 4–4 draw at Firhill, which I think was one of the tensest and most thrilling games I ever watched. I remember the whole summer was sunny that year but the perspiration running down my face that afternoon was not only caused by meteorological factors. The replay was the next night at Firhill and, despite the usual heroics from ex-Celt Willie Miller in goal, Celtic won 4–1, with a double from Fallon and goals from Peacock and Walsh. After beating Raith Rovers in the semi-final, they qualified to meet Aberdeen at Hampden.

The following side was selected to play that day: Hunter; Haughney and Rollo; Evans, Mallan and Baillie; Collins, Walsh, Fallon, Peacock and Tully. The mere recital of their names brings back pictures from so many long-ago Saturdays. I was at Hampden that day and I remember being annoyed that Sean Fallon, a forthright Irish full-back of no great subtlety, was again selected at centre-forward. I considered him a claymore rather than the rapier I preferred. Then again, his was the style of the great Jimmy Quinn and the even greater McGrory, match-winners both. So who was I to complain? Besides, it lined him up with another pair of Irishmen, or rather Ulstermen, Bertie Peacock and the redoubtable Tully, so there should have been no problems of communication. We all knew that Sean was a favourite of Bob Kelly's and that was an end of the matter. Unfortunately, Fallon didn't see much of the ball in the first half, and when Hunter collided badly with a goalpost Benny Yorston put the ball into an empty net to put Aberdeen one up.

It got worse when the head-bandaged Hunter couldn't stop a long-range volley from ex-Celt Tommy Bogan and Aberdeen were two up. I could feel my heart sinking, but I reckoned without Charlie Tully. I should have known. He wandered over to the right in search of the ball and, almost on half-time, he got a shy and impertinently threw it against the retreating back of Davie Shaw, the Aberdeen left full-back, and referee Mowat awarded a corner. Shaw protested strongly, but Tully had already run to take the corner; he crossed the ball in perfectly and Fallon put it in the net right on the whistle. I can still hear the crowd's gasp at Tully's impudence and its outcome.

In the second half, it was all Celtic. Tully, fired up, ran amok, sending Fallon through to score again and setting Jimmy Walsh up for the winner. It was a Tully exhibition and I was delighted to see yet another all-time great at the peak of his form. There was a silly and trivial controversy after the game when Celtic discovered that one of the leaping salmon that served as handles to the cup had come off. In the course of further investigation by a silversmith, it was found that the cup, far from being brand new, was a second-hand clean-up dating from 1912, when Provan Gas Works beat the Glasgow Police in a local competition. It was quite laughable and no one laughed louder than Charlie Tully.

I recommenced my theatrical career in June 1953 with the Wilson Barrett Touring company in *The School for Scandal*, but I found it hard to concentrate on rehearsals because Celtic had just won the highly prestigious Coronation Cup, staged to coincide with celebrations for the coronation of Queen Elizabeth II of England or I of Scotland, depending on which side of the border you viewed the new television's pictures.

John Bonnar was our new goalkeeper and Jock Stein, signed from Llanelli in December 1951, was now at centre-half. Bobby Collins had come in on the right wing, but the most important change was at centre-forward, where Neilly Mochan, signed from Middlesbrough only three days before, was rushed into the side for the quarter-final against Arsenal at Hampden. The Arsenal players, having watched Celtic play in the Charity Cup final, were unimpressed and considered their match against the Scots a walkover.

Celtic's form had not been good in the League and they knew themselves, on current form, not to be in the same league as Arsenal, literally and metaphorically, but their pride had been hurt and they were determined to at least make a game of it. They ran onto the park with teeth clenched. Arsenal opened in leisurely and arrogant fashion until Evans intercepted an over-confident pass and sent a long ball forward to Walsh, whose shot was just wide of the post. This gave Celtic an unaccustomed confidence and they surged forward, cheered on by the 60,000 crowd, of which I was one, roaring with all my new-found actor's projection. Bobby Collins scored the only goal of the game directly from a corner kick, thanks to the notorious 'Hampden swirl', as the wind on the pitch was called. The scene was now set for the semi-final against Manchester United. I remember I skipped rehearsals to see this one. I was just one of a 73,000 crowd.

Celtic stormed the United goal for the first 20 minutes without success, until Tully took a hand and set Peacock up for a thundering volley and the first goal. There was no more scoring in the first half and I was sure United would come out in the second half with all the big guns, like Viollet, Rowley and Pearson, blazing. They did, but it was that man Mochan who did it again, with another deftly delivered ball from our Charlie. He ran through from the centre circle and slipped the ball past Crompton in the Manchester goal. Jack Rowley, the Manchester centre-forward, did score near the end, but Celtic held out and we were in the final. I was under contract at the Citizens Theatre, but I wasn't in their current play, which meant I had Saturdays free and was therefore able to see the game.

This was at Hampden on 20 May against Hibernian, who had demolished a good Newcastle side. The Edinburgh club at that time featured the most feared forward line in Scottish football, the legendary 'Famous Five': Smith, Johnstone, Reilly, Turnbull and Ormond. Gordon Smith on the right wing was a real star, as was 'Last Minute' Reilly, so called because of his propensity to score important goals in the last minute of the match, most famously against England at Wembley. Ormond was no slouch, either, and was to be a Scotland manager after his playing days.

Celtic had only one change, Willie Fernie for Tully, who had pulled a muscle in the semi-final. Tully was irreplaceable, but if you had to, Fernie was the next best thing. An exquisite ball player, he was to make his claim to greatness in the future. Meantime, he ran out in front of 117,000 spectators that day at Hampden. I was unable to get in at the Celtic end because of overcrowding, and the police sent us all round the gates to the Hibs end, where I just scraped in. Luckily, we shared the same colours. If not close family, we were very near cousins.

It was a long pass from Stein to Fernie and a flick on to Mochan that brought the first goal, a drive from 30 yards, just on the half-hour mark. The Celtic support went wild and I found it hard to be quiet at the other end. Just on the interval, Gordon Smith cut through the Celtic defence and his chip gave Reilly the opportunity to equalise, but Bonnar dived to save, and Celtic hearts started beating again.

The second half was one of the longest I had ever to survive and the entire 45 minutes was a shameless testimony to goalkeeping at its finest. John Bonnar was superb and the ex-Arbroath custodian could only be described as inspired. The hitherto erratic goalkeeper had the game of his life. The clever Hibernian forwards created chance after chance, but Bonnar, not the tallest of goalkeepers, was equal to everything they rained in on him – direct shots, crosses, headers close in – and on the only occasion he was beaten, McPhail was there to head off the line. Totally against the run of play, and two minutes from the end, Evans released Fernie to lay it in the path of Walsh for Celtic's second goal. Celtic were obviously destined to win that day. Thanks to 'that bloody Bonnar', as Willie Ormond called him, they did, and the Coronation Cup joined the rest of the silver in the Celtic Park Presidential Room, formerly the Trophy Room.

In season 1953–54, they won the League and Scottish Cup double, the first since 1913–14, and I hardly saw a match of it. After a whole boyhood of living in hope, with only tales of the Exhibition Trophy to sustain me, I was deprived of the sight of Celtic as victors because I had married a fellow student, the most beautiful girl in the Glasgow College of Drama, Sheila Cowan, from Fife, and moved with her to Bristol and the Old Vic Theatre, there to be 'Englished'. This was a necessary part of my career progress, but the occasional glimpse of Bristol City or Bristol Rovers when I didn't have a matinee did nothing to compensate for what I was missing of my beloved Celtic in their new-found pomp. Sheila had hardly heard of Celtic; she preferred badminton. Her family came from Kelty, which was not far from Cardenden, where John Thomson had been raised. When I told her this, she said, 'Who?' I didn't even bother to answer.

Being in the West Country, there was no *Sunday Mail* every week as there had been in Germany, my mother having thought I had grown out of such childishness now that I was a married man. Why didn't women then understand these things? The truth was the Celtic fever was even worse the longer I was away from Glasgow. Denied the comfort of at least the weekly results and comments, I felt the full pangs of withdrawal symptoms. This was a condition I had to learn to endure and I applied myself to it heroically albeit, in the end, vainly. The club was too much in me, it went too deep, to discard in a moment. I had to find ways of maintaining contact, however tenuous, until I could get back to a proper physical relationship once more. I needed to hear the grunts and see the sweat and feel that thud at the heart – my heart.

So, by way of radio and the back pages of English newspapers, conversations with itinerant Glaswegians and phone calls home to Glasgow, I managed to keep up to date. Jim was now playing for Portsmouth, following a misunderstanding with Celtic prompted by an everyday encounter between my uncle Phil in Baillieston and Jimmy Gribben, the well-known Celtic scout, who lived in the area, when they met in the street one day.

'How's young Jim daein'?' asks Jimmy. 'He wisnae at the Park last week.'

'No, he wisnae,' says Phil. 'He's doon at Portsmouth the noo.'

'Portsmouth? No' wi' Pompey, I hope?'

'I think so. They asked him tae come doon and hae a look, that's a'. Their scout, Hugh Bone, I think it wis, wis ay aboot the hoose.'

'Aye, I heard that,' muttered Jimmy.

'Aye, Jim's there the noo wi' Tom an' Mary. His mum and dad, like.'

'Aye, I jist hope we'll see the boy back. He could be a guid yin.'

'Aye, right enough,' says Uncle Phil.

That was all that was said, but it got back to Celtic Park much enlarged no doubt, and when Jim returned to training a week later Mr McGrory was waiting for him. He didn't stand on ceremony.

'I hear you were wi' Pompey last week.'

'Aye,' said Jim innocently. 'It was great.' Jim was thinking of the sun on the south coast and the free holiday he had given his parents.

'Did you sign anything?'

Jim had to think for a minute. 'Yes, I did –'

'WHIT?'

'It was just a –'

'Never mind whit it wis. You were morally bound to us. Right, that's it. Collect your boots and clear off.'

'But, Mr McGrory –'

It was no use. The normally easy-going Celtic manager abruptly ended the interview. That was how Jim was lost to Celtic. It broke his heart. All he had signed at Portsmouth was a receipt for hotel accommodation.

Never mind, he went on to enjoy a few seasons with Portsmouth, who not many seasons before had been English champions and were a power in football. He later rejected a move to play in New Zealand, whose Football Association was then run by an old-time Celtic supporter, and chose to move to York City, where he established himself as captain. Towards the end of his career, he joined a Greek team in New York before transferring to an Italian team in Toronto, where he finally hung up his boots, at the age of 40, and opened a pub. Jim had a full life in sport, even though he didn't really do justice to the boyhood talent that Celtic saw. It might have been different had he stayed with them. Every Catholic boy in Glasgow and the west of Scotland, in all Scotland even, with any football talent at all hoped to pull on a Celtic jersey. It was almost a categorical imperative and Celtic took it for granted that it had first call on this great surge of talent available annually. Rangers felt the same about players of the Protestant persuasion, which gave them a distinct numerical advantage when it came to potential manpower.

I still can't get rid of the feeling of regret that I didn't see Jim play in a Celtic strip, even if it were only to see him as a proxy me. I've had a lot of good moments as a player in the theatre, as a playwright in my study, even as a playboy in the big, outside world but I would have given all of that to say, 'I once played for Celtic.' I realise that this is only romantic nostalgia for the days of my youth, but for me it is more of a 'lostalgia', a word coined by my friend, Bob Adams. It is no less real for all that. There have, after all, been many 'one-game' players in Celtic's history, ranging from the famous Walter Arnott of Queen's Park, against Third Lanark in 1895, to my namesake Chic Cairney, against Raith Rovers in 1949, around the same time I might have seen Jim play at Celtic Park.

Who knows, he might have been in the first team by 1955 when Celtic ceded the League Championship to Aberdeen. This prompted the Celtic supporters' sporting welcome to the Dons at Parkhead on 16 April, with an extended ovation that startled the Aberdonians with its unrestrained generosity.

This was not the first time the Celtic support was to win plaudits for its sportsmanship in defeat and, as one of them, I am particularly proud of that fact. I wasn't there on that particular Celtic Park occasion to see Celtic beat the new champions 2–1, both goals scored by Hooky McPhail, back at centre-forward, but I was gratified to read about it in Bristol, where, only a couple of months before, I had made my debut as a father during a run of *The Merchant of Venice*. It was a beautiful girl, so we couldn't name her John McPhail Cairney. We called her Jennifer.

Big John, once our leading light, was now in decline. The team was discovering a new spirit under the determined captaincy of Jock Stein, but for all the promise of this phase it gave me one of my biggest Celtic disappointments. I had now moved to London, having got a swanky agent and the offer of a line of TV work. Sheila and I found a flat, or rather half a house, in Buckhurst Hill in Essex and for the first time had a television set. I remember the first thing I saw on it was young Shirley Bassey from Cardiff singing pop songs the way Celtic fans now sing 'The Fields of Athenry' – slowly and with feeling.

The great news was that I was able to see the Bhoys play live courtesy of the BBC on the Saturday of the 1955 Scottish Cup final against Clyde; the match was relayed from Hampden, since it didn't clash with the FA Cup final played two weeks later. I couldn't wait for this first-ever televising of the event. I switched on and sat back. Nothing. I thought there must have been a sudden snowstorm in Glasgow on that April afternoon, for the screen was filled with snowflakes. I could hear the voice of Kenneth Wolstenholme, the English commentator, but I couldn't see anything. I jumped up angrily and, like a true Luddite, banged the top with my fist and pummelled the sides. Nothing happened, the storm grew worse and I bellowed in frustration. At this, Sheila told me to be quiet, I would waken the baby. Fearing a worse storm than silent snowflakes, I grabbed my jacket and ran all the way to the pub at the crossroads and arrived to hear from the apathetic barman that 'Keltic' were leading 1–0 at half-time.

'Who scored?' I asked eagerly.

'God knows, some Scotch fella, I suppose. What'll it be, then?'

Over my beer, I gave my full attention to the commentary and learned that Walsh had scored from a Fernie pass, that Collins was the star man so far and that Clyde were lucky to be only a goal down. I drank down my beer and felt well content, which surprised me. I didn't drink beer. I was a Guinness man. What did it matter? For the moment, my Scottish Cup was full and running over.

I don't know what was said in the Celtic dressing-room at the interval, but for some reason they came out with Fernie and Walsh drawn back, which pushed Evans and Peacock further back. Perhaps the intention was to defend their lead. To me, the hand of chairman Kelly could be seen here and it wasn't a winning one. So it proved. The defence, marshalled by Stein, defended well, but the rearranged forward line was inept and the crowd knew it. They became quieter and quieter, almost willing a Clyde goal as a protest against the changes.

It came in the last minute from a corner, when Bonnar, blinded by the late-afternoon sun, mistimed his jump and the ball went in between Mike Haughney and Frank Meechan on the goal line. They couldn't believe it, nor could Bonnar, nor the Celtic supporters, nor this lone viewer in the pub drinking his beer. I ordered another one to drown my sorrows and the next thing I heard was the barman. 'Ain't you got no home to go to?'

When I got home, Sheila didn't even ask the score. All she said was, 'You smell of beer.' I sighed and took myself off to bed.

I had a feeling of foreboding about the replay. Even from 500 miles away, I could sense that the initiative had passed to Clyde, who were cock-a-hoop about avoiding defeat in the first game. In that strange way that happens in football, the psychological advantage is often worth a goal start and Clyde came out in midweek feeling they had already won. Inexplicably, McPhail was at inside-left to accommodate bulldog Fallon and, astonishingly, Walsh was moved to outside-right, displacing the hero of the first game, Bobby Collins, who was dropped. No one could understand why potential winners like Collins and Mochan were not played.

It appeared that it was all Celtic for most of the game, and while they perspired for corner after corner and while shot after shot hit the post or went over the bar, Clyde were inspired to hold out until Tommy Ring broke away to net in a goalmouth melee what proved to be the only goal of the game. Ring, who was in my year at St Mungo's, put in the final touch in a replay that Celtic ought to have won. When Tommy went, as usual, to have Sunday lunch with his mother and the family a few days later, his brothers, all fanatical Celtic supporters, wouldn't speak to him, nor did they for the rest of the week.

By this time, I was in films and under contract to the Rank Organisation. I had to read about Celtic whenever I could and wherever I was sent on location. It was difficult to get the *Sunday Mail* in the South of France, where I was filming *Ill Met By Moonlight* with Dirk Bogarde. He had gone to school at Allan Glen's in Glasgow before the war but had no interest in football, even less in Glasgow. 'I hated the place,' he said, so I never bothered mentioning Celtic again and kept to the script. Not every film star at the time had Dirk's antipathy to sport. The late, lovely John Gregson, with whom I appeared in *Miracle in Soho*, filmed entirely at Pinewood Studios in Buckinghamshire the following year, was a Liverpool fan but had a natural soft spot for Celtic. John was a good Catholic, whose two sons were at Ampleforth, a famous Catholic public school. Everything in him pointed to a Celtic bias. I also became friends with a set rigger who once played for Chelsea. He loved to chat on football matters, so my balance of life was restored. He was an Arsenal fan. I never, ever told him that my second football team was Tottenham Hotspur.

The phenomenon of the twentieth century was the rise of the moving picture from a sideshow novelty to the prime source of entertainment for the masses, much as television is today. What is less considered is how professional football has had much the same evolutionary development, from a public school playing field's diversion into what is acknowledged to be the world's favourite spectator sport. Although more people may go fishing than play football, more spectators watch football than any other sporting activity.

What is it about it that attracts these millions? First of all, it is accessible. You can play it anywhere there is a piece of level ground and room to put up goalposts or put down jackets at either end. You don't even need a referee; all you need is a round ball and 22 youths, male or female, who can run about and will agree to the basic rule, which is not to touch the ball or any opposing player with your hands and to put the ball into the opponent's net. This is why it is known as 'the simple game'. Another reason for its total appeal, and why it has survived today as an entertainment industry, is that it is truly cosmopolitan. You can easily believe that, if we ever get to Mars, it will be a football that will be kicked into space, not a golf ball. Who knows, in the far, far future, there may even be a Cosmic Cup. The game will always continue to grow. It's like the ball itself, it has no edges, it just goes round and round. Wherever a game is played, you will always find somebody watching, and you can take it that they will have a bias towards one side or another.

That is possibly the biggest fascination, that we can choose our own sides to play not only for themselves but for us watching. They are our proxy figures. Players ought not to take that responsibility lightly, for they can not only make our day but change our lives by one thunderbolt shot or soaring header. We can carry that one sporting moment in our minds for ever and savour it again and again as, in Wordsworth's phrase, 'emotion recollected in tranquillity'.

In the following decade, Celtic appeared unsuccessfully in two Scottish Cup finals, in 1956 and 1961, when they lost to Hearts and Dunfermline respectively. Meantime, they took their revenge on Clyde in the 1955 Glasgow Cup competition, when they won 4–0 at a canter, with Collins restored and Mochan scoring a hat-trick. Lessons had been learned, but would they be remembered? Celtic went on to meet Rangers in the final, which they drew 1–1, hitching up their shorts again for yet another final replay. This time, Fallon was in his rightful place at left-back and the forward line now read: Eric Smith, Fernie, Jim Sharkey, Collins and Mochan.

The high-scoring game (5–3) that resulted was the consequence of the contest between two clever, contrasting centre-forwards – Sharkey for Celtic and Don Kitchenbrand for Rangers – playing against two tactically aware centre-halfs in Stein and big George Young. It was the traditional contest between youth and age, between innocent energy and calm control, and on this day the young bloods won out. Kitchenbrand scored one of Rangers' three and Sharkey two of Celtic's five to win the game and the Glasgow Cup.

During this period, I saw Celtic games while I was on family visits to Glasgow. There was always a standout player in the team, a glint of gold among the brass. Jim Sharkey was such a player. He was an original. Whenever he got the ball, he would try for the unexpected. Yet Sharkey was a puzzle. An exceptional player in every respect, he was lithe, smart and comfortable with the ball at his feet, as all great players are. He began his career, like many East Enders, in half-a-crown street games on any patch of open ground, so he was professional early. He was spotted by Celtic and farmed out as a provisional signing to Rutherglen Glencairn as an inside-forward but was signed up fully by Celtic at the end of 1954. However, he made his first real impression as the latest in a long line of post-war Celtic centre-forwards. He might have been the answer to their prayers, but whatever it is that bedevils wonderful players, whatever jinx haunts the hugely talented, Jim Sharkey never really got the reward his gifts deserved. He was a Celtic natural. A Bridgeton boy, he was steeped in the club's ethos and grew up in the Sacred Heart parish, an area that reaches right back to the very beginnings of the Celtic story. His idol was Gerry Padua McAloon, a wartime Celt, also from Bridgeton, who was the occasional gleam in a very dull forward line. From him, Jim learned the famous double shuffle, a much-practised gambit that he was to make his own with Celtic.

Sharkey had everything that a footballer needs to make it in the big time: style, confidence, ease on the ball and the impudence to 'play' at the game with panache, much like McInally but with twice that great player's application. He was in fact a precursor of George Best, but without that player's offstage peccadilloes. In short, he had it in him to become an all-time Celtic great, but there was some intangible element in him that militated against his full development. This is seen in so many players, but in Sharkey's case it was highly marked.

The cause may have been a smash in the face that he had in a game against Greenock Morton in early 1956. It was so serious that the injury caused severe blackouts, which lasted for months. He came back eventually to full training and it seemed that he might win his way back to his old flair, and the Celtic support, already recognising in him the genuine article, hoped that it would be so.

However, a purported misdemeanour by Sharkey at Seamill, where Celtic normally prepared for big games, was reported to chairman Kelly. Jim was immediately censured and dropped for the upcoming

Scottish Cup final against Hearts. His place was incongruously taken by full-back Mike Haughney. This haphazard, if not bizarre, method of team selection was often at the cost of the side's effectiveness, and never more so than in this case. Stein, the mainspring of the side, was injured, as was Collins, the dynamo of the forward line, so the latter's place was taken by an unknown Billy Craig and Evans went to centre-half with Haughney stepping in where Sharkey should have been. This make-do-and-mend team was only announced to the players hours before the kick-off, so they had little time to get used to its irregularity. As a result, they went onto the field untypically uncertain and hoping that their raw talent would suffice.

This was a big ask against the Hearts forward line, which contained Conn, Bauld and Wardhaugh, a deadly trio at the best of times. Urged on by Dave MacKay and John Cumming at wing-half, the famous three persecuted the unfamiliar Celtic defence at will, but it was Hearts winger Crawford who scored in the twentieth minute and stunned most of the 133,000 crowd. They had waited a long time to see their team go west into the spotlight and now they were enjoying it enormously. Crawford scored again to increase their lead, due to Bauld's freedom to move out to the left wing at will and cross for the outside-left, who had moved inside to score. This was the area where Haughney, the full-back, should have been, instead of at inside-right in the forward line, where Sharkey's place was. It was a big price to pay for a small fault. Celtic had lost a second successive Scottish Cup final.

Sharkey tried to make his peace at Celtic's post-match dinner, but Kelly refused to listen to him and Jim knew that his days were numbered. He was transferred to Airdrie in November 1957 and one can only say that Airdrie's gain was certainly Celtic's loss. He was a sensation at Broomfield, and Airdrieonians referred to him as the 'Airdrie Tully'. He gave his Celtic colleagues a hard time when he played against them, but, being the likeable fellow he was, he was cheered by the Celtic support for his efforts as much as by Airdrie's fans.

Thanks to Sharkey, the Waysiders reached second place, if only for a brief time, in the Scottish League. By now, Sharkey was restless and had begun the great dance down that happens to players of his temperament. He eventually left Airdrie because they apparently accused him of not trying in a game against Celtic. To add to his worries, he broke his ankle playing for Raith Rovers against St Mirren and missed the rest of the season. He retired to become a porter at

Pembroke College, Cambridge, an untypical end to an untypical career, but then everything about him was unexpected. He was atypical but no worse for that. His career pattern was eccentric but not erratic. A trivial error, or rather one man's reaction to it, took him off a pathway that would surely have taken him to the stratosphere.

I have given this space to Sharkey, despite his unfortunate fading away, because he was potentially a true Celtic great, one who was not really given his time. He was not a Kelly Babe, he was a Kelly victim.

CHAPTER FOUR

Sing a Song of Celtic

Malcolm MacDonald, Right-Half
The finest all-rounder on Celtic's books,
With delicate touch and quiet good looks,
He could play well wherever selected,
A Celtic great, as Fate had directed.

No Celtic supporter can ever forget Jock Weir's final-game hat-trick at Dundee on 17 April 1948, which saved Celtic FC from the threat of relegation for the first time in their history. It was one of their most famous victories, but it was also the day of their greatest shame. They had avoided a great humiliation. The relief itself was akin to that of another Mafeking to those of us exiled from Scotland. I was in training at RAF Padgate in Lancashire at the time and that night I went into the NAAFI and got very drunk. I ended up standing on top of a table singing every Celtic song I knew. I was glad to be rid of the tension, but I didn't know I could sing.

Cut to January 1956: the *Daily Herald*, a Labour Party organ, carries a headline in its show-business column stating 'John Cairney, the new voice of 1956', and in the same year a columnist in *Woman* magazine expressed the view that my singing voice had in it 'all the warmth of Italian sunshine'. If you are surprised to read such things, believe me, I was astonished, but then I was completely taken aback by how quickly 1956 and 1957 were turned into two years of song. It happened thus.

I was cast as a Malayan student, Jan Vidal, in a film for Rank called *Windom's Way*, starring Peter Finch. In one scene, I had to address a huge crowd of other supposed Malayans in the back lot at Pinewood. They were made up entirely of waiters from London: Thai, Chinese,

Japanese, Korean, Jamaicans and a few real Malayans (anyone who didn't need dark-brown make-up applied the way I did). According to script, I was inciting them to rebellion, but the extras were more inclined to break into song than into revolt. I often joined them at lunch and that's how I met Sammy San.

Sammy, a slight, slim Malayan, brought his guitar to the shoot every day. At the first chance, it would be out and he would be strumming chords softly and expertly. Often he would play his traditional melodies and I was able to add lyrics to these on the spot; that way, we would attract a little ring of listeners in the break times. One day, one of these was one of the film's producers. Unknown to us, he got the sound man to make a tape recording of one of our improvised duets. Sammy and I could both harmonise and his light tones suited my ruined Irish tenor.

Some time later, this recording was played by the producer at a party in London. It was heard there by Jeannie Carson, a charming singer/actress with whom I had worked at Elstree on a film for American television. Jeannie was intrigued and asked to have a copy so she might play it to a friend of hers, Norman Newell, who happened to be an A&R manager at HMV. This inadvertent networking is how whole careers are made, and that was how Sammy and I found ourselves at the Abbey Road Studios in Hampstead one evening, in the company of Geoff Love and a couple of top-flight guitarists, making an extended-play record of four of our own songs.

Its release in 1957 led to a lot of unexpected engagements. I was on *Top of the Pops* singing 'Alone' with Ted Heath and his orchestra. Because of the complicated orchestration, I couldn't hear my entry. So I took my cue from the bass player and somehow we managed to get through it before a studio audience of apathetic teenagers. At the end, I had the feeling that Cliff Richard was quite secure with his Shadows.

Nevertheless, Sammy and I did have some success at live shows, and I was once recognised in Soho after we had been interviewed on the *Tonight* show with Cliff Michelmore, but the BBC preferred Robin Hall and Jimmy MacGregor, who followed soon afterwards and stayed on the programme for years. Sammy and I were offered a musical tour nationwide, but the very thought of singing the four same songs every night appalled me, so I decided to take early retirement from pop singing.

After this unplanned musical interlude, which at least got me membership of the Songwriters' Guild as a lyric-writer, I got back to acting in films. I learned to ride a Vespa to play a murderer for Anglo-Amalgamated in *Marriage of Convenience* and then went into army uniform to be a singing private soldier for Associated British in *Girls in Arms*, in which I sang to Carole Lesley, so the recording session paid off. One way or another, I just moved from job to job through the late '50s, which pleased my agent but interfered enormously with my keeping up with things Celtic.

Wherever I was, I would make sure I heard the Saturday teatime football results on BBC radio. This meant listening in from Maidenhead, where we now lived. By a kind of osmosis that all genuine football enthusiasts will know, I heard enough during my new-found prosperity to keep my Celtic appetite whetted and eager for more. For instance, I learned in May 1956 that they had signed yet another new centre-forward, Billy McPhail. I immediately saw him as I remembered him, tall and aloof and smartly dressed, in the corner of our St Mungo's playground. He appeared to me then as somebody beyond my standing. A sixth former belongs to another world from that of a scruffy second-year underachiever whose only school abilities were drawing Spitfires on the blackboard and reciting Celtic football teams of the past.

Billy was captain of the 1st XI and looked it. Even then, he had all the hallmarks of the successful athlete: lithe, confident, good-looking, neatly dressed; in all, the boy most likely to succeed. All this, however, was nothing compared to his relation to big brother John. This gave Billy in our eyes the status of a near-deity in the playground, an image not at all diminished when he left school to join Queen's Park and train as a hairdresser. Because of his skill with the comb, he was known in the Celtic team when he joined them as 'Teasy-Weasy', a fashionable figure in the trade at the time. This didn't deter Billy from becoming accepted in the side. He brought with him a reputation as a goal-scorer, not only with the Spiders but with Clyde, whom he joined next. Now it was third time lucky, and he was with Celtic, where he should have been in the first place.

Here he would soon find himself teamed with Sammy Wilson, at his shoulder at inside-left. Sammy was imported by chairman Kelly in May 1957 on a free from St Mirren. Kelly always had an eye for a bargain and he quickly snapped him up. It did not take the former Renfrew Junior long to make a good pairing with McPhail. The latter's ability to head-flick a ball into Wilson's path in the penalty area drew quick dividends in the goal department and the pair were included in the team for Celtic's defence of the League Cup. The 3–0 victory over Partick Thistle in the replayed final of October 1956 had been Celtic's first success in the competition.

Dating from its beginnings in the wartime Southern League Cup, with its sectional structure allowing for four finalists, one from each section, to fight it out after playing each other twice, the League Cup offered a losing club a second chance to progress to the final play-off rounds. Celtic were never happy with this formula and, prior to season 1956–57, had rarely succeeded in getting out of their section. Now, for the second time running, they had reached the final, where they would face their nemesis, Rangers.

Little did they realise that this game, scheduled for Saturday, 19 October 1957, was destined to be hailed as one of the greatest in the annals of the club's history and that the players involved in it would, as a result, enter collectively into the pantheon of the Celtic great. It came to be known in folklore as 'Hampden in the Sun'. There were songs written to commemorate the occasion, there was a whole book written about it, but such was the scale of the thing that only an operatic score by Verdi or a symphony by Mahler would do it justice, and it would take a Shakespeare to put it into words.

This is by no means fanciful. I have it from several Celtic supporters who saw the game, level-headed professional men all, who have declared solemnly to me that they were sure that day they had died and gone to heaven. The bare facts are these: Celtic and Rangers met at Hampden Park to contest the final of the 12th Scottish League Cup and the teams selected were as follows.

Celtic
Beattie; Donnelly and Fallon; Fernie, Evans and Peacock; Tully, Collins, McPhail, Wilson and Mochan

Rangers
Niven; Shearer and Caldow; McColl, Valentine and Davis; Scott, Simpson, Murray, Baird and Hubbard

Referee: Mr J. Mowat (Burnside)

The scene was set, the cast was chosen and the audience was in its place. Even the weather conspired to assist in the performance, a bright afternoon sun shining down from a cloudless blue sky, and the supporters of both sides were already sweltering in anticipation. The curtain went up as the referee blew for kick-off and, in a shirt-sleeved atmosphere that more befitted the Mediterranean than the Clyde, the drama began. I wasn't there, but my heart was where I ought to have been – in the Celtic end at Hampden.

I could easily imagine how they felt as they waited for their team to face Rangers – foreboding, dread, anxiety, nervousness – pick what word you will. The simple truth was that Celtic, in our experience, were never expected to beat Rangers. Certainly, we'd had our moments against them, but in the long haul it was generally Rangers who came out on top. This is what made the incredible events of this October afternoon all the more astonishing. I am indebted to Messrs Tom Campbell and Pat Woods, Celtic scholars both, and to their excellent history of Celtic's first 100 years, *The Glory and the Dream*, for its detailed account of this magnificent occasion, as indeed I am for all historical facts, names and places mentioned in these pages.

From the start, McPhail had the beating on the ground and in the air of his funny Valentine – John Valentine, newly signed from Billy's old club Queen's Park. They may even have been teammates in their youth, which was perhaps why Billy had complete mastery over John. The Celtic forwards sensed this immediately and laid siege to the Rangers goal in the first quarter of an hour, with both Tully and Collins hitting the woodwork with George Niven, the Rangers goalkeeper, well beaten. The Celtic crowd were fired up by this promising start and began to think that this might be their day for once. In the 23rd minute, McPhail rose in the penalty area for another cross and glided a cleverly headed pass into the path of the onrushing Wilson, and Slammin' Sammy crashed into the net for goal one. Joy mixed with relief at the Celtic end. Only 77 minutes to hold out now for a win.

That was our mindset then. A second goal would be too good to be true. But when Collins thundered a 30-yard free kick against the bar, a feeling of 'you never know' spread through the green-and-white brigade. Unbelievably, Celtic continued to dominate as half-time approached, but it looked as if they would have to carry only a slender 1–0 lead into the second half. Again, McPhail got the better of

Valentine, but this time on the turf, and he lofted a high ball into the path of Neilly Mochan on the left wing. The winger went surging past Ian McColl and Bobby Shearer to cut in and blast an unstoppable volley past Niven into the far corner of the net. Goal number two with two minutes to go to the interval.

At the break, the Celtic contingent was babbling in disbelief. Their team was so much on top they should have scored almost at will. Dick Beattie had almost nothing to do. Evans was strolling. Tully and Mochan were rampaging on the wings, and Collins was always menacing, but the sensation was McPhail at the spearhead and his uncannily accurate distribution at speed. He surely deserved a goal. However, the man of the first half was unquestionably Willie Fernie, who seemed to come of age during the game. If Evans strolled, Fernie walked, precisely and almost daintily picking his way effortlessly through Rangers legs and totally controlling the game from the kick-off to the half-time whistle.

That was what thrilled the supporters – not so much the two-goal lead but the swaggering manner in which it was achieved. This was the template laid down by the club's first manager, the Willie Maley way – cavalier football played in the Celtic style, with gaiety and elan, attacking all the way and not giving the other time to counter-attack. The supporters hadn't seen this sort of total, all-round effectiveness for years and were still pinching themselves. Perhaps the players were, too, in the dressing-room. More of the same was all that was wanted now.

One supporter, with a few half-time beers in him, raised a fist containing a couple of pounds and called to those around him, 'Two tae wan that Cel'ic get a penalty, Tully'll take an' score wi' a fuckin' scissors kick!' Laughter all round.

That was the keynote of the second-half, laughter – and joyous incredulity. Never in the lives of those present had Celtic shown such a disdainful, virtually arrogant superiority over their great rivals, and the Parkhead faithful lapped it up. They had waited long for such a day in the sun, but Celtic – and McPhail – weren't finished yet. Fernie began again where he had left off and was the clear architect of a second-half rout. Rangers were thoroughly demoralised and had no answers. Celtic had five standouts up front and they continually put the heavy-footed Rangers defence under question.

The *Sunday Mail*, that faithful football chronicle of my younger days, carried the headline 'Gers Were Lucky Not to Lose Ten'. What a day of Celtic joy! It went on to say that the match had been a victory for 'pure, unadulterated football' adding that 'there is no limit to what pure football can achieve'. The report held that, apart from Niven, Rangers had had not one success on the day, while Celtic had had eleven.

With the second half not yet ten minutes old, Wilson's cross found McPhail and he got his first goal and Celtic's third. Ten minutes from the end, Billy ran from the halfway line to score his third and Celtic's sixth. Mochan had tapped in for number four at seventy-four minutes and with only a minute left Celtic got that penalty the supporter had foretold. Fernie stepped up to take it and calmly put Rangers out of their misery. By the way, the score still stands as a record for a national cup final in Britain.

The Rangers goal was hardly noticed. It was scored by inside-forward Billy Simpson, while Evans was off the field with an injury. The Celtic support sportingly cheered the effort. By that time, it made little difference. They acknowledged that the goal was Rangers' fee for turning up so that Celtic could give them a masterclass in team effort and all-round football. Fighting broke out among the Rangers support and Mr Mowat stopped the game to let the police deal with some very unhappy men. The final whistle was a signal for the Rangers fans to shuffle out of Hampden ashen-faced and shaken, and for the Celtic fans to stand there singing as the sun began to set over Mount Florida. It was a day that could only end in song, and thousands of Celtic voices rose into the air in a spontaneous Handelian hallelujah that possibly owed more to Harry Belafonte.

> Oh, Hampden in the sun,
> Celtic seven and Rangers one,
> All sing hail to the bhoys in green
> For the finest football ever seen.

It may not have been that, of course, but in the excess of that great moment, who can blame them for thinking so? I have very few regrets in my life, but one of them is that I never saw this particular game. It was what my whole childhood dream had been about, what the empty wartime years had yearned for. I would love to be able to say, 'I was there.' Instead, I was in Maidenhead, spending the morning buying furniture before hurrying home to get the result on the radio. I couldn't believe it. I was sure there was an error, but when I checked and was reassured, I opened a bottle of St-Emilion and drank it all on my own, slowly and happily. Hilaire Belloc would have understood:

> Wherever a Catholic sun doth shine
> There's always laughter and good red wine.
> At least I've always found it so,
> *Benedicamus Domino!*

After such a feast could only come a famine, and so it was. Within a year, the wonderful team had disintegrated, first by retirement, which was inevitable, then by injury, which was unpredictable, then by transfer, which was deplorable. Fallon went sideways, as it were. He came off the team sheet but was kept on the books as assistant manager to McGrory. That made for a triumvirate of good, earnest, Celtic-minded men with not an ounce of management flair among them, as far as I could see. The results were to speak for themselves during the seven empty, Lenten years that were to follow.

The case of Charlie Tully was entirely different. He retired to begin a useful managerial career in Ireland and with him went most of the colour that was in Celtic in his time. Charles Patrick Tully played to the crowd and how the crowd loved it. When Danny Kaye appeared at Hampden before the Charity Cup final in 1950, Charlie joined him for a spontaneous bout of repartee, in which he more than held his own with the American comedian. Tully went for the jocular, and his foolery often blinded people to the fact that his football skills were on a near-genius level, as he showed on so many occasions.

The decade that was his with Celtic is recognised as the Tully years and his right to be judged as a genuine Celtic great cannot be denied. Tully stories abound and everyone has their favourite – whether it's his taking a corner at Falkirk and being told to take it again because the ball was not on its proper mark, retaking the kick and scoring again, or his telling Alf Ramsey, the England full-back, who was to mark him that day, that he (Tully) had a ticket for the stand in his pocket if he (Ramsey) would rather watch the game from there, as he (Tully) would see that he (Ramsey) would never get a kick of the ball. There are so many stories like this about Tully and they typify the man. He helped this legend along by playing as cast, being the clown prince in an arena where he was a rightful king. Tully died in his sleep at home in 1971, at the age of 47, and his funeral in the Falls Road, Belfast was a municipal occasion. No one would have enjoyed it more than Charlie.

Tully had been recommended to Celtic by one of their own players at the time, big John McPhail. Hooky had gone to Ireland to recuperate from a throat infection and he took the chance to go up to see the other Celtic in Belfast. Tully impressed him at once and when McPhail came back to Celtic Park he mentioned to trainer Chic Geatons that there was a man in Belfast worth taking a look at. Chic mentioned this to McGrory, who passed it on to chairman Kelly, and Charlie was at Parkhead before Hooky's throat got better.

Another McPhail was Tully's teammate in the sun, big John's younger brother Billy. He was a Celtic prince of another kind from Tully, more in the handsome, Prince Charming category, but suspect knees and headaches brought his career to a premature end. He was unlucky, too, in succumbing at too early an age to Alzheimer's, a disease some believed was precipitated by the very thing that marked him out as a player, his heading skill. It was a sad, lingering end for a player who had shone so briefly, but so brightly, in a game that will never be forgotten by so many.

Nor will Fernie, Evans and Collins be forgotten by supporters. Yet each of them was gone so soon after their epic triumph, each a casualty to the board of directors' reluctance to pay their labourers a wage worthy of their hire. Fernie went to Middlesbrough, Collins to Everton and Evans to Chelsea because, overall, the deals looked good on paper. This has been a fault of the Celtic board from the earliest days: good book-keeping has come at the cost of poor performances. Apparently, the chairman had been heard to remark about the younger McPhail after his first few games, 'I think I might have made a mistake paying two and a half grand for this fellow.' Billy's Hampden performance paid that back at a stroke. Thus a great team fell into ruins, not like Athens or Rome, a noble structure whose day had passed, but as a football work of art at its peak.

It's not that there weren't some near misses by the survivors, but there were no big hits. Quarter-finals, semi-finals and finals were played, even a semi-final of the European Cup-Winners' Cup in 1964, but nothing was rewarded except for a Charity Cup and a Glasgow Cup, both once desirable prizes but now considered very small fry as trophies. I could only watch from afar. Close up would have been unbearable. By this time, I was in my 30s and going from picture to picture with Rank.

I was in *A Night to Remember*, a film about the sinking of the *Titanic*, with the amiable Kenneth More. The 'sea' scenes were shot at Ruislip Lido in London with model boats. I suddenly found myself fully clothed in deep water. Nobody ever asked if I could swim. I couldn't, but I acted it sufficiently. However, I lost my cap in one take and had to dive under the water to retrieve it. I put it back on my head and let the water run down my face. I knew I had to return the hat to wardrobe. The director liked what I'd accidentally done and asked me to do it again. I did so, in the freezing water, but, in the end, it was pointless – that sequence was cut from the finished film. On the whole, I was glad to be involved in this wonderful titanic adventure. I wish I could have felt the same about the good ship Celtic.

It went sailing on, still afloat but making heavy weather of it all. Captained ostensibly by manager McGrory it was in fact steered by chairman Kelly, assisted by bosun Fallon, and manned by apprentice seamen, some of whom would prove able, but not yet. A course was set by those upstairs that was stubbornly held, even if it appeared to be going against the tide. However cavalier they may have wished to be in the old Celtic style, there was more 'oops' than 'hoops' about this squad, and it would leave Celtic trophy-less for a decade. Roundhead Rangers, meanwhile, having recovered from being exposed to the Celtic sun at Hampden, went from strength to strength with ruthless thoroughness. They were now virtually untouchable at the top in Scotland and they intended to stay that way.

The main difference between the two great rivals was in management style, training practices and calibre of player. Bill Struth, the team's previous manager, had moulded the Rangers of the day. He was in the Willie Maley mould, more of an athlete than a footballer. Like Maley, he was also a firm disciplinarian, even to the extent of demanding a code of dress for his players, which included the wearing of a bowler hat when on Rangers business. Some players had to stuff their bunnets in their pockets, but they concurred with the rules. It was all part of Struth's way of lifting the club image to ensure that the players felt superior even off the park. The Rangers rules were strict and rigidly enforced. Training was supervised by Struth himself and was thoroughly carried through by competent professionals. Rangers' current manager, Scot Symon, although more flexible, followed in this tradition.

Of the team itself, most were seasoned footballers of wide experience and others, like Valentine, were new. Whether experienced or not, for Rangers players, football was their business and they were just as anxious as their directors to make a profit. Each player on the books soon found out that the best way to do that was to keep on winning.

Celtic's players, on the other hand, were generally left to get on with it. They often reported for training in their dungarees and removed them to do endless, mindless circuits of the track, with little sign of formal supervision from manager or coaching staff. This allowed senior players to break off at a far corner for a quick puff of a cigarette or to take a little-earned breather. My brother, Jim, who trained with Celtic around that time, told me that what team practice they had was done hurriedly in five-a-sides behind each goal area when a player could steal a ball from the pavilion. Otherwise, no balls were allowed. It really is hard to believe – training without a ball. It's like rehearsing a play without saying the words, and it explains much about Celtic's unenthusiastic performances throughout this era and why they kept on losing.

In an article for *Weekly News* in October 1960, Chic Geatons, Celtic's long-suffering trainer, finally gave way to his frustration and spoke his mind. Chic had been a good player for the club and he might have been of help as a trainer-coach had he been allowed freer rein. Clearly, this was not the case. He wrote:

> The question I ask myself is this: if Celtic are too much at the mercy of one man's whims and fancies, is there anybody around with courage to stand up and insist on a new deal for the club? It is all wrong that the chairman should take over so much managerial direction; the chairman should be the chairman, the directors the directors and the manager should manage.

Chic had served Celtic well as player and part-time coach, then as full-time coach, but increasingly he resented the office intrusions, and he resigned. He had played at the highest level with the club and knew their traditional, attacking, toe-to-toe play, which was based on making speedy triangles moving up the pitch; he now saw it replaced by safety-first punts from the back and hopeful crosses into the penalty area. Since the players' average age was so young, there were no senior players to growl behind them or offer shouted instructions. The Kelly

Babes were lost in a wood of their board's making and, just like their supporters, were waiting for better days to come – or, in football terms, the return of a lost art: team play.

Ironically, it was during this drab time for my team that I became friends with the painter Sir Stanley Spencer, who lived in Cookham Rise. With Rank's help, I had bought a house there and I met the famous painter outside my own front gate when my little daughter, Jennifer, wanted to see the baby in the pram he was pushing. The 'baby' was a kettle of water and the pram held all his outside painting gear. Sir Stanley had loved his wartime years on Clydeside as a war artist in the shipyards, even though he didn't understand a word the workers were saying. He did say he heard the word 'football' mentioned from time to time, 'generally preceded,' he said, 'by another F word'. And he laughed his unusual high-pitched laugh. I liked Stanley Spencer.

I told him the story of Seton Airlie, one of our many home-brewed wartime centre-forwards who might have done well had he stayed in Glasgow but the army took him to London, where he turned out for Chelsea alongside Peter 'Ma Baw' McKennan of Partick Thistle. Seton was tempted to stay in the south of England after the war but got an offer from Cannes in the south of France and couldn't resist it. He settled into the Continental style and quite unexpectedly made a friend of Pablo Picasso, whom he met at Golfe-Juan, where they both lived at the time. Pablo, being Spanish, knew his football, and he also knew the football player from Carmyle, whom he invited to join him at the wedding of Rita Hayworth to the Aga Khan. Not bad for a Celtic centre-forward, but Stanley was unimpressed. He didn't approve of Cubism.

In September 1960, I came back to Glasgow to play Hamlet at the Citizens Theatre. (I had returned a little earlier so that I could see a game at Celtic Park.) Hamlet says of himself:

> Is it not monstrous that this player here,
> But in a fiction, in a dream of passion,
> Can force his soul so to his own conceit,
> That from her working all his visage wann'd;
> Tears in his eyes, distraction in's aspect,
> A broken voice, and his whole function suiting
> With forms to his conceit?

If you substitute 'body' for 'voice', then you have some sense of how a football player might feel trying to deal with the demands made on him. The player on the stage has to work to make his effects in the play look easy. Similarly, the player on the field has to 'rehearse' in training, so as to make his skills effective in the game. For the actor-player, to perform Macbeth might be considered as a Scottish Cup win; to play Hamlet is to reach the peak of the acting repertoire. The equivalent for the football player might be the final of the European Cup. For the actor, the World Cup is a King Lear.

Professional players know these heights in their own game and the good ones aspire to this standard. It's the same way with the actor. For me, it was a long way from an East End tenement in Glasgow to the battlements at Elsinore. A nice irony of the time is that, just as people queued up to see *Hamlet*, I queued up to see Celtic. It didn't matter to me that the pulse was weak; the body of Celtic was there, still alive in me.

There was no queuing at the gate this time. It was a seat in the stand, no less. I was ridiculously excited – and I was so disappointed. I had come home to play in a tragedy, not to sit and watch one, and it was a real tragedy seeing so much young football talent being put to such little use on the field. They were running about like so many deer, full of raw energy but lacking in professional purpose and poise. Only young Bertie Auld on the wing and Paddy Crerand at right-half had any suggestion of having antlers.

Typically, Auld was allowed to go to Birmingham, despite McGrory's strong protests. This could have been partly due to Auld's not meeting Mr Kelly's standards of altar-boy behaviour on and off the pitch. Bertie was inclined to give as good as he got, often before he got it, but this did not detract from the fact the he was a helluva good player, loved by the fans but maybe not by the chairman. Many years later, Bertie confided to me when we once met in Nova Scotia that he 'didn't knock it off with Mr Kelly'.

Paddy Crerand was a Gorbals boy whose heart and soul were with Celtic from his days at Holyrood Senior Secondary and he couldn't wait to sign for them in 1957. He had the same competitive temperament as Auld. Both in the same team would have been any manager's dream, but it was also a combustible risk. Paddy was considered early in his career to be one of the best half-backs in the world and was frequently sought by other clubs, including Real

Madrid, no less. Despite his public proclamation that he would never leave Celtic for any team or any amount of money, he left to join Matt Busby at Manchester United in 1963. According to his book *On Top with United*, a half-time row with Sean Fallon in the dressing-room during a Rangers game left him dissatisfied and unhappy. Yet when he was told, on returning home from Mass one Sunday morning, that he could leave Celtic, he burst into tears. He pleaded with McGrory to let him stay and went off to Manchester still looking back to Parkhead. He ought to have been retained so that he might have taken his place not as a legend at Old Trafford but as a Celtic all-time great.

This high-handed treatment of quality players was seen no doubt as high-minded by Kelly, but it cost Celtic so much over the years in a way that meant so much more than morals or money. The supposed youth policy at Celtic was palpably not paying off. Inconsistency was the killer; important results were not achieved. The promise was there in so many of the young, bankable players, but not all of them delivered on their promissory talents.

Celtic signed their 'babes' for next to nothing and hoped for the best. Certainly, they would get their money's worth out of several before the decade was out, but it was a dubious policy at best and tried the trust of the support severely. Supporters gathered outside the players' entrance to vent their displeasure, not at them but at the directors. They were not happy when the directors paid no attention. Nevertheless, being Celtic supporters, they still continued to pay their money at the turnstiles. This was the famed Celtic loyalty. The board, however, did sanction the signing of more experienced players in the face of the increasing criticism of their youth emphasis. The only success of the veteran intake was Ronnie Simpson. He had been a boy goalkeeper with Queen's Park before going on to play with Third Lanark, Newcastle United and Hibernian. Son of the Rangers centre-half of pre-war years, Ronnie (or 'Faither' as the Celtic players called him) had a lot of playing years in him yet – as had some of Kelly's kids, but their hour, and Faither's, had not yet come.

Nor was the Messiah quite ready either. Jock Stein, the man who was to answer Chic Geatons' prayers, had left Celtic in 1960 to go and ply his post-playing trade as a manager. Like Chic, Jock had learned his football on the field, via the older players he'd played with at each stage. There were no sophisticated courses or diplomas in his day. Your football apprenticeship started with your first kick of the ball and, for men like Stein, it didn't really finish until you hun␣

Born into a Protestant mining background in Lan␣ young Jock had little option but to go down the pit, wh␣ played football when he could, with a miner's grit and de␣ He signed for Burnbank Athletic in 1938 but actually first ␣ Blantyre Victoria, where, after four years of working hard and ␣ harder, he was signed by Webber Lees for Albion Rovers in Coatb␣ ␣ge. This was where I first saw him play, in 1944 against Celtic; it was the same match in which Bobby Evans made his debut at outside-left.

At this time, Jock was a good workhorse footballer rather than an obvious thoroughbred, but he already showed a capacity for work and a willingness to learn something about all aspects of the game. His good physique cast him in the defender's role, but it was a good place to get an overall view of any game and the wily Stein kept his eyes open. He knew football was his only chance of leaving the pits for good.

In 1950, he saw an advert for 'players of proven ability' placed in a newspaper by Jack Goldsborough on behalf of a Welsh club in Llanelli. It went on to say that 'transfers were no detriment . . . but only top players need apply'. Despite his wife's misgivings, Jock applied and won a place alongside good pros like Dougie Wallace, the former Clyde centre-forward. It wasn't the most prestigious career move, but it was another rung in the ladder, one that would lead him only eighteen months later to Celtic Park, where he was to remain for the next seven years – much to the surprise of his Lanarkshire friends and the delight of his wife, Jean, who was only too glad to be back home in Scotland.

It turned out that Jock had been recommended to Celtic by old Jimmy Gribben, the Bargeddie coalman, who had been interested in my brother's career. It was thought that Jock might be just the man to bring on the reserves, but the injury situation with the existing defenders was such at the time of Jock's arrival that he was rushed onto the team at centre-half, and he stayed there for the rest of the season and beyond. Flanked first by Evans and Joe Baillie, he began modestly and slowly asserting himself, so that by the following season he was seen as the linchpin of the team, in a half-back line that now read Evans, Stein and Peacock.

In 1953, he was made captain. As Celtic went from strength to strength, so did Jock. As a player with Albion Rovers, he only ever won one medal – in the Lanarkshire Cup – although he had another

,ootball prize to show, a leather wallet. This was won in 1945, when Jock was unexpectedly drafted into a Celtic team when they were a man short for a summer five-a-side tournament at Cliftonville. Jock happened to be at the ground. Now here he was, as captain of that same Celtic, lifting the Coronation Cup eight years later. The following season, he led the Bhoys to their first double in 40 years and in that same year was capped for the Scottish League against the English League at Stamford Bridge. It didn't matter that they were beaten 4–0; Jock had made his point. He had been formally recognised by his peers and was now safely beyond the pithead.

Unfortunately, in 1955 in a game against Rangers at Parkhead, he injured his ankle so badly that he was forced to retire not only from that match but from the game itself. He limped off to take charge, two years later, of the Celtic schoolboys and reserves, who would soon be playing at Celtic's new training ground, along the London Road going east towards Belvidere Hospital, only a short walk from Celtic Park. An old football pitch lay between Westhorn Park and Dalbeth Cemetery, and Jock persuaded the directors to buy the site as an extra training resource. It was a piece of forward thinking and the first hint of the latent Stein managerial instinct.

His reserve charges won the 2nd XI Cup in 1958 against Rangers, triumphing 8–2 on aggregate, but by that time Jock had moved to Dunfermline, in March 1960, as manager. These are the mere bones of the Stein career to this point, but the larger legend was now on the make, at which time, personally, I got a big fright.

On Wednesday, 3 April 1963, the telephone rang in the bedroom at Maidenhead. It was a priest's voice from Glasgow telling me my father had died following complications after an operation for ulcers. These were a result of his time in England during the war, when he was in the London Blitz and on the south coast during the buzz-bomb rocket scare that followed it. He had never been the same since he'd returned to Glasgow to spend his early retirement doing the *Glasgow Herald* crossword at the kitchen table, playing bowls at Westhorn Park along the road from us and having the occasional nine-hole round of golf on the Letham Hill course up at Riddrie. He found retirement tedious and I really think he died of boredom, at the age of only 54. That very night, I had made my London Theatre debut as Jack Absolute in Sheridan's *The Rivals*, with Fay Compton, but my understudy took over on the second night while I flew home for Dad's funeral. The next morning, I opened the blinds on the window that looked out onto the street and watched a sea of men's flat caps filling Williamson Street as they gathered to walk to the cemetery. From two storeys up, it was like looking down on a football terracing.

It reminded me that life went on across the road at Celtic Park and that Stein and Kelly, for all their differences as men, and particularly as football men, continued to talk to each other. In the next few years, while Celtic continued with their suicidal youth policy, Stein made bricks without straw at Dunfermline. This was noticed in other places, and Hibs, Newcastle United and Wolves all made overtures to the rising manager. Hibs won and Stein moved his new authority to Easter Road. Whatever else he was, Kelly was no fool and at a covert lunch at the North British Hotel in George Square, he put it to Stein that there might be an opening for him at Celtic Park, sharing managerial duties with Sean Fallon. Stein declined. Negotiations stalled. Stein returned to managing Hibernian but quietly and confidently made plans for his eventual return to Celtic. Through a friend, he contacted Bertie Auld in Birmingham and asked if he'd like to return to Celtic. 'Like a shot,' said Bertie.

This rare action, of the manager of a club making contact with a player of another regarding his return to yet another club is another instance of the cunning and instinct for precise planning for which Stein was to become famous. He was always looking ahead, and at that moment he was looking no further than that chair at Parkhead. He knew his appointment – when, and not if, he got it – would be a tremendous breakthrough on so many fronts and would whip up a storm both for and against, but he wasn't above making a little history.

Stein trusted in his long-practised gambler's instinct and kept his cards close to his chest. For Jock, it was the manager's job or nothing. Meantime, Kelly was also further considering the matter. It was a tricky decision. He knew the board's concern. This man was a Burnbank Protestant and had grown up as a Rangers supporter, but he was a non-drinker and married to a Catholic (even though Jean had 'turned' for him). Incidentally, he was also the best managerial prospect in Britain.

Finally, the chairman made up his mind. Without any consultation with his fellow directors, he met with Stein again to offer him the post of Celtic manager. Jock was delighted, but his first thought was for the iconic McGrory. He couldn't hurt such a man. Kelly reassured him that Jimmy would become Celtic's first public-relations officer. When he told Stein he wanted him to take on Sean Fallon as co-manager, Stein initially refused outright. There was a stand-off, until the ungloved left hand of the Celtic chairman reached out and patted Stein's shoulder, saying, 'Very well. It's all yours.' A momentous decision had been made. It had to happen and it did.

On 31 January 1965, it was officially announced that Mr John Stein was the new manager of Celtic Football Club. Rather than being met with misgivings – after all, he was the first non-Catholic manager of Celtic – the appointment of Stein to take the team into the new era was greeted with loud cheers. The support knew how much the team needed on-the-ground leadership instead of edicts from above. A new surge of confidence swept out from the dressing-room, down the tunnel, across the pitch, into the Jungle and onto the terracing. Even before Stein put on his Celtic tracksuit, the effect of his Messianic coming was shown in the results. The haphazard hopefuls suddenly blended as a team on a snow-covered pitch at Parkhead to beat Aberdeen by the astonishing score of 8–0.

I heard that result on my transistor radio in the tiny dressing-room in the tenement building that was the old Traverse Theatre in St James' Close in Edinburgh. Only a few days before, I had given the world premiere of *There Was a Man*, a solo play on the life and works of Robert Burns by Tom Wright, directed by Gerald Slevin. It was scheduled for a week's trial run, but I played it for a month, and at the following Edinburgh Festival, and, one way or another, in one form or another, all round the world. Frankly, it totally ruined my conventional career, but it gave me a fantastic life and a whole new direction as a solo actor.

I returned to the West End in London to open with Burns at the Arts Theatre to a surprisingly successful run, which I remember only for the fact that my London producer, Tony Marriott, was being booked for parking outside the theatre by a Scottish police constable in the London force, and when I told the policeman I was playing Robert Burns in the theatre that very night, he said he had a good mind to double the fine. Thanks to a good reception otherwise from the London critics, they asked me to extend the London run, but I had already been invited to take the show to an international Festival of Solo Artists in the Theatre St Pierre in Geneva. This was a move into the solo world of people like John Gielgud, Emlyn Williams, Micheál

Mac Liammóir, Roy Dotrice and Hal Holbrook, who were the giants of that time. I was to fill in the vacant Thursday and, understandably, *Genève Soir* had a headline reading '*Qui est John Cairney?*' When I repeated the show in Vevey, I was thrilled to see Charlie Chaplin with his family in the theatre box, but when I glanced up during the action, he was sleeping, and when I took my bow at the end, he was gone. But then he was nearly 90.

The return of Jock Stein had a similar career-changing effect at Parkhead. The pre-Stein Celts had promise, but that was all. They needed a firm, knowledgeable hand to fulfil that pristine promise, and with the hour came the man. It was as if big Jock had halted them in their course and completely changed their direction. He would put them – and Celtic – back on the right road. Suddenly, some lines from the Burns script applied:

As I cam ower by Glenap
I met an ancient woman,
Wha bad me yet keep up my hert
For the best o' my days were comin'.

Sevenpenny gate days, with brother Jim.

In the RAF during
National Service.

Recording an EP for HMV.

An early film, *Time for Me to Go Now* with Jeannie Carson at Elstree Studio

Windom's Way, playing Malaysian Jan Vidal, with Peter Finch.

In Berkshire with my
mother, Mary Cairney.

Strolling along Piccadilly with Jim.

On a mountain-top in France
in *Ill Met by Moonlight*.

Phoebus in *Cleopatra*, filmed in Rome.

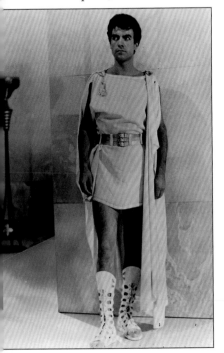

Playing *This Man Craig* in the TV series

The very first production of *There Was a Man*, at the Traverse Theatre.

The Celtic *Quizball* team in action (courtesy of Jim Craig).

WILLIE WALLACE

JIM CRAIG

JOHN CAIRNEY

A Kiwi wedding day with Alannah.

Playing Robert Louis Stevenson,
with Alannah as Fanny Osbourne,
at the Byre Theatre.

As 'Theatre at Sea' with Alannah.

At Celtic Park, where the sevenpenny gate used to be.

Jimmy McGrory: goal opportunist par
excellence (© the McGrory family).

Jimmy Delaney: my star pick of them all
(courtesy of the Scottish Football Museum).

Malcolm MacDonald (second from right):
the complete all-round footballer (© Press Association).

Willie Miller: bravest of the brave
(© Press Association).

Danny McGrain: a class act
(© the Scottish Football Museum)

Tommy Burns: Celtic passion
personified (© Getty Images).

Paddy McCourt: a master of
the unexpected (© Getty Images)

CHAPTER FIVE

A Serenade from Stein

Billy McNeill, Centre-Half

King Billy he was, though it mightn't sound right
For a Celtic legend, but I still see the sight
Of his tall figure soaring high
To score with his head in the Hampden sky.

If it were true that I had just struck gold in one half of my life by finding Burns to perform, then it was just as true that in the other half Celtic had struck oil in deciding to rebuild its house on the rock that was Jock Stein. On 9 March 1965, he formally returned to Celtic Park. With the news, I felt an extraordinary feeling of totally unsupported optimism. I was balanced again and walked with head held high. Big Jock was back and the gallus chanter would soon get Celtic back on song, I had no doubt of that as a supporter. I was also supporting a growing happy family, but continuing to concern myself with the affairs of a football club. When I could, I travelled to see them play. This is what being a supporter means; you support.

When working in London, I caught the sleeper from King's Cross or Euston so that I could arrive in time to have breakfast at my mother's in Dennistoun before going off to witness another defeat or yet another draw at Parkhead. The return sleeper trip prior to Stein's arrival would nearly always be dismal. This might seem meaningless to those who are not cursed with the Celtic obsession, but my fellow sufferers will know what I mean. 'What a waste of money,' my mother would mutter as she waved me off.

I wonder what Stein's mother thought of her son John's new job and how the whole Stein family in Burnbank took it. His own father, still

97

a Rangers fan, saw the benefit of his son's going to Parkhead as a career move but deplored it in every other way. Why couldn't it have been Ibrox? The Protestant pubs in Burnbank thought the same, while the Celtic minority there rejoiced. Down the pits, the miners argued the pros and cons just as Stein himself had foreseen. He lost a lot of friends at this time, but I think he gained an exceptional inner purpose. He knew what he was doing. He had struck out to become his own man. Balladeer Stein would call the tune now. The supporters were singing already. And so was I.

I recorded a single of Bing Crosby's 'Please' with 'Deep Purple' on the other side and I think it sold only to the more loyal of my relatives. They should have asked big Jock to make the recording, because he had a very pleasant singing voice and a surprisingly wide repertoire. He was certainly top of the pops at Celtic. Everyone came round to the appointment – players, supporters, even the most partisan of directors. All Stein said to the players was, 'I'll do my very best for you. All I ask is that you do your very best for me.'

That they did was proved by a determined Scottish Cup run that saw them face Stein's former managerial charges, Dunfermline, at Hampden in the 1965 Scottish Cup final. The team selection here led to the first test of the Stein–Kelly relationship, a 'contest' that was not fully resolved in Stein's favour until January 1966. Stein had selected Bobby Murdoch at right-half and Kelly protested that Murdoch, whom he had spotted as a 12-year-old, was an inside-forward not a wing-half. Stein's reply was a polite 'You'll see on Saturday what he is.' Murdoch, of course, was a natural at right-half and played a big part in Celtic's victory, due entirely to Billy McNeill's 'Captain Courageous' header from a Charlie Gallagher corner in the dying moments. I still have a newspaper picture of Billy, half-hidden by the crouching figure of Bobby Lennox, almost regally delivering the header over the advancing Dunfermline goalkeeper. It was a golden moment and it heralded the start of the new era. It was a wonderful start for the new order at Parkhead, but what nobody knew was that it was the beginning of something bigger than any of them had ever imagined.

No less significant was Stein's points win over chairman Kelly in the Murdoch matter. He may have won the first battle on the field, but it was equally vital that the new manager should win the larger war at the boardroom door. Big Jock was obviously not going to be a McGrory-style rubber stamp and nothing was to deter his first ambition, which was to restore Celtic to its rightful place as a leading British football club. And after that, who knew? Why not the world? Meantime, the importance of the cup final result was not lost on him. He said later, 'It wouldn't have gone as well for Celtic had they lost this game.' The youngsters who delivered on that important day, Saturday, 24 April 1965, were: Fallon; Young and Gemmell; Murdoch, McNeill and Clark; Chalmers, Gallagher, Hughes, Lennox and Auld. The spine of the great team to come was already there in the half-back line and they had in their manager a man who knew now that there was only one way to go and that was up.

He started off in his Celtic Park office by having a large, framed photograph of Billy McNeill being borne aloft by his teammates after the game, placed so he could see it at all times. The picture of these young, triumphant faces would be his talisman. For many of them, Mr Stein had been their first mentor when they arrived at Celtic as schoolboys. He had overseen them into the reserves and hadn't they won his first cup for him? He, more than anyone, knew the latent quality that was there, and like the miner that deep down he always was, he knew he could dig it out. He had hit on a rich seam and couldn't wait to get his big hands on it. Practised gambler that he was, he knew that the odds, for once, were in his favour.

Winning the League Championship was his first target. That would be his clarion call to the football world, his declaration that a new Celtic was in the making and a new kind of manager was at the helm. The big obstacle in his path, as always, was Rangers, and the problem was how to deal with their relentless methodology and physical prowess. They could be grim, but they were also good, and manager Stein had to prepare his prancing colts accordingly. He stressed that they should keep it simple but keep it strong, not dirty or underhand but straightforward and direct.

While he recognised that there were other hurdles in the League steeplechase, Rangers, as far as Stein was concerned, represented the Becher's Brook. It had to be got over and he plotted to this end. Minute appraisal of every opponent was made as a matter of course, but he made a very special study of Rangers, down to a detailed dossier on every player at Ibrox. He regarded them as the only team Celtic had to beat to win anything. He hated losing to them, even though he had once supported them, but realistically he knew they would always stand between him and his goal for Celtic – to make them the very acme of a modern, professional football team.

To open the new offensive, Stein in his now recognisable battledress, his tracksuit, was already in the thick of it on the training ground. First to arrive in the morning and last to leave at night, he was the omnipresence in everything Celtic, always available to players, directors, journalists, other managers, friends of friends and anyone else who ventured near the ground. He was particularly sensitive to the needs of the supporters, who in his mind were the mainstay of the club.

Stein loved the supporters. He wasn't so far removed from being an ordinary working man himself. He knew he might have gone back down the pit after Wales if Celtic hadn't come for him. He had a lot to be thankful to old Jimmy Gribben for. 'No one knew more about football than Jimmy Gribben,' said Stein. When Stein strode through the door of Celtic Park on that marvellous 'homecoming' evening of 26 May 1967, he headed straight for the boot room to give his old mentor the first feel of the European Cup. It was payback time. Similarly, he would see the Celtic supporters rewarded. He saw their presence at the park as the sole reason for the footballer's existence, much in the same way as an actor in the theatre needs an audience. Each is necessary to the other and this mutual dependence must never be ignored or neglected.

A football supporter brings himself to the match much as a member of the audience attends to watch a play. Each enters as an individual member of the public, but if the 'play' experience works well, these individuals will soon find themselves bound in a collective, subject to a larger will than their own and going with it as it ebbs and flows with the action. This is highly therapeutic; I can vouch for that. It does one good to let off steam, to enjoy a pretended delight or a sham anger you can feel for the moment, knowing that by night-time it will be no more than a memory. There is a huge psychological interaction going on in the sheer mass of human beings reacting to what they see and feel. This can only be beneficial, as long as each component individual remains in his or her place of awareness.

An audience 'knows' an actor is acting. He is not 'real' but only pretending. The football player is performing, but not pretending. He can't be other than real, for there he is before you on the field. He must deliver on the day, he must justify the hours of training, he must entertain the crowd. Oddly enough, Jock used this theatrical analogy when he urged his young players to entertain their vast following. As he told them in his characteristic way, 'They've worked a' week, they need to be cheered up on a Saturday, no' demoralised. They get enough o' that at work. Away an' enjoy yourselves an' let them enjoy theirselves too.'

It was a simple directive, but beneath its *Sunday Post* style lay a highly sophisticated approach to team management. Stein never missed a trick. Everything was tried: blackboard lectures, TV clips, newspaper cuttings, training experiments with several balls at once, one-to-one conversations with each player, sing-songs, card schools – above all card schools – and all this with gentle, avuncular comments or jokey asides or, when necessary, coalface language that would blister the dressing-room walls or bring on an electrical storm around the Barrowfield training pitch. 'Hey, you sir!' would bellow out from the terracing and the player concerned would know he was for it, but afterwards, away from the dressing-room, there was often a quiet word of encouragement.

Nothing was left to chance. As a real gambler, Stein didn't believe in chance. You studied form, you got all the facts on the case that you needed, you checked on the latest info and, having made your choice, you went for it with all you had – and hell mend those who didn't. The first priority for any side, in Stein's eyes, was team spirit – and it was this *esprit de corps* that he worked towards, which was why he encouraged card schools, especially Solo, and the rowdier the better. The Glasgow element in the squad, which was most of them, needed no advice here.

During the detailed coaching lectures, nobody dared interrupt or question; all they had to do was take it in. In everything, he was almost pugnaciously purposeful and he made this very clear to anyone with all six feet of him. His was a massive presence. He appeared a great bulwark of a man who could float with ease in the deep water he so often stirred up. The big man's energy was immense and it seemed to renew itself exactly according to his use of it.

He appeared to relax only in the easy atmosphere of the after-match bath with the boys or the team-bus singalong. When did he get a rest? What was his energy source? What was this dynamo like at home? He had moved Jean and their son and daughter to Glasgow's South Side, but that was not a public matter. His family life was sacrosanct and he made sure it stayed that way. He was reputed to be very good at bowls, but few ever saw him play. Stein had two good personal friends at this time, both called Tony, both bookmakers and Celtic supporters of the traditional type. They loved the man they called 'the Big Barra' and he appreciated them for the link they gave him to the punter on the terracing. This was a key ingredient in his public relations.

For my part, I couldn't wait for real Stein time to begin. It did not start all that well. In the last game of the season, only four days after their dramatic cup win, Celtic went through to meet the same Dunfermline, who trounced virtually the same Celtic by 5–1 at East End Park. It was then that the cuddly bear Stein showed his teeth. In the dressing-room afterwards, he took a vicious bite out of the team, naming them contemptuously one by one while they sat with heads bowed in shame. He spared no one and no words were strong enough to make his meaning clear. When he stopped for breath, some of the players thought he had finished and stood up, at which Jock bellowed, 'Get back on your fucking arses! I'm no' finished yet!' And he wasn't. When he did, they were like jelly, and later they were ladled silently onto the team bus for a very quiet trip home to Glasgow.

Even though they lost 2–1 to Rangers in the first Old Firm game of the new season, 1965–66, they had played well enough and this gave Stein hope. There was no verbal assault this time. They didn't need it; the Dunfermline tirade was still simmering. However, it had had the desired toughening-up effect and this was clearly illustrated in the way they battled through the ties of the League Cup during the following season to face their nemesis, Rangers, again in the final. No casual approach now for this autumn confrontation, for that is exactly what it was – a brutal, unflinching, man-to-man exchange that should have been staged in a Roman amphitheatre, not at the demure Hampden.

A record crowd for a League Cup final of 107,609 saw Ian Young's first tackle on Willie Johnston. It made them gasp. I was in Glasgow for a BBC television programme and didn't have a ticket. I turned up at the front entrance on spec. Luckily, the doorman recognised me from TV and called down one of the Celtic directors, who gave me a pass. This was promotion indeed. I sat and peeked over the directors' heads at the game. This was a lot better than standing on tiptoes in the Jungle, trying to peer between two hefty shoulders.

So I saw it for myself. Johnston went down as if bulldozed. I was relieved to see him get up. This was the key moment and it set the tone for the rest of the game. I've never been so tense at a game of football.

I was almost too scared to breathe as players clattered into one another like dodgem cars, giving and getting a bruising with every tackle, all the finer points of the game forgotten. The referee ran about like a Red Cross man, forever waving for attention to the wounded. I remember thinking, 'I'm not enjoying this.' I had never felt that way before, even when we were at our dismal worst.

Such a meaty game had to be decided by penalties, and so it was, one obvious, for hands by Ronnie McKinnon of Rangers, and the other controversial, because of a tackle on Jinky Johnstone from behind, but since both were netted by John 'Yogi' Hughes, it somehow sweetened the savour of raw meat that the game itself suggested. Even though Young of Celtic scored an own goal, it wasn't enough to deny my team their second cup in the year and Stein his first major win over 'the enemy'.

I should have been delighted, but I wasn't, and I rose to leave as Celtic came out to parade the League Cup before their rapturous support. As soon as the team appeared on the track, the enraged Rangers supporters invaded the pitch, and for the first time that autumn afternoon the Celtic team retreated. So did I. I couldn't get rid of the unaccustomed sour taste in my mouth and took the train back to London in a kind of huff.

This cup success was matched by a foray into Europe for the Cup-Winners' Cup and a tie against Dynamo Kiev, whom they beat 3–0 in the quarter-final first leg at Celtic Park. Everyone looked forward to the return tie, which meant a journey to Tbilisi in Georgia, because the Ukrainians' home ground was unplayable in January 1966. I never even thought of making the trip and as it happens it was a very good thing. From what I have read of it in *The Glory and the Dream* and in Archie Macpherson's excellent Jock Stein biography, as well as what I have heard from my friend Jim Craig, it appears to have been a bit of a mess from beginning to end.

It looked as if Celtic were the victims of a Russian conspiracy to demoralise the Celtic party throughout, in ways that had nothing to do with football. First of all, they objected to Celtic's usual choice of Aer Lingus for their air travel and insisted they should be rerouted via Moscow, thus adding to an already lengthened journey. Even so, Celtic managed a 1–1 draw and thus added a snowbound European lustre to their emerging status as a club on the rise – but then they had to get home again.

There was a two-hour catering delay at Tbilisi and a further five-hour technical delay at Moscow, during which no one was allowed to leave the plane. This was followed by an unexpected stopover in Stockholm because of freezing rain, and the next morning, because of yet another technical fault, Aer Lingus had to divert another plane to bring the players and the Celtic party back to Prestwick. A bus was waiting to take them to Celtic Park, where they arrived at 11 p.m. The players were immediately thrust into a loosening-up session by Stein until after midnight and were eventually allowed to make their way home in the early hours of the morning. It was home from Russia with something less than love.

Jim Craig mentioned that one good thing at least had come out of the Russian expedition. He had been ordered off at Tbilisi when the left-winger he was marking punched him; Jim ran after him and, in his own words, 'gave him a mouthful'. The referee then sent off the winger and Jim – who hadn't even touched the Russian. After the game, Stein advised Jim to apologise to the Celtic chairman for being sent off. Jim was indignant. 'Why should I apologise for someone punching me in the mouth? I was sent off for nothing. It's the referee who should apologise.' Stein said nothing, but when the team was picked to play Hearts the next day, Craig's name was not called out. Jim sat the game out in the stand, where director Desmond White wondered why he wasn't playing. 'Chairman's orders, I suppose,' said Jim, remembering big Jock's warning, and sat back to watch his travel-weary, jet-lagged teammates lose to Hearts.

White tackled Stein on the matter and learned that the dropping of Craig was a sanction imposed by Bob Kelly himself and not Stein's idea. White was furious and called a special meeting of the board, where he tabled a motion that there should be no interference by any member of the board, on whatever grounds, in the team selection made by the manager. This was carried. From that day, Jock Stein had full control of all playing matters – and that was official.

His strong hand was exactly what was needed at this stage of the Championship. By February, Celtic had lost to Stirling Albion at Stirling, but they were not to lose another game in the League all season. However, Rangers were doing just as well and Celtic would have to rely on their rivals losing unexpectedly to have any chance of the Championship. Happily, Rangers obliged on a couple of occasions, which meant that at this stage it was neck and neck for the title. Nerve was the thing that was needed now, and a cool head. Mr Stein had both.

Meantime, Celtic took revenge on Hearts in the Scottish Cup and also beat Liverpool in the first leg at Parkhead in the semi-finals of the European Cup-Winners' Cup. However, Stein was worried that the side did not have the same kind of buoyancy it had shown earlier in the season. If they retained the Scottish Cup, winning the League Championship would give them the treble – an undreamed-of prospect only the year before. It was a big ask. It was more probable, however, that they would win the Scottish Cup and the League than that they would have any further success in Europe. In the second leg at Liverpool, it was the denial of a goal by Bobby Lennox in the last minute of the semi-final that put them out. Stein was furious that a perfectly good strike had been disallowed for offside. Nevertheless, in the bigger picture, if he had to be beaten by anyone, he was glad it was by his old pal Bill Shankly. Still, first things first, and that meant home affairs in Scotland.

They had reached the final of the Scottish Cup, where they were due to meet Rangers. They held them to a 0–0 draw, but in the replay they were narrowly beaten by full-back Kai Johansen's winning strike with 20 minutes to go. They had nothing left now to play for but the Championship, which at least would mean a shot at Europe's most prestigious competition. That was certainly something to play for. There was only one problem – Rangers.

Jock knew on this return that he had the better playing side, but because of their youth and relative inexperience they were troubled by that old Celtic curse, inconsistency. As in the past, they were world-beaters one week, the next week well beaten. He knew the only way to cure this was to give them a self-belief that would allow them to trust in the collective talent they shared between them. To help find this magic formula, he wasn't afraid to make changes, to experiment, and he told them so. He worked on the overlap with Craig and Gemmell. Auld was given a new role in midfield and encouraged to play the general in the McMenemy manner. Simpson had been first choice in goal at one stage in the previous season and revelled in his second chance with Stein. Murdoch grew in stature match by match and captain McNeill was already there. Johnstone and Lennox owned the two wings. Perhaps the most significant new face was that of Joe McBride from Motherwell. He was the first signing Stein had made before the season began. He was to become a killer centre-forward in the McGrory mould. But would the mix be ready in time?

They left it late. On Saturday, 7 May 1966, in the last minute of the last match of the season, destiny finally blessed them. Bobby Lennox somehow prodded the ball into the net with his shin just before the final whistle, with an inch-perfect pass from Jim Craig. The goal meant that Celtic had pipped Rangers by two points to the title, their first since 1954. It was a sweet triumph for Stein and his draconian methods. Twelve years he had waited, and now his team had made their intention clear – to take the ball and, between them, kick it fearlessly into the future.

At Glasgow's Central Station, the scenes on the platform as the train steamed in from Motherwell were like those of a victorious army returning from a campaign, these drably clad, exuberant partisans of the streets howling out their joy in spontaneous cries of 'Cel-TIC! Cel-TIC!' That one word said it all for them. They had waited a long time for this. Many were openly crying. When I heard the result by phone that night in my Berkshire home, I remember punching the air triumphantly and accidentally knocking over an open bottle of Nuits-St-George. It didn't matter; I had already tasted a headier nectar.

Celtic embarked on a tour of Canada and the United States, preceded by the close-season break in a first-class hotel in Bermuda. This might seem an ideal luxury holiday to many, but to the players the idyll became nothing more than an exotic training ground. They might have been doing their sit-ups under a burning sun, but the routine was strictly Barrowfield. Stein made sure of that.

He also showed a capacity to take the initiative in other areas. When the Catholics in the party, which meant most of them, had gone off to Sunday Mass in Hamilton, Bermuda, the non-Catholics would just hang about listlessly not sure what to do with themselves. Stein didn't like this – it made for division – so he acted. Ronnie Simpson was sent off to find a Protestant kirk on the island, and Stein led his minority contingent there for an hour and no doubt crooned a hymn or two. This was all part of his painstaking method of building a team from the foundations. He would try anything if he thought it would lead to greater efficiency on the pitch.

He never missed a chance to innovate and the players would often wonder if they could keep up with every novelty he produced. Some were discarded at once with a loud guffaw, but other experiments were persevered with, and if they were seen to work, then they were gradually absorbed into the training system. The thing was to keep moving forward, and to do so confidently.

On the tour, some of their matches were to be against quality teams of the calibre of Bayern Munich and Tottenham Hotspur, as well as local sides eager for the chance to pit their wits against the new Scottish League champions, League Cup winners, Scottish Cup finalists and European Cup-Winners' Cup semi-finalists. Fortunately, they had Jock Stein on their side. He was named not only Scottish Manager of the Year but also British Manager of the Year. He didn't let this double compliment affect him in any way. He was in his element in the exotic environment as supervisor of all things, professional and social. He continued his close study of each player, probing to find the smallest chink in their performances that might be worked on to aid team effectiveness. He reasoned that they wouldn't be with the club if they couldn't play, but to play together instinctively and spontaneously was the key to fuller achievement, and he made achieving this his overriding goal.

This trip might have been part holiday, but that didn't stop his football brain from ticking over. The Stein shop never closed. The man was a complete professional; he was also a natural and astute psychologist. He knew when to let the guard drop and be one of the lads. This was where his easy singing style came to the fore, and these relaxed, social sessions with the group did much to offset the tensions that the special training talks and tactics sessions in the tropical climate could create. The ringmaster with the whip could just as easily revert to being master of ceremonies.

A further temptation to the players was the well meaning but intrusive and time-wasting attempts by the Celtic diaspora to meet, greet, touch or merely gawk at their heroes. These new rich, successful Canadians and Americans were once little Glasgow boys who didn't have much chance to see Celtic teams who had won anything, so this was as big an experience for them as for the players. These immigrants lavished hospitality on the team at every opportunity and Stein, tactfully as ever, and often wittily, turned it away whenever he could. He pretended not to see his players look on ruefully. This was how Stein developed a disciplined bonding and he could see already that it was beginning to work.

This was proved when the team beat Spurs in Toronto in a manner that underlined the fact that this was in no way a leisurely summer exhibition match. It only emphasised Stein's utter hatred of losing any game anywhere at any time. The new intensity of this emergent Celtic team was proved when they met Bayern Munich in San Francisco. The player opposing Stevie Chalmers on the left wing suddenly punched the Celtic player in the jaw. Stevie immediately got up and chased the offender behind the goal and thumped him in return. He was joined by a group of Celtic supporters who pulled Chalmers off and would have dealt with the German player themselves but for the intervention of Stein, who dragged Chalmers away and dispersed the would-be attackers. It was this prompt response to whatever situation arose that marked him out as a manager of high order.

Earlier in the trip, he had taken the whole team off to the Aqueduct Park in New York for the races, where a trophy called the Celtic Plate was competed for. Stein was in his element here and his love of the horses and betting came to the fore. Some think he may even have lost a year's bonuses on this one afternoon, but no one could have guessed that from his happy demeanour. It was a time for total celebration and party they did until they were homeward bound again for Glasgow.

When they returned to Celtic Park, it was to find that the old Jungle had been razed to the ground and in its place was a more modern enclosure. This was a fitting metaphor for the new season about to start. The old, rusting, leaking, decrepit shed represented the team as it had been. It had served its purpose but had not done too much for the comfort or condition of the supporters it sheltered. Now a new team had been proved in the North American tour and it shone with all the promise and attraction of the remodelled enclosure, which now welcomed a rapidly increasing number of Celtic fans.

Suddenly, Celtic Park was a hot ticket and the joke among the supporters was that you had to queue the night before in order to get a good view on the day. The truth was the new enclosure was the shape of things to come and a season ticket was well worth considering. Suffice to say the boys' gate gradually disappeared in the new admission rearrangements. All this hinted at a move towards the inevitable corporate control that was to come. However, during this period the support didn't give much thought to such off-the-park developments. We had a new team to hail; that was why we piled in at the gate. This was going to be our year. I couldn't have been a Celtic fan at a better time, and Saturday afternoon was sacred to their worship. 'Fan' is drawn from the word 'fanatic', although I think in my case it derived more from 'fantasy', because that was my Celtic world for so long. I was carried along on mythic tales from the past and sustained by impossible dreams for the future. My mindset Celtic wasn't a real thing at first; it was built up in my imagination over the years and gradually grew into something very real indeed.

'I think we could win everything in front of us. I think this could be a season to remember.' Stein actually said this to his players, not once but many times, in so many words. In so doing, he imbued them with such confidence that they went into every game wondering how much they would win by, not whether or not they would win. As always, the Old Firm was back in business, but this time it was the junior partners who got in with the first winning strikes.

The first encounter came in the Glasgow Cup and victory was achieved at Ibrox in a runaway 4–0 rout, which incorporated a Bobby Lennox hat-trick. Celtic triumphed again in the League with a 2–0 win at Celtic Park. Auld and Murdoch each scored within three minutes and the team sat back and soaked up everything Rangers could throw at them to win round one. This was nearly getting monotonous – except that it wasn't, it was marvellous. The League Cup final (referred by my boyhood friend Tiny Wharton) was then attained in a canter through the section play, and once more the Light Blues faced up to the inexorable green-and-white tide. A Bobby Lennox goal decided it, this time from a Joe McBride header back across goal.

They then showed their fighting qualities by coming from behind three times to beat Dunfermline Athletic 5–4 at East End Park thanks to a McBride penalty. The gods were obviously with them, and Stein knew that when the going was good you ran with it as fast as you could. The supporters were running as hard as they could just to keep up. It was unbelievable: half the season gone and already two cups in the bag and ahead in the League. They were in the European quarter-finals and were already favourites for the Scottish Cup. It was all too good to be true.

In London, I was running around the various television studios in shows like *The Avengers* and *Dr Finlay's Casebook* hardly able to concentrate on a single line of script, convinced that my Celtic bubble was going to burst at any moment. In my experience, it always did just as it was getting serious, but this team was different. These were

Glasgow samurai, going quietly about their deadly business, killing off opponents with professional ease. They were helped by occasional strokes of luck, such as Berwick Rangers knocking Rangers out of the Scottish Cup in a sensational result at Berwick. On returning from a tense European semi-final tie in Prague, Celtic found themselves facing a strong Aberdeen side in the final at Hampden. A further stroke of luck was that big Jock had stolen Willie Wallace of Hearts from under Rangers' nose, just before Joe McBride, his leading goal-scorer, went down with a serious knee injury. This meant that the team he sent out at Hampden that April afternoon in 1967 had that winning look that was to become increasingly familiar in the weeks and months and years ahead; in fact, they were to become iconic, for these were the cubs that were to become the world-famous Lisbon Lions.

Celtic supporters in the modern era know these names well and recite them reverently just as I did the team that began Kennaway; Hogg and Morrison, and my uncles knew Thomson; Cook and McGonagle, and my grandfather could recite Shaw; McNair and Dodds etc. These teams were a roll-call of Celtic aristocracy and they resound like a litany through the story of Celtic's growth in the twentieth century. Stein's young gladiators deserve to be in that number. And here they are in team order:

Ronnie Simpson
Faither, the elder of the squad, was the kind of goalkeeper who used whatever part of his anatomy came to hand to keep the ball out of his net. In this, he succeeded admirably. He exuded an air of calm around the penalty area and this gave his defenders confidence.

Jim Craig
Jim came to be known as 'Cairney' because of my playing the eponymous role in *This Man Craig*, a BBC series in the '60s. Stein dubbed him with my name in training and it stuck. This was a compliment to me, for Jim was a sound, fast and clever full-back, who was very strong in the tackle and master of the overlap.

Tommy Gemmell
Another master of the overlap, with a lethal shot to match, as his remarkable goal-scoring record showed. Tommy was worth a sixth forward in any game, but it was as an intimidating defender, right or

left, that he made his mark. He was afraid of no one, not even Jock Stein.

Bobby Murdoch

Known as 'Sam' after Samuel B. Allison, a well-known Glasgow demolition expert. That might have fitted Bobby's strength in the tackle, but he was also a master of the long, match-changing pass and got a lot of vital goals as well. He could strut through a match – and often did.

Billy McNeill

'Cesar' was Celtic through and through and it showed. A gentleman player in every sense and born to be a leader of men, he earned that place by exemplary captaincy and a consistent header of winning goals in important games. He was the genuine pivot of the team.

John Clark

John was a Kelly Kid who never made it as a right-half but immediately clicked when Stein moved him to the left. He was a quiet, unshowy performer, but he was an invaluable link in a defensive system that often employed him as a sweeper at the back.

Jimmy Johnstone

Jinky was anything but unshowy and his greed for the ball was not always understood by his teammates, who were hungry for it themselves. Yet they forgave him everything when he turned on one of his mesmerising runs down the right and won yet another game for them.

Willie Wallace

Called 'Wispy' because of his initials W.S.B. (William Semple Brown Wallace), but the nickname also acknowledged his dexterous antics around the penalty box. He was brought in as a goal-scorer by Stein and he fully lived up to his billing. A Stein favourite.

Steve Chalmers

Steve could run all day and was the ideal team player, forever at the service of whatever tactic was selected for the day. Like McNeill, he was courteous to a fault, but when the going got tough on the field, Steve got going.

Bertie Auld

Bertie, a hard but skilful performer, was often his own worst enemy, but he was a friend indeed to Celtic when something out of the ordinary was required. He was a genuine cavalier in the Celtic tradition and, although a joker, he could put his highly individual skills to good use.

Bobby Lennox

Bobby never had any hesitation in cutting through a defence at speed. His ability to score on these runs made him a Celtic goal-scorer second only to the great McGrory. Modest and unassuming, he knew his own worth and showed it often.

These, then, were the men who ran out to face Aberdeen and take the third piece of silverware in this miracle season. Stein asked Chalmers to go right as often as possible and take his marker with him, thus leaving the middle free to allow Wallace to score twice and win the Cup for Celtic. It was as easy as that, or at least this exceptional team made it seem so. There seemed to be no weakness in their line-up, and if one appeared it was swiftly dealt with either by manager or players. It began to look as if they might very well make a clean sweep this season. Even the press in England was beginning to take notice. Some even visited Glasgow to see for themselves.

This was something I couldn't do. I was working in London on the series *Man in a Suitcase*, for ITV. The episode was called 'Essay in Evil' and all I got was kicked in the back for my troubles in a filmed fight with the leading man. It was hard to keep my mind on anything other than the coming together of this great Celtic side and whether it could survive the last stages of the European Cup. I followed their progress meticulously. They disposed of Zurich methodically, again due to Stein's foresight. He said Zurich would play tight and rely on a breakaway. They did, and that allowed Gemmell to come surging through in the second leg to score twice. Tommy was especially keen that night because he had put a bet on Celtic's winning.

After Zurich, Celtic played Nantes and won through to face a much more impressive side, Vojvodina from Yugoslavia. They proved to be a very competent side indeed at home. 'The best team we played in the tournament,' Stein was later to say. They beat Celtic by a goal. This time, Gemmell was the culprit as he fluffed a back-pass to Simpson, letting the Yugoslavs in for the only goal of the game. This set up a very tense, blood-pressure-raising second leg at Parkhead, which tested the nerve of everyone present. After an hour of evenly contested play, the Yugoslav goalkeeper fumbled a ball. Quicksilver Chalmers was first to react and jabbed the loose ball into the net.

Even after that, the Slavs held on, fighting for a replay in neutral Rotterdam as Celtic pressed continuously and the minutes mounted up. Then training tactics paid off. Charlie Gallagher took a corner on the right and two Celtic players ran out of the penalty area, taking their markers with them, allowing Billy McNeill to run into the empty space provided and head into the net for the winner. Pandemonium as the 70,000 crowd vented their relief in the most prolonged cheering ever heard at the stadium. I was listening on the radio and when that goal was scored, I danced round the room on a balloon of euphoria. It's the kind of feeling a supporter lives for, a hopeless, helpless giving-over to sheer joy.

It had been a near thing. Vojvodina were good, so it was all the better that Celtic should beat them at this stage, if only by a goal. The experience was invaluable and would stand them in good stead. According to Tom Campbell, one veteran reporter was heard to mutter on leaving the new press box built over the old Jungle, 'Aye, Jock cut the margin fine the night.' Archie Macpherson quoted Tony Queen, who had said to him afterwards that it 'almost wrung the soul out of me'. There speaks the true supporter.

Still buoyed by that hard-won victory, Celtic overcame Dukla Prague at Parkhead by 3–1. Remembering his team's previous frailties, Stein determined on a purely defensive formation for the return in Prague. This time, only Chalmers was left up front and everyone else was pulled back. It was not Stein's style at all, but it was horses for courses. Once again, it was a Stein gamble that paid off and Celtic were in the final at Lisbon. The date for the match against the mighty Inter Milan had been announced as 25 May 1967. This once-in-a-lifetime occasion couldn't be missed. I immediately made plans to be there, no matter what.

I reckoned without BBC regulations. I was in Glasgow for BBC2 in the second series of *This Man Craig*. I occasionally got an episode off, to give me a much-needed rest, or one with little to do, so that I could at least have a breather. I looked at the advance schedule, praying hard, hoping for the chance of an 'out'. To my delight, I saw that I was free and could get to the game in Portugal. However, when I mentioned my plans to the producer, he was adamant that I couldn't take the risk of leaving the country while playing the lead role in a continuing series. I even thought of appealing to David Attenborough in London, the BBC2 boss at the time, but, lovely man that he was, I knew his hands would be tied. In deep grief, I resigned myself to watching it on the box.

I flew home on the midnight plane to Heathrow. By match time the next day, I had all three television sets in the house switched on, the big one in the sitting room, the medium one in our bedroom and the tiny one in the kitchen. Sheila had agreed to take the children and the dog out so that there were only four of us in the house when the match kicked off: the cat, Celtic, Inter Milan and me. I uncorked a bottle of Chilean white wine and, with shaking hand, poured myself the first glass and sat back on the couch.

I had hardly swallowed the first sip when Jim Craig was adjudged to have committed a foul in the penalty area and we were down 1–0 in the first ten minutes. I went upstairs to see if a change of set would bring us luck. I stretched full length on the bed, tense in every muscle as the Inter Milan iron defence took over. At half-time, I went down to the kitchen and made myself a Nescafé while the cat and I waited for the restart. I must admit I had misgivings. I found myself leaning on the kitchen counter, peering into the nine-inch TV. I had meant to go back into the sitting room, but I was transfixed.

With 63 minutes on the clock, my pal Jim Craig sprinted clear and rolled the ball back to Tommy Gemmell, who had come barging upfield to take it in his stride. He thumped it majestically past the Italian goalkeeper. My coffee cup went flying and I nearly went with it. 'We're going to win,' I shouted at the cat. She scampered off in fright into the sitting room. I followed her to see the rest of the game on the big television. I dived onto the couch, sending the cat scurrying back into the kitchen, just as Steve Chalmers deflected a Bobby Murdoch shot bound for the net to lift the roof – and the European Cup. I jumped up, raised both hands high, let out a roar – and burst into tears.

CHAPTER SIX

Comes the Fall

Bertie Peacock, Left-Half
A Northern Ireland shamrock crossed with a thistle,
Bertie could play till the final whistle.
An eager beaver in any position,
A worker-player in the best tradition.

It matters little now who actually reached the summit of Everest first in 1953, the Kiwi Hillary or the Sherpa Tenzing; it only matters that the top was reached by their mutual efforts in the final stages. It is the same thing with Stein and Celtic and their attaining their football Everest of 1967. Was it through the manager's contribution to team morale and efficiency or solely to the side's efforts on the pitch? I like to think that, as with the mountaineers, it was a fortunate combination of both.

Shankly's famous statement to Stein – 'John, you're immortal now' – seems a mite exclusive. He ought to have gone round every player in the dressing-room and said the same to them, for each of their names has entered into mythical territory and the legend of the Lisbon Lions has even been perpetuated by having the title writ large in red in the new stand at the eastern end of Celtic Park. This later overhaul of the stadium did much to improve the spectators' conditions, but in a sweep it obliterated the old parameters of the ground. This included, at the London Road end at Kinloch Street, my first route of passage to Celtic, the sevenpenny gate.

Now the London Road Lambs had become the Lisbon Lions. It is good that these young men and their mighty deeds should be commemorated, but I feel a tinge of regret for those players who were part of that miracle year's squad but didn't make it to the winning XI: John Fallon, the goalkeeping substitute, who didn't play, but at least he was there; the late Willie O'Neill, full-back, who ceded to Jim Craig because of a change in tactics; John Hughes, who had performed well in earlier rounds, but whose personal relations with Stein were strained at that time; Charlie Gallagher, whose corners were so rewarding but who was also omitted; Joe McBride, who was riding so high on the scoresheet, but knee injury finally forced his withdrawal, allowing Willie Wallace to step in. But 'that's fitba', as Jimmy Delaney so famously said.

An *annus mirabilis* is hard to follow in any sphere, and so it proved for Celtic. Even the most powerful meteor has to fall to earth eventually. Had Stein had a sense of theatre, he would have retired there and then at his very peak and been revered thereafter as a football god. Instead, although he had no contract to fulfil (he never had a contract at Celtic), he felt a moral duty to see his squad made ready to do battle again. Another season waited. His immediate task was to prepare his favoured group for the prospect of getting back to work at less Olympian levels.

First, there was a show match at the Bernabéu Stadium in Spain against Real Madrid for the benefit of their former centre-forward, the iconic Alfredo di Stefano. There was nothing at stake here except prestige, but Stein valued that even more than any trophy. He knew that a win against what is regarded still as the best team in the world would put his team immediately on that level, but at the same time he did not wish to put his brand-new Lions at risk so soon. He had his own reasons not to gamble on seeing that team lose, so he made two changes, bringing in John Fallon for Ronnie Simpson and Willie O'Neill for Steve Chalmers, with appropriate positional adjustments. This seemed justice enough, for both played well, especially Fallon, and Celtic, incredibly, ran out winners, thanks to yet another Lennox hit following a great run by Jinky Johnstone. The Stein cup overflowed. Then it was back to auld claes an' parritch.

The League Cup of 1967–68 beckoned and this time Rangers loomed in their group. For their first meeting at Ibrox, the gates were closed on nearly 95,000 fans, of which perhaps less than half were Celtic-mad, and the other, greater half were just as lunatic. There is another similarity between the two great Old Firm armies: they are both colour blind; one sees only blue, the other only green. Celtic took the lead from a first-half Gemmell penalty, but Penman equalised with a late free kick and the draw led to a very tense replay at Parkhead. The latter game hinged on a missed penalty by Rangers' Johansen when they were leading 1–0 with ten minutes to go. This escape fired Celtic up and they proceeded to run riot, with goals from Wallace, Murdoch and Lennox, to seal a very satisfying result for the Celtic end.

I was one of them again, having been up in Scotland that year for the end of the second series of *This Man Craig*, and was able to make myself available Saturday afternoons to see most Celtic games in that season. It was good to rub shoulders with the other supporters in the enclosure again, to talk that special football language that begins with a chatter of excitement before the game starts and goes on in virtually a running commentary, which grows hysterical or muted according to how the game's going. The half-time Bovril never tasted better.

This game at Celtic Park was particularly pleasing in that it was, in the parlance of sports journalism, a game of two halves. So many events in life have this Jekyll-and-Hyde propensity, where some occurrence, however small, can turn a whole unhappy sequence right round to make it memorably enjoyable. When Johansen stepped up, so full of certainty, to take that penalty and hit the bar, it was just such a moment. I can remember the feeling of euphoria even now, so you can just imagine that reaction multiplied thousands of times over among the Celtic support. I knew then, in my bones, that not only would we win the game, we would also retain the League Cup – and we did, beating Dundee 5–3 on 28 October.

The strain of maintaining such a high level week in, week out was bound to tell and it showed in the early exit from the European Cup at the hands of Dynamo Kiev. This was followed by a woeful chapter of unsavoury happenings in South America in search of the supposed 'World Club Championship'. Stein thought it would prove to be the final cherry on the cake. Instead, the episode had all the feeling of milk that had gone off. In retrospect, it made the most combustible Old Firm match look like a game of dominoes.

Celtic won the first leg at Hampden Park through a McNeill header from a corner by Hughes. It was a match that gave ample warning of Racing Club's win-at-all-costs approach. On their arrival in Buenos Aires for the return leg, the whole Celtic party felt they had been put under arrest, the police presence was so strong. It was supposed to be for their protection, but they didn't enjoy that. Most Glaswegians, by instinct, are uneasy in continued police proximity. The sense of intimidation was all round them and did little to make them relaxed. The players were well used to the reaction of hostile fans, but this was fanaticism of another order altogether. It was only another football match, but this environment was not friendly. It was openly political, it was hate, it was war.

In the return leg (and in the play-off later in Montevideo), every Celtic player, at least once in the game, and Jinky Johnstone several times, was kicked, punched, elbowed, spat upon systematically and always when the referee's head was turned the other way – and all the time being viciously taunted and verbally abused by the partisan Racing Club fans. Nobody needed to know a word of Spanish to get their meaning.

It would be a downright lie to describe the proceedings as a sporting contest in three matches, so we will pass over the whole shoddy display and merely say that Racing Club concentrated entirely on a crude defence and negative tactics to stop Celtic playing football of any kind in Buenos Aires and won 2–1 on breakaways. Simpson was struck on the head by an iron bolt thrown from the crowd before kick-off and had to be replaced by John Fallon. Johnstone had to wash his hair at half-time to clear it of spittle. The dressing-room atmosphere was brittle.

The score meant a third game had to be played, in Montevideo. Celtic ought to have flown home in the face of such disgraceful tactics, but Stein's blood was up and his pride was hurt. He still believed football would win out. He was so wrong. Three Celtic players were sent off, as were two from Racing Club, and still the game, if it can be called that, went on. The referee seemed to be living in a space of his own. He could have been in the Tardis with the door shut. The Celtic players could only take so much, hence the sendings-off. Finally, Tommy Gemmell acted for all of them when he went storming over to Norberto Raffo, the chief offender, who was laughing openly at his latest foul, and gave him a hefty kick right in the bollocks. The Argentinian screamed and big Tommy walked off. The ball was on the slates from then on, as we say in Glasgow. Bertie Auld was fouled, yet he was the fourth Celt ordered off. Bertie, who couldn't speak Spanish, told the referee in his own way to 'Fuck off' and stayed on till the bitter end. And it was bitter for Celtic.

The records show that Celtic were beaten 1–0 but really the only thing that lost was football itself. Television pictures were beamed right round the world showing Stein remonstrating with Gemmell after his action, and Celtic were written off as Glasgow hooligans, especially by the English sports press. But any Glaswegian will marvel at how restrained the team were for so long. They had to snap and Gemmell only did what many of them would have done, except perhaps Bobby Lennox, but then he came from Saltcoats.

The English reporters present were perhaps still resentful of Celtic's being the first British club to lift the European Cup and were taking every opportunity to belittle the Scots. Archie Macpherson tells a lovely story about how the plane carrying the press back to Britain was delayed by fog at the airport and the journalists were going over the events, with some regret from the Scots and glee from the English. One of the group, a prominent English broadcaster, had been particularly scathing about the Glasgow team in his reports home and continued to blame them for their uncontrolled and unprofessional behaviour, completely ignoring the obvious provocation. In his opinion, the Argentinians deserved their well-won victory. This was too much for an eminent member of the Scottish press who went up to the haughty Englishman and floored him with a single punch to the jaw. End of story.

At the BBC's sports celebrations for 1967, Celtic were named Team of the Year, and deservedly so. However, Stein was never to forgive the BBC for focusing their coverage of the South American debacle on his remonstrating with Gemmell after that player's deliberate kick at Raffo. It made dramatic television, but it gave entirely the wrong impression, which wasn't helped by the commentator's remarks. Jock continued to moan about it. He was a darker Stein since South America. He knew his team would have won in style had they been allowed to play and this always rankled with him. He may have felt he was to blame for pushing them too far and now he realised that the only way to get over it was to win yet another Championship.

The sadder but wiser Celtic contingent returned bonus-less but determined to aim for the League Championship. This meant another duel with Rangers in the League. Celtic had already lost their first League clash 1–0 and Stein knew that Rangers would not lose too many games as they came into the final straight. However, he also knew he had the better team. So did we supporters, and we all waited for them to prove it. By the New Year, there were only two points in it and the whole support was holding its breath.

In the spring of 1968, a strange thing happened. Rangers were due to play Celtic in the semi-final of the Glasgow Cup and Celtic waited to fix a date. Instead, they received a formal letter from their opponents ceding the tie, 'due to a congestion of fixtures'. This was unheard of. Rangers were a point ahead in the League, and also still in the Fairs Cup. For them to shy away from another Old Firm clash was unbelievable, especially to their own followers, who had to take a merciless ribbing from their Celtic counterparts. Celtic went on to beat Clyde 8–0 in the final to take the Glasgow Cup. Rangers were repaid for their cautious tactics by losing in the Scottish Cup and Fairs Cup and were now level with Celtic in the League. To add to their misery, Aberdeen beat them in the last game of the season and Celtic went on to retain the League Championship by beating Dunfermline, who had just won the Scottish Cup. Celtic had played 32 games without a loss and had won 16 in a row.

This is the stuff of champions and I was one of the few at that time who thought the second Stein side was a better football team than the redoubtable Lions. To say this aloud would have been unthinkable at this time, as the Lions had been put on an impossible pedestal.

The second series of *This Man Craig* was drawing to a close and they wanted to do a third, but I demurred; it was too punishing a schedule to keep up. I knew how Rangers felt with their fixtures piling up on them. Besides, STV had asked me to write and star in a six-part series on the life of Burns, which I couldn't refuse. It involved research in Scotland and that meant my being on Celtic's doorstep again for next season. I signed the contract gleefully and drove north to Glasgow.

I was there to welcome new signings Harry Hood and Tommy Callaghan and see the introduction of the home-grown defender Jim Brogan and that idiosyncratic genius George Connelly. They all soon made their presence felt in the squad. Big John Hughes got back to form again and wee Jinky was on fire on the right. The whole team was ablaze, with Lennox and Wallace interchanging at will and causing havoc wherever they went. Soon the League Cup was back on the sideboard, after a scintillating 6–2 win over Hibs in the fire-damaged Hampden. The hoses didn't dampen the Celts charge through the season, which culminated in the 1969 Scottish Cup final victory over Rangers, their first since 1928. Connelly showed his real class in this 4–0 win and I was sure he was a player who was heading for the heights.

The 1968–69 Championship had been won five days earlier at Kilmarnock when Gemmell scored to give us the necessary draw. Kilmarnock was a good augury for me because of its Burns connections. The Burns series had already gone out on Scottish Television and was well received by viewers. Now I was back in Scotland for further work on a Burns episode for ITV's *Sunday Night Theatre*, but I was more concerned with my other kind of theatre, which meant attending at Rugby Park on the evening of Monday, 21 April. Having spent so much time in Ayrshire filming for the Burns series, it was like coming home driving to Rugby Park that night. I remember the match less for the score (2–2) than for the fact that I was recognised by a group of young Kilmarnock supporters who threatened to turn over my car after the game. I don't know whether it was because they knew I was a Celtic supporter or because they, as Ayrshire lads, didn't like my portrayal of Burns. At any rate, I was saved by a crowd of Celtic supporters, who formed a ring round the car and allowed me to drive away.

I returned south for another episode of *The Avengers*, which meant I was back to catching up with results in the Sundays or listening to Radio Scotland on my car radio, which was the only way I could receive the station in Maidenhead. I spent hours sitting in my own drive trying to follow the games as the car windows misted up. It got very thick inside the Saab as I heard of Rangers' win at Ibrox in the 1969–70 League Cup, but it cleared up a bit when Celtic won the return game, with Gemmell scoring to set Celtic on the road to a fifth successive triumph in the competition. At this time, only these Old Firm games mattered in the winning of major domestic trophies. With all respect to the other clubs in Scotland, a fixture with them was really a practice run for Rangers and Celtic. That was the way of it then and it still is.

Because of the incontestable superiority of the Rangers–Celtic axis in Scottish football, I have always been an advocate of a British League, so that these two giants of Scottish football can meet teams nearer their own level more regularly. This would raise not only their own standard of play, by making them open to consistent challenge, but it might also go some way to diffusing the inescapable focus on their rivalry, which only sustains the imbecilic sectarian emphasis. Scots could then join to cheer on their own goliaths as representatives of Scotland against the Manchester Uniteds and the Arsenals on a regular basis, which would be to everyone's good.

If such a National Football League of Great Britain should come to pass, it would enable the teams not at this elite level to compete more equably at a slightly less stressful pace, always allowing for promotion and relegation. It would then be possible, if not probable, that Elgin City could meet Manchester City, if they played well enough long enough. Such utopian hopes belong more to the pipe dream than the pipeline and are unlikely to come to pass in my lifetime.

My concern for season 1969–70 was whether Celtic could keep up the pace they had set themselves. Advances had been made on all fronts, but were marred by the usual Old Firm 'incidents'. When Jim Craig accidentally put the ball through his own net in a Scottish Cup tie, he was 'congratulated' by a Rangers player. This caused mayhem. Arrests were made among both sets of supporters, and both captains were called before the SFA to explain matters. This was merely talking, not action, and nothing changed the fact that Celtic won. The pressure was still on, but Celtic's suspicions of SFA and refereeing bias against them began to grow from this time, especially when the official in charge of the 1970 Scottish Cup final appeared, to all Celtic supporters at any rate, to gift Aberdeen the trophy. They were a good team, but it is much easier to win when you have an extra man like Bobby Davidson.

Jock Stein was incensed and let his feelings about the referee be known from the top of the Hampden stairs to the bottom. He called for a full investigation of the referee's performances, but all he got for his pains was a token fine for his outburst, which possibly amounted to a tacit admission by some that he was probably right. However, the Celtic luck was about to turn – upon the toss of a coin, of all things.

In the European Cup, Celtic had disposed of a lot of quality along the way, including the great Benfica. They met in the return leg in Lisbon with the home team having to score three to draw, which they did, sending the match into extra time, by the end of which there had been no further scoring. They then retired to the pavilion with the tie still undecided. The referee called the two captains together to toss for it. Billy McNeill was not noted for his gambling skills and looked to his boss for help, but Stein only said, 'You're on your own here.' Billy had to guess correctly not once but twice, the first time to see who would make the deciding call. In both cases, Billy guessed rightly and Celtic were through to the quarter-finals in a manner that pleased nobody. Fortunately, they went on to beat Fiorentina, which saw them cast to play Leeds United, the English champions, in the semi-finals.

When I heard this, I felt so disappointed. The English champions against the Scottish champions would have made an excellent final for the 1970 European Cup. Not only that, it was a managerial contest between two thinking managers, Don Revie and Jock Stein, both then at the top of their respective games. It would never get any better than that. But it was not to be. However, Celtic got by at Elland Road by 1–0, through an effort by George Connelly that was deflected by a Leeds player past his own goalkeeper, and Celtic expectations were high for the return at Hampden on 15 April.

I was in London in a TV play for *ITV Playhouse* and of course I was talking about nothing else but this great football match I'd been hoping to see, but I hadn't been able to get a ticket from the 134,000 available. One of the cameramen heard me going on about it and told me his young brother had a Leeds supporter's ticket but, like hundreds of other Leeds fans, had decided not to go. I got him to phone his brother right away, because I knew any spare tickets would be snapped up immediately by success-hungry Celtic fans. This is why I found myself standing on the terracing among a lot of Englishmen. Oddly enough, I was playing a Yorkshireman in the play I was rehearsing, *Mixed Foursomes*. I didn't mention this to the guys around me, but I got some good tips for my English accent.

Another coincidence was that the key to this absolutely unforgettable exchange was the battle of wills and skills that went on in the centre of the field between the 'mixed foursome' of three Scots and an Irishman. They were Murdoch and Auld for Celtic and Billy Bremner and the Irishman Johnny Giles for Leeds United. It was like a whirlwind game of chess in the middle of the field and it was fascinating to watch these four wily footballers fight for the ascendancy. Billy Bremner drew first blood on the quarter-hour with a thundering shot from long range. John Hughes was playing himself into the final, but it was the 'Flying Flea', Jimmy Johnstone, who was rampant. He toyed with Terry Cooper and Norman Hunter, the two most feared defenders in English football, as if they were junior trialists, but nothing came of his complete mastery of the right side of play. Given the speed and the quality of play from both sides, the first half flew by in minutes, it seemed. At the interval, my English match companions were chortling, and even generous in their praise of Celtic. I could only agree.

The second half had hardly started when Auld picked up a short corner and crossed for John Hughes to head the equaliser. Only minutes later, Leeds had to change goalkeepers because of an injury to Gary Sprake, and another Scot, David Harvey, took over. At once, Johnstone was rewarded for his night's work when he turned a ball back into the path of the running Murdoch who, without pausing, sent a thunderbolt past young Harvey to win the game.

It was a wonderful goal, an exhilarating game, and at the end of it I couldn't resist a mighty cheer, which caused one of the Yorkshiremen to exclaim to his pals, 'Ee, the lad's one o' them.' He was so right. I never felt more 'one o' them' than I did that night. It was a truly epic struggle, tough without being testy, strongly contested without being at all dirty, but, above all, well played in every sense of that phrase. I was right; it ought to have been the final.

The actual final could not have been more contrasting. Perhaps Celtic had paid too dearly for that memorable semi-final. They were not the same team at all against the Dutch champions, Feyenoord, at Milan three weeks later. Unlike before Lisbon, Celtic were the clear favourites to win the cup for the second time and nobody disagreed with the bookmakers. Stein had tried to warn the team against underestimating Feyenoord, but a Glasgow zest, a gallus swagger, appeared to have overtaken the whole squad following that marvellous Battle of Britain with Leeds.

The atmosphere was altogether too relaxed. Players, surrounded by journalists, were even accused of being more intent on striking sponsorship deals than discussing tactics. This, however, was a European Cup final. They should have known that, like all really big occasions, it would be a 'oncer' – having no precedent and making its own rules. The Stein plan this time was to let the side play their natural game. As Stein said to reporters when asked how the game would go, 'We'll see.'

I didn't see it, however. The night the match was on I was professionally involved myself. I was actually recording a TV play in London and rather preoccupied throughout the evening, with little time to think of anything else. Like everyone else, I thought that, after Celtic's performance against Leeds, it was a foregone conclusion. When someone told me the result after our recording, I was thunderstruck. I still couldn't believe it when I read all about it in *The Times* the next morning: 2–1 after extra time for the Dutch. It was a very unappetising breakfast that morning. The team that didn't make it this time was: Williams; Hay and Gemmell; Murdoch, McNeill and

Brogan; Johnstone, Wallace, Hughes, Auld and Lennox. George Connelly was 12th man.

This was still a good team for all that, with plenty of good players in the line-up, but something must have been missing on the night. Even though Celtic scored first, through another Gemmell screamer following a free kick, Feyenoord equalised through Rinus Israël almost immediately, and Celtic dropped their heads and their guard. According to the reports, Feyenoord dominated the second half as Celtic uncharacteristically wilted. Brogan and Johnstone were injured but played on. Only Auld was substituted, for Connelly, in the latter stages. They survived until extra time. Hughes might have scored in the first few minutes but had no luck. Instead, it was Feyenoord who scored, two minutes from the end, after McNeill had used a hand to try to prevent the ball reaching the dangerous Ove Kindvall, who nevertheless managed to net and broke Celtic hearts in the process. Instead of a second Bannockburn, it was Celtic's first Flodden, and it was hard to take. Even though it was a very narrow defeat, and after extra time, it was still very deeply felt by the players and by those of us reading about it.

The Scottish press reaction was bitter and blame was poured on the players for lack of effort, but Tom Campbell and Pat Woods put it succinctly when they wrote in *The Glory and the Dream*, 'The serpent of complacency had crept into Paradise.'

The case of champagne waiting at the hotel was left undrunk and the next morning there was a very long wait at Malpensa Airport, from nine o'clock in the morning until five o'clock at night. That would have done little to lift everyone's spirits. It would have been a very solemn homecoming for all of them. By the way, the play that I was recording the night of the match was called *Requiem*. Enough said.

Pelion was piled upon Ossa when, after these epoch-ending events in Italy, Celtic, minus Jimmy Johnstone, who was on agreed 'home leave', went straight into an unfortunate exhibition tour in Toronto, New York, Boston and Bermuda. In contrast to the team that had made the previous bonding trip across the Atlantic, the tour that had heralded the new-look, winning Celtic, this jaded, disappointed, travel-weary 1970 version of Club Celtic were on a hiding to nothing. Manchester United beat them 2–0 in Toronto and a pugilistic Bari team tried to kick them off the park in a hard-won 2–2 draw in the same city, only five days after their savage encounter in New York.

These spoiling tactics angered Stein so much that he leapt out of the Celtic dugout and into the Italians', where he lifted their coach to his feet and punched him to the ground. He then left him lying and the others staring while he collected his bag from his own dugout, walked out of the stadium to the airport and flew home on other business, having made his point. He did not see Bari walk off the park in protest at the 'poor' refereeing, which no doubt had tried to curb the Italians' tendency towards assassination.

This left the team in the charge of the assistant manager, Sean Fallon, who tried to control a group of young men who were trying to climb out of a sequence of bad results that were not always their fault. All this was too much for the Celts. Taking advantage of the boss's absence, they revenged themselves on these dispiriting happenings by taking full advantage of generous hospitality at that Celtic hub, Kearny, New Jersey.

Fallon felt obliged to send the identified ringleaders of the social whirl, Auld and Gemmell, home on the first plane. Discipline was restored. I think the truth might have been that they were still suffering reaction from that needless defeat in Milan. A turning point had been reached for team and manager, and Stein would have his work cut out to bring his charges back to the high levels so recently displayed against Leeds. It could be argued that those halcyon days were already over.

A hint of things to come was evident in the delayed Glasgow Cup final against Rangers in early August 1970, when Stein fielded seven reserves in a comfortable 3–1 victory. However, the Ibrox club gained their revenge in the League Cup final, where the 16-year-old Derek Johnstone scored the only goal of the game. 'The right result,' said the *Celtic View*, correctly in my opinion. I was now reading this publication more regularly, having been engaged to do a series of plays at the Lyceum Theatre in Edinburgh, where I was happy to meet with fellow actors and fellow Celtic supporters Jimmy Grant and Joe Brady, who were even more Celtic-mad than I was, especially wee Joe, now, alas, gone to his Maker.

Joe had been brought up in the Calton (now called Merchant City East by estate agents) and had begun at the boys' gate like me. He did a long stint on *Z-Cars* on television, and had he still been in uniform instead of sitting at a dressing-room mirror between shows on a Saturday, he would have arrested himself for a breach of the peace, such was his language and behaviour when he heard Celtic had just lost again. Jimmy, being a Highlander, or rather an Islander, was much more courteous and just swore softly under his breath. I merely sighed, but it was wonderful to share Celtic with these two for the run of *Willie Rough*.

Oddly enough, because of Saturday matinees, I saw less of Celtic while I was based in Edinburgh than I did when I worked in London, which was perhaps as well, as they were going through what was, for them, a slump. It was baton-changing time, but the baton hovered uncertainly while changes were being considered. Some of the Lions had retreated to a corner of the cage and some, like Simpson, had left it altogether. Gemmell was eyeing the bars warily, as if looking for a means of escape, and even Jim Craig was thinking more and more of dentistry. Young cubs like Davie Hay and Danny McGrain were already prancing eagerly and the name of another was being mentioned more frequently: Kenny Dalglish. Their time was nigh, but Stein was being canny.

While I waited for this next Celtic to emerge, I was similarly engaged in rebuilding. I had bought an ancient ruin in Pittenweem, dating from 1590. With the help of the National Trust, I was making it into the new Cairney family home. It was more than a matter of just moving house again. By this time, I already had a beautiful stately home on four acres by the banks of the Thames at Bray, which was more than adequate, but, just like my team, I was now nearly forty and in need of change. With more work offered at the Lyceum and the Burns tours growing every year, I decided to renovate the Earl of Kellie's Ludging and move up to Fife. Kellie Lodging, as I called it, was well worth it, and the sale of Braywick Cottage in the south paid for it all, so the move was duly made. I settled back into my favourite armchair and, from my study overlooking the North Sea, opened my copy of the *Celtic View*.

The magazine had been started in 1965 by Jack McGinn, later to become a director of Celtic, to give the supporter a voice, a forum in which to express his opinions on the running of the club and its impact on team performances. A few years later, I met Jack in the Duke of Touraine restaurant at Parkhead. Knowing of my Celtic allegiance, he wanted to chat. It seemed the BBC were considering beginning a sports quiz programme, to go out from Manchester, involving selected football clubs and a celebrity supporter of each. Would I consider being Celtic's choice?

I was highly flattered, but pointed out that Celtic had many supporters more celebrated than me: Sean Connery, for one (a Celtic supporter at that time), and Rod Stewart, for two. Jack said he had tried both, but they were too busy; seriously, though, he would like me to consider it. I didn't need to think about it and said he could give my name to the BBC. Because of *Quizball*, I became the only man to play for Celtic without kicking a ball for them.

In due course, I was delighted to meet with my fellow members of this new Celtic team. I was surprised to find how personable and articulate Billy McNeill was and that he was as commanding a presence in the studio as he was on the field. Willie Wallace was the other player on our side. I gather 'Wispy' was there because the original choice, Celtic's other university graduate, John Cushley, was unfit to travel to Manchester, and Wallace happened to be at the ground that day and took Cushley's place. The second university man at Celtic Park, Jim Craig, was also unavailable, and his place was taken by his father-in-law Jimmy Farrell, who happened to be my lawyer and also a Celtic director.

This was the team that went to Manchester for the first season of the programme. We lost after extra time to Nottingham Forest. The formula was that we were asked four questions ranging from easy to difficult. I think our mistake was that we played too safe and kept mid-range instead of going for the Route One Question, which naturally earned more points. Next time, however, we had Jim Craig on the team and that made a difference. Jim was a mine of information on all sports and much else, I cornered the arts queries and Billy dealt with science matters. 'Wispy' didn't say a word, but he still got his £100 fee. Thanks mainly to 'Cairney' Craig, we went Route One all the way and beat Sunderland 3–0, West Bromwich Albion, who had won the competition the previous year, 2–1 and Hearts, after a very close game, 3–1, and Celtic took the silverware. It was fun being around all the footballers from the different clubs. I met Jim Baxter, who was there as a spectator with Pat Crerand, and all the beautiful football wives, not to mention the other celebrities, many of whom, like James Bolam, were actors I had worked with. Altogether it was a great time and not at all like work.

We came back for a third season and won, with this man Craig again on form for us; Billy wasn't bad either. Wispy still hadn't opened his mouth on transmission, so we arranged that we would leave one question to him whether he liked it or not. The question was Route Three, I think. It was 'Who or what is garryowen?' We all knew it was a kick from the hands to score over the posts in rugby but looked at Wispy to respond. He gulped, pressed his buzzer and whispered tentatively, 'The racing correspondent of the *Daily Record?*' It got the biggest laugh of the night. Wispy retired defeated, but he laughed about it later, and got another £100. We went on to beat Manchester City 5–0, Aberdeen 4–3, another tight match, and, finally, Everton 7–5, to win another *Quizball* Cup.

Shortly afterwards, we were invited to face a challenge from an England Football Select and I lost it for us by trying to be too smart. The question was not difficult: 'Who wrote the opera *Carmen?*'

'That's easy,' I called out, and put my finger on the buzzer, but Bobby Charlton, as alert as he ever was on the football park, pressed his first and shouted, 'Bizet!' The question master awarded him the winning point.

Jim and Billy gave me stick in the hospitality room afterwards. I said I was meaning to make a rhyme: 'Easy – Bizet.'

'Smart-arse,' retorted Jim.

Billy put his hand on my shoulder and said quietly, 'As the boss keeps telling us, John, keep it simple.'

It was back to the real world again.

At the beginning of the 1970–71 League campaign, Celtic were aware that they could repeat the famous six-in-a-row sequence won by the Celtic side that had dominated Scottish football before the First World War. That was a long time ago, and it was a much harder feat to attain in modern times, but the spur was there. The Stein machine was still, despite tinkering with the moving parts, in good working order. It had to be, for new teams were coming to the fore in the chase for the Championship, like Aberdeen, for instance, who had a strong, young side and were at the top of the League at the turn of the year by a point. For once, there was no challenge from Rangers, who were eight points behind Celtic at the time and ended up fifteen points adrift. The Copland Road brigade was faltering so much that many expected that when Celtic met them on 2 January 1971 it would be a mere formality. It was a lot more than that. I was there that day and in a way I wish now I hadn't been.

It was goalless for most the game and I can recall being frustrated, standing high up at the Celtic end of Ibrox, wondering if my team would ever score; they had had most of the game but couldn't find the net. It was not only freezing but a wet Govan mist seemed to be hanging over the park. Maybe the Celtic players couldn't see? Then, a minute from the end, the wee man Johnstone scored and we thought we had the match won. So did many of the Rangers supporters, for we could just see them moving up to the top of their terracing on the way out. But with only seconds to go, Colin Stein headed into the net to tie the game 1–1. We howled in despair and, as the Rangers fans erupted in jubilation, we turned away to make our slow, dejected way out. To have thrown the game away on the last whistle was so typical of the old Celtic I knew.

Suddenly, there seemed to be a commotion on the terracing straight across from where we were filing out. We stopped to look as figures were seen running across the field and up the track beside the stand, all heading in the one direction. What was going on? It was hard to see in the mist.

'Must be a fight or somethin', said somebody.

'No' among their ain, surely?'

'Ach, the Huns wid fight wi' anybody,' added somebody else. We left them to it.

It took forever to get clear of Edmiston Drive. I'd got through town and into Duke Street before I thought to turn on the radio and see if I could get the Aberdeen result on *Sports News*. The first thing I heard was a female voice:

> News has just come in of a serious accident at Ibrox Stadium in Glasgow, where, because of unusual crowd pressure on Stairway 13 at the Copland Road side of the ground, barriers are said to have given way resulting in some casualties as spectators were crushed in the ensuing fall onto the steps. Further information will be given on this as information comes to hand. It has been announced that . . .

I reached over, switched off the car, then sat in the dark outside my mother's flat, hardly able to take it in. Those guys on the steps, I mean, they were just at a match. I found my mother with a cigarette in her mouth. She was up to high doh.

'How terrible for a' they poor men,' she said. 'It was oan the television there, but I coudnae watch it. I hid tae have a cigarette. A' they bodies lying on the track. It wis awfy tae watch. Some o' them nae mair than wee boys . . . Are ye gonnae take yer coat off?'

A sombre voice was saying, 'I understand there have been fatalities, but the number of dead has not yet been disclosed . . .' I couldn't answer my mother. I just stood there, staring at the television.

'I'll put on the kettle,' my mother said.

CHAPTER SEVEN

This Old Firm Business

Jimmy Delaney – Outside-Right
Deadly in the goalmouth,
Speedy on the wing,
Jimmy Delaney on the ball
Was indeed a wonderful thing.

What has become known as the Ibrox disaster was, sad to say, not the first occasion at the Rangers ground that involved a loss of life. The first occurred on 2 April 1902. A new wooden stand-cum-terracing extension had been erected at the ground to cope with the large crowd expected for the biannual Scotland against England international. Ten minutes into the game, the flimsy structure collapsed, the inadequate planking gave way and hundreds of spectators plunged to the ground below; 26 were killed and 587 severely injured. It is thought that the wooden planks couldn't take the sudden surge of weight as spectators moved forward to get a better view of Bobby Templeton, who was playing on the right wing for Scotland that day. Templeton later became a Celtic player.

The second Ibrox disaster was on 16 September 1961. Two people were killed and forty-six injured when, at the end of an Old Firm League encounter, a barrier broke on Stairway 13, the very same exit that would feature in that unfortunate third catastrophe after the game that I attended in 1971.

A nurse from the St Andrew's Ambulance Association, on hearing of it, said, 'Oh, not again!' It all came out in great detail the next day in the newspapers: sixty-six killed – thirty-three men, thirty-one teenagers, a boy of nine (Nigel Pickup from Liverpool) and a woman.

133

She was Margaret Cameron, God rest her soul. It is not known where she was in the pile-up at the foot of Stairway 13, lying flat on the ground dead or sitting up dead or still standing dead, but dead they all were. In addition, 145 people were injured. Not only Glasgow was mourning the dead. These Rangers supporters came from all parts of Scotland; five young teenagers were from Fife and young Master Pickup came from Liverpool. But they were all in the mortuary now and sixty-six homes were mourning husbands, fathers and brothers trapped and one female suffocated by the bent metal barriers.

To read about it in the light of day made it almost unbelievable. I had to keep reminding myself that I had been there. It was a football match, for God's sake. Then there were all the stories.

Russell Leadbetter, in *The Herald*'s Saturday supplement on 11 December 2010, reported William Mason's story:

> I started down the slope but was lifted off my feet, and I remember beginning to slowly fall forward. Halfway down, the crowd stopped but there was no let-up in the pressure. It was unbearable. I remember the sensation of being crushed as I lay almost horizontally. I managed to free my upper chest to breathe. I think I was trapped for around forty-five minutes. I remember hearing people shouting and bawling, but they gradually fell silent. I was suffering from a lack of oxygen and desperately wanted to sleep, but someone near me kept slapping me in the face – he knew it was important I remained awake. I don't know who he was. There was no communication. Eventually I was hauled out bodily by the police, who carried me down to the pitch. I remember it was freezing cold. The sky was dark and the floodlights were still on. I couldn't move or talk, I was still in shock. Somebody was going along the pitch checking the people who were lying on it, 'Dead ... dead ... dead ... he's OK.'

Forty years on and he still had the pictures in his mind's eye:

> The bodies were taken on stretchers into what I'm sure was the away dressing-room. That's where I was taken. I now know that everybody was dead. There was no moaning or groaning, absolutely nothing, and I thought at first I was dead. The guy next to me sat up and lay back down again. The nurse came over and checked him,

then she covered him up. I had seen him sitting up, and that's when I started crying. That's what triggered it. I was still in shock and couldn't move, but I was in floods of tears. The nurse must have seen me. She said, 'This one's alive, get him out of here.'

It was another 17 years before Mr Mason went back to a match at Ibrox.

In the days following the tragedy, communal church services were held in the city at the Presbyterian Glasgow Cathedral and at St Andrew's Roman Catholic Cathedral, where both clubs united to remember what they called their absent friends. Players from both clubs attended these services, all looking like schoolboys in their black ties and suits. For days afterwards, Glasgow was in a kind of daze. I kept thinking, 'What could anyone have done?' All I could do was write a few lines of verse.

> If I could I would have reached a hand
> Across the pitch and beyond the terrace
> To that other place
> Where you, my fellow football fan,
> Reached the span of your allotted time
> Too soon upon the sound of cheers,
> Leaving us to hear the whistle
> With chilled hearts
> And faces hot with tears.

The late Matt McGinn, folk singer and dear old friend of mine, wept openly when he heard the news from Ibrox and wrote a song about it.

> New Year bells had been ringing,
> All Scotland was singing,
> The old year had died, and the new had been born,
> As the news of disaster, from Ibrox came spreading,
> The news that would cause a whole nation to mourn.

> Two great goals had been scored, in the last dying moments,
> Jimmy Johnstone for Celtic, for Rangers young Stein,
> Their supporters all cheered them with voices of thunder,
> Unknowing what waited on staircase thirteen.

135

Sixty-six people died, some in flower of their manhood,
When the fences gave way, and the barriers bent,
Seasoned Glasgow policemen, their faces all tear-stained,
With brave efforts endeavoured, far worse to prevent.

All of Glasgow enjoined for the first time in history,
In the Glasgow Cathedral, no Billy, no Dan,
But the Old Firm united, to pray for the victims,
Of a tragedy set in the memory of man.

New Year bells had been ringing, all Scotland was singing,
The old year had died and the new had been born.
As the news of disaster from Ibrox came spreading,
The news that would cause a whole nation to mourn.

* * *

Before you can even begin to talk seriously about Celtic, you have to consider Rangers. It's like Gilbert and Sullivan, Laurel and Hardy, salt and pepper, knife and fork. They go together, if not quite like love and marriage, and together they have driven a two-horse carriage through Scottish football since the first kick of a ball between them in the late nineteenth century. On 15 April 1904, the *Scottish Referee*, prior to yet another Scottish final between the two, showed a cartoon of a tramp holding a placard reading 'Patronise the Old Firm' and the collective term has stuck.

It was intended as an uncomplimentary reference to their propensity to carve out all the available soccer prizes between them, within Scotland at least – a tendency that persists to this very day. It can be seen on the one hand as a double blessing, a mark of the high quality at the top of the Scottish game, or, on the other, as a twin curse because of their monotonous domination in season after season. This would be acceptable were this winning rivalry confined to playing-field matters, since it could only improve the two teams' respective standards of play. Unfortunately, each club has come to represent considerations other than football and this can only be to the detriment of their respective sporting achievements.

For better *and* worse, this famous football marriage has produced the twin towers of prejudice that still stand tall, glowering at each other, secure on their hidebound foundations, their windows reflecting a mirror image of the other. Two mighty structures that, between them, ought to be the pride of Scotland, yet too often, in the football sense at least, are its shame and disgrace. Why is this so, when by far the greater majority of each support is tolerant, understanding and decent, and completely respectful of the other?

In Scottish eyes at any rate, Rangers and Celtic symbolise the underlying sectarian divide that still exists in Scottish society, however much it is politically swept under the carpet. For very shaky historical reasons and even more dubious religious ones, Rangers are held to be the upholders of the old Scottish order of things and Celtic are the 'foreigners' and a threat to the Protestant establishment. Rangers are proudly Glasgow Rangers, whereas Celtic are considered more as belonging to Ireland and all things Irish, even though both teams ply their trade within the same city.

To many Scots, Rangers are 'us' and Celtic are 'them'. For the Celtic supporter, of course, the very opposite is true. That this bias is idiotic and unsubstantiated goes without saying, but it is one that is deep-rooted in the west of Scotland psyche and ingrained in the minds of those who see in Celtic's Irish origins a threat to Scottish patriotism and a very real danger to the state of the nation. They consider that the Celt's first loyalty is to the Vatican and after that to the Irish Republic, as represented by the militant IRA, and that God comes to him only in the person of the local parish priest. Heaven is available at the price of a penny candle and hell is to marry out of the faith.

Such arrant nonsense has been perpetuated for years and, although much less obvious in modern times, it is still there, simmering under the surface. It only needs the slightest spark to set the cauldron bubbling. So much so that it invests the ordinary event of a sporting fixture between the two clubs with ramifications that have nothing to do with football. A win or loss in an Old Firm match can achieve the status of a national disaster and a game between Celtic and Rangers is sometimes viewed less as a football match and more as a bloody battle to be fought to the death.

The image comes to mind of a Rangers–Celtic match I saw at Ibrox when I was a student in the early '50s. A Rangers supporter on the terracing was provocatively waving a large Union Jack and the police tried to remove him or at least the flag from the crowd. A riot broke out in the area and within minutes mounted policemen were thundering across the pitch to reach the scene. I remember the thrill of seeing the horsemen, galloping hard, with batons raised and hearing the thud of hooves on the turf. It was like something out of *Henry V*, but the only breach to be observed was the waving of a flag.

The Union Jack, however, is just another physical expression of the Rangers supporters' claim to a unique 'Britishness', which is just as ludicrous as their usurpation of our mutual National Anthem as their exclusive club chant. It defies belief that the average supporter at the Copland Road end lives with a deep concern for the Royal Family and that the Queen is at the very centre of their lives, so why is the National Anthem sung out lustily from the terracing as if it were a love song? Celtic do much the same, of course, with 'The Soldier's Song', but at least it's a better tune. Such overt differentiation on both sides only inflames the rotten wood at the bottom of the pile. The Irish sing easily and naturally. It was little surprise that when they banded together at Parkhead they sang. At first, it was hymns, then Irish folk songs, then football songs based on these rhythms, and 'Let the People Sing' emerged as a typical melody for the whole Celtic support. If they were Irish songs, they were politically motivated, not sectarian.

In the beginning, the Irish troubles had no bearing on troubles at Celtic Park or Ibrox. It was the importation of Protestant Ulster artisans from the Harland and Woolf shipyards in Belfast during the First World War that brought irrelevant implications, like King Billy and the Orange Order, to a head. These other Irishmen, who, historically, once were Scots, brought with them their banners, drums and flute bands and a whole paraphernalia of prejudice against Roman Catholics. A Masonic element was also there but discreet and not always obvious to the uninitiated and certainly not to wee boys lining up at the sevenpenny gate. Ibrox suddenly found itself welcoming a whole lot of new supporters, complete with patriotism for the throne of England. This new invasion coincided with the football dominance of Celtic's first great team before and during the First World War. It was at this time that the sectarian chants originated, born out of frustration and envy.

This is a matter of historical fact and not an indication of bias or prejudice. Of course I have a bias towards Celtic, but I do not ignore the obvious. It takes two to quarrel and each faction here is as much to blame as the other for this misplaced and excessive partisan hatred.

Even the players play under the burden of this false responsibility to the blue and the green. As Tommy Burns so aptly put it, 'In Glasgow, if you play for Rangers or Celtic, one half of the city hates you and the other half thinks they own you.' The more sensible among both supports find the safest way is to laugh about it, like when two Celtic supporters found themselves in St Peter's Square in Rome when Celtic played a friendly against Lazio. Said the first, Pat, in a tactful whisper, 'Who's that on the balcony with Charlie Tully?'

Rangers have their equivalent, as witness Bill Paterson's excellent *Tales from the Back Green*. Bill was brought up in the East End, not far from Parkhead. As a Rangers' supporter, he was in the minority. As he says in his book:

> Instead of a walk to Paradise with the green-and-white hordes that passed our close, we had to ride on a tram into town and travel several stops on the underground to reach our alleged Valhalla at Ibrox Park. And for a while I did.
>
> 'There'll be sad hearts in the Vatican tonight,' was the poetic image conjured up when Rangers did well or Celtic did badly and I used to imagine a papal enclave sitting round the fire on a wintry teatime checking their pools coupons from the Scottish Home Service results.

Behind the joking, however, there is still, unfortunately, a sad strain of seriousness. Bill's allegiance to Rangers came to an end when he and his father witnessed a melee between the respective supporters outside Ibrox. As his father said, 'Never again,' and both reverted to the family loyalty to Third Lanark.

The grimmer aspects of the rivalry refuse to go away. Echoes continue to reverberate in the mindless chanting accompanied by drumbeats in a cacophony that mars the atmosphere of every ground where either team plays. Despite the combined efforts of FIFA, the SFA and even government agencies, no matter the fines imposed and the stated intention of each club to eliminate it, the poison still persists. This sort of thing adds nothing to the game.

I can remember, as an 11-year-old, the crossover drill at half-time when the sets of supporters at Celtic Park changed ends, depending on which goals the sides were playing towards, by walking through the Jungle. Celtic supporters always started looking east towards the Springfield Road end and at half-time many supporters changed over to make sure they had a good view of the goals going in. The Rangers supporters did likewise, going in the opposite direction. The Jungle represented a kind of no-man's-land through which both sets of supporters had to pass. Of course, there were raucous shouts and heavy banter, but I have no memory, at that time, of vicious chanting or slogans in our ears as we crossed. Rising above the shouts was the call from the vendor, 'Duncan's Hazelnut, penny a bar!' The idiot minority from both sides was perhaps kept in check by the fact that they were threading their way through a temporary neutral territory.

I grew up thinking of Rangers as naturally superior to Celtic. I had to reduce the whole Ibrox identity to a shadowy 'them' in order to cope in my boy's way with what I thought was their ruthless efficiency. It was the only way to make the austere image they had in my mind more manageable. Rangers players weren't ogres; they were more like phantoms in my young head. Tall, forbidding and remote, they were encased in a kind of mist that shrouded their magnificent stadium, which stood like an intimidating fortress on the south side of the river. We had to take the tramcar over the Clyde to get there. It was like crossing the Rubicon and coming upon a foreign land.

Rangers were a considerable power in the unofficial world of wartime football. I can remember their names even yet; they were branded into my subconscious. Jerry Dawson was in goal, Dougie Gray and Tiger Shaw were the contrasting backs, Dougie being the gentleman and Tiger being anything but. Little, Young and Symon were the half-back line and the forward line was Waddell, Tory Gillick, Thornton, Duncanson and wee Caskie, who had been signed from Everton. Rangers seemed to have found a way of keeping their players through the war years by enrolling them in reserved occupations, like those very same shipyards that hatched the original trouble during the First World War – although it must be said that their centre-forward, Willie Thornton, was a serving soldier and won the Military Medal for bravery. His colleagues and opponents in the Old Firm exchanges of that time might have earned similar commendations for valour on a different kind of battlefield.

We must try to remember that Rangers were also Celtic's first chosen opponents and relations between the clubs were cordial until the infamous 'double drawn' Scottish Cup final of 1909, when official misunderstandings about a replay after the first drawn game led to a bloody riot among both sets of spectators and as a result the Cup was withdrawn. However, the rioters were united in their opposition to officialdom and the trouble had no roots in sectarianism.

There was nothing specifically Protestant or Masonic about the Rangers team as far as I was concerned as a boy. They were better, that was all. They were the Roundheads and we were the Cavaliers; they ruled the roost while we flapped aimlessly around the farmyard. Our lot at Parkhead then were warmly acknowledged as 'us', so their many football sins were forgiven. Yet there was always something likeable about their very earnestness or was that just my own bias showing? All I know is that I didn't really care whether our players were Catholic, Protestant or Hindu, I just wished they could play.

My boyhood view was that Celtic were never supposed to beat Rangers and that even a draw was held to be a kind of victory for us. They were invincible in my eyes and even when I got to know them in my adulthood, I was always surprised by how engaging and likeable many of them were. Big George Young was so admired by Celtic supporters for his gentlemanly conduct and fair attitude throughout his career that they gave him a dinner to mark this. Willie Woodburn, their formidable centre-half and George Young's predecessor, used to service my car when I lived in Edinburgh. 'I was tempted to let your tyres doon,' he used to quip.

When I was in Canada on a Burns tour one winter, I met a Glasgow man long emigrated to Toronto who acted as if he'd never left the place. He said to me as I signed his programme, 'You know, you're the first Cath'lic I've ever spoke tae.'

'What?' I was incredulous. He came from Glasgow; it seemed very unlikely.

'Honest, that's right enough,' he insisted. 'We just never met any somehow.'

A great truth might lie under that simple statement. For all his business acumen and dollar success, he was still fundamentally ignorant about the other half of his home town. Did he think we spoke Latin in the house or what? His final comment, as he left, laughing, clutching his programme, was even more profound. 'I always thought ye hid tae be rid-headed tae be a Cath'lic.'

In the days of my passing quasi-celebrity, my dear friend Andy Stewart and I, in a bid to defuse the cretinous antics of the small sections of each support, tried to arrange via John Greig and Billy

141

McNeill that on the Saturday of one Old Firm game at Parkhead, I, as a known Celtic man, would sit in the Rangers directors' box and Andy would sit among the Celtic men. I duly turned up and took my place, receiving as I did loud verbal abuse from both green and blue sides. I glanced to my right to see how Andy was doing. There was no sign of him. He later said he had been delayed at the BBC. My only consolation was that I won a fiver from John Greig on the result. Andy and I still remained the best of friends. Although raised in Arbroath, he was born in Glasgow and was always a Rangers fan. He and I were fellow students at drama college and had many 'interesting' football discussions in the common room. Our mutual pal Johnny Grieve used to referee. He was a Partick Thistle supporter.

I grew up thinking that the whole world was Catholic, only because my whole world was. I was shuttled between home and church and school, feeling entirely safe and secure in that blinkered web of cosy kinship. I saw no need to look outside that confining circuit. Orthodox Jewish boys must wear the same kind of protective family armour. As a young boy, however, my Proddy street friendships became a good balancer for me. They helped to give me a kind of perspective on this needless and unnecessary Catholic–Protestant divide that so sorely bedevilled our bit of the city. The Gibsons, the Murrays, the Robertsons and the Weirs whom I knew in Williamson Street were a handy antidote to my lot, the Coyles, Prestons, McNamees and McIlhattons within the family networks in Parkhead, Shettleston and Baillieston.

Celtic comes to most boys down through the fathers. My own certainly introduced me, but in a sense he left me to it. His attendance at Celtic Park was intermittent, but my uncles, Phil and Hughie, were more constant and they were the companions of my early spectating. It was as if one were being passed down an unbroken line of Celtic support and it would be a sin to leave a gap. Not that you have to be a Catholic to support Celtic. Far from it, but it helps. Rod Stewart is a known Celtic fan, but then, as the son of a professional footballer, he knows his football. Sir Sean Connery was taken to his first Celtic match by his father, Joseph, when he was just wee Thomas Connery from Fountainbridge in Edinburgh. He followed them faithfully until his playing of 007 in the James Bond movies introduced him to golf and that sport took over the rest of his leisure life. When he eventually resumed his interest in football, it was to Ibrox he went, which lost the actor a lot of Parkhead fans, but then what he forfeited on the Celtic swings he gained on the Rangers roundabouts. This change of loyalties I gather was due to Connery's friendship with the Rangers chairman at that time, Sir David Murray.

Stein, the iconic creator of the Lisbon Lions, had something of the same experience when he opted to return to Celtic as manager. Half of Lanarkshire took umbrage at this rejection of former affiliations, which was also due to Stein's unexpected good relationship with a chairman, Sir Robert Kelly. Friendship is no bad basis for any emotional decision and, who knows, a change of heart like his might even do some good in the long run. There have even been accounts of Rangers supporters converting to Celtic, but it didn't mean a change of passports or a need to attend Sunday Mass. Many of other faiths and persuasions around the globe have done the same but in Glasgow, even now, to be associated with Celtic in any way is to be tainted, as they would say, with the Papacy. In Glasgow, the question, 'Whit school did ye go tae?' has no educational relevance whatsoever.

It is one thing to acknowledge the club's legitimate Catholic origins but Celtic players don't have to wear dog collars nor their supporters flaunt rosary beads. Religion has been made the excuse for so much divisive and abhorrent social behaviour, and this is not always fair. It is assumed in Glasgow that if you are born a Protestant you are required to support Rangers no matter your own football leaning; the same goes for Catholics and Celtic. This fact has proved to be of sound commercial value to each club, they can count on it, but it has no moral force or legality. There is no doubt, however, that being a Celtic supporter in Glasgow, and a Catholic in Scotland, is to feel marginalised and in a minority. Yet what a margin, what a minority.

A vast swathe of men and women, as well as boys and girls, are still united by a series of events both on and off the playing field all the way back to that first gathering of followers around the open space off Janefield Street. It gives them a sense of being part of that original community, in the sense of family, that still obtains in the grass-roots support of today, but they must rise above the utter nonsense of a deliberately fostered religious divide that has cut deeply into the body of the game they love. The extreme elements among both groups of supporters must call pax soon and end this farcical situation where the pursuit of outdated, irrelevant vendettas takes precedence over football priorities, otherwise they may damage football in Scotland fatally.

I remember receiving another invitation to attend as a guest yet another Rangers–Celtic game, this time at Ibrox. I had met someone at a Burns supper who had influence then at Rangers and he was of the same opinion as I, that there should be more mixing between the two. Which was why I found myself sitting next to a Rangers legend, Bob McPhail, and sharing a blanket with him, since it was a very cold Saturday afternoon. This very famous player had played beside Jimmy McGrory of Celtic in a well-remembered Scotland game that produced the first 'Hampden roar' after one of McGrory's goals. We talked of this and of other great games he was in and it all reminded me that I was a Scotland supporter as much as a Celtic supporter. Well, maybe not quite as much. He laughed when I told him, 'When Scotland lost, I cried until Sunday, but when Celtic lost, I didn't dry my eyes until Tuesday.'

While we were talking, I couldn't get over the sight of a section of the enclosure opposite us containing a group of Rangers supporters who spent the entire game taunting the Celtic support to their right. The Rangers section, comprising mainly adolescent boys, occupied a whole block right at the edge of the Celtic end and spent the entire match singing their ribald songs, shouting obscenities and maintaining a constant stream of invective against the green-and-white scarves encased in their own section. As far as I could see, on this occasion, the Celtic fans paid no attention but kept their focus on the football they had come to see. The singing and shouting Rangers, however, did not even give the pitch a glance. It was as if the need to chant had been bred into this faction and the game itself was less important than their practised inanities. When I pointed this out to Mr McPhail, he shrugged and said, 'I pay no heed to that sort of stuff, and if it gets particularly annoying, I just take out my hearing aid.'

Oh, that all solutions were as simple. Celtic won that match but the memory that remains is of the Rangers youth choir being given over entirely to invective.

Even as a boy, I was aware of this more extreme section of their support. I was once standing on the pavement somewhere on Polmadie Road when my pals and I were heading to Hampden for an Old Firm cup final. We were waiting to cross the road when a Rangers supporters' bus stopped right in front of us and I found myself looking straight into the eyes of a young Rangers fan of about my own age. I was on the edge of a grin and expected more or less the same reaction from this boy. Instead, his mouth twisted into a snarl and through the dirty window pane I could see the lips form into every obscenity he could think of. I couldn't lip-read but I got his meaning, and it wasn't friendly.

However, it was not what he said, or what I thought he said, that stays in my mind but the look in his eyes. It was an expression of hate, real hate. I had never met unashamed hate before. This is not to say that Celtic are blameless in this respect. I'm sure there are Celtic buses had many occupants had the same eyes, only hidden under a different colour of cap. This was instanced in the May 1999 Old Firm game, when referee Dallas had to receive attention from the ambulance corps after being struck by a missile thrown from the Celtic end. Four other Celtic supporters invaded the pitch to confront the referee. At the end of the match, which was won by Rangers 3–0, more missiles were thrown at Rangers players as they left the pitch.

Both clubs are trying their best to address this constant eruption during and after games. Celtic's Bhoys Against Bigotry, Rangers' Follow with Pride and the cross-clubs Sense over Sectarianism have attempted to reduce the provoking sectarian chants and the outbursts of violence that they produce. But, even with the good will of everyone involved, including civil and government authorities, they still don't quite know how to root it out.

More than 60 years after my first experience of the rivalry, that same baseless ill-feeling pervades extreme factions in the west of Scotland and fuels the sectarian sickness that blackens the good name of football. Neil Lennon, the current Celtic manager, had a parcel-bomb delivered to him at Celtic's training ground at Lennoxtown on 26 March 2011. A few days later a similar liquid-based device, designed to cause 'real harm' according to local police, was also sent to Celtic's lawyer, Paul McBride QC, at the Faculty of Advocates in Edinburgh and to ex-MSP Trish Godman, a prominent Celtic supporter, at her constituency office in Bridge of Weir. It was her staff who alerted the police. This letter-bomb action was not the work of underground military forces or political regimes but the calculated efforts of a small pocket of venom, probably a couple of deranged individuals provoked to such insane acts by sheer bigotry and a background of hatred against Celtic and all things reputedly Catholic. It was clearly beyond a football matter now. It had become a question of social disease and would be dealt with by the appropriate state authorities. To paraphrase Winston

Churchill, 'Never in the field of football history have so many suffered so often from the actions of so few.'

I have an actor friend, John Shedden, who came from Lerwick many years ago to study drama in Glasgow. Because he liked football, he went to Celtic Park one Saturday and saw Henrik Larsson. Jack was knocked out by the whole Celtic style of playing. He has supported Celtic ever since and is still a Celtic season-ticket holder. 'I'm not a Catholic,' he told me. 'I'm not even a Protestant – I'm a Shetlander! But I love football and I love the way Celtic play it. It's as simple as that.' And so it should be.

Postscript: I recently took a walk in Queen's Park with Alannah, and we saw coming towards us on the path a man with his young son. He was wearing a Celtic strip and his little son was sporting a Rangers jersey. A mere hopeful glimpse, perhaps, but it had in it a vision of the new order that might yet come to pass.

CHAPTER EIGHT

To Manage Somehow

Kenny Dalglish, Inside-Right

All Kenny's eloquence lay in his feet
But there he spoke for the man in the street,
He gave them a glimpse of football's art
Why did he and Celtic have to part?

In September 1971, chairman Sir Robert Kelly died of cancer. This was a seminal moment for Celtic in that it lost a major figure in its story, linked by family to its very beginnings. Despite his abrupt manner, he tried only his best for the name and the game that Celtic played. He also had the wisdom to see in Stein a saviour figure, and the intelligence to give him his head. For that, all of us were grateful.

Robert Kelly had lived long enough to see Celtic attain the holy grail of the European Cup and also to make it to six in a row in the Championship. They made a forceful run in to the League by drawing with Aberdeen and beating Ayr United to secure the flag. This made the last game of the season against Clyde on May Day 1971 something of a spring party for all, and Stein, well aware of this, decided to field the Lisbon Lions for the last time to ensure the uniqueness of the day.

This Man Craig had prevented my travelling to Lisbon, so I couldn't miss this one. Dammit, I did. I was rehearsing *Elizabeth R* with Glenda Jackson in north London. I liked Glenda, but if it had been a choice between Celtic and her, Celtic would have won hands down. However, the director, Roderick Graham, had called a Saturday rehearsal. Wouldn't you know it, it had to be that very Saturday. A Saturday rehearsal is nearly always a camera run-through, so I couldn't even slip out to the nearest radio. A crowd of 35,000 saw the Lions play that day. I grieved for a week that I wasn't one of them, especially as they won 6–1.

Thereafter, the famous team began to splinter: Simpson had already retired, Gemmell was transferred to Nottingham Forest, Murdoch was soon to leave for Middlesbrough, Clark to Morton, as did Chalmers; Wallace and Hughes went to Crystal Palace and Bertie Auld joined Hibs. Most of these players left reluctantly. They had a lot of playing years in them yet, they loved being at Celtic, but they were no longer part of the Stein plan. That was the nub. His primary concern was football, not personal relationships. Perhaps he thought over-familiarity would weaken his authority. There was no doubt he could be brutal in his decision-making. He had been given the reins but there were times he used them like a lash.

I got a sense of this thunder in his make-up when I was introduced to him at Celtic Park. It was one of the few times I was a guest at a game, and the party I was with suddenly came face to face with the team as they were preparing to go down the tunnel from the dressing-room. Bertie Auld saw me and called out, 'Hey, Cairney, shouldnae you be at Somerset Park?' That was the ground of Ayr United and was Bertie's allusion to my Burns association. Just then, Stein came out and Bertie said to him, pointing to me, 'Hey, boss, d'ye know who this is?' Stein glanced at me, muttered something like, 'Aye, I know fine,' and turned away to talk closely with Jimmy Johnstone. I had my hand all ready to have it shaken but put it back in my pocket and hurried away to find my seat. Stein had plenty on his mind without worrying about stray actors.

Metaphorically speaking, the door of the dressing-room was opening to let in the 'Quality Kids' already waiting in the corridor, and Stein's hand was already on that door handle. Lou Macari was one of the new signings, in place of Wallace. He proved his worth by scoring the opening goal in the Scottish Cup final replay victory over Rangers on 12 May 1971. It was my mother's 62nd birthday, so I'd been in Glasgow anyway and was able to see the game at Hampden before taking my mother to dinner.

The big disappointment was in losing out to the Dutch club Ajax in the European Cup, but they were a great side and were just beginning their own golden era in European football. There were rumours that Manchester United were after big Jock as manager but the deal foundered on the suggestion that Sir Matt Busby would still be there as director of football, whatever that entailed, but still a backroom influence. It might also have been down to Mrs Stein's reluctance to leave home again, or perhaps there was another cause – his desire to keep faith with the Celtic supporters. I like to think that this was so, for he loved the ordinary bulk at the heart of the support, and on their behalf he felt he still had great things to do at Celtic Park.

Through all these winning years, Jock Stein *was* Celtic and every Celtic supporter knew that. I was only one of many. Yet I remember at the same time having a feeling that his whole heart was perhaps not in the managerial chair as much as it once was. It was only natural that such a long strain of success should take its toll. At least with failure, you are put out of your misery at once, but Mr Stein was now beginning to appear the victim of his own extraordinary longevity at the top. The man's stamina was extraordinary. He still put in the hours on the training pitch, on the road to see other matches, and on the phone to anyone who was willing to talk Celtic. Calls for his services had come not only from Manchester but from Leeds and, most unexpectedly, from the other side of the city.

The approach supposedly made by the public-relations officer of Rangers, Willie Allison, to negotiate Stein's possible move to Ibrox around the end of the '60s was highly intriguing. That would have illuminated Burnbank, but it would have caused an eclipse over Celtic Park. Stein's father might have been delighted, but his son might have been a little more aware of what the more sinister extremes of the Old Firm rivalry needed. He fretted about the anti-Catholic bias he saw at the BBC and the SFA, and he once told Archie Macpherson, 'All kids should go to the same school.' This man Stein might have done great things at Ibrox, but obviously he must have declined the approach, if indeed it did happen, for he was still at Parkhead for the start of the 1971–72 season.

Celtic started off the League campaign in style by beating Clyde 9–1 at Parkhead and then Rangers twice in quick succession, laying down an early marker for their retaining the Championship. Their seventh successive title owed much to the presence of another new kid on the block, Kenny Dalglish, who had endeared himself to the Celtic support by his calmly taken penalty in a League Cup tie at Rangers. Nonetheless, not even this fresh talent could prevent the shock that lay in store in the final of the League Cup. Partick Thistle, led by Dave McParland (later to be involved backstage at Parkhead), beat them convincingly by four goals to one. Of course, Celtic's goal was scored by Dalglish.

I was glad I was spared the humiliation, as I was in London recording *Jackanory* for BBC television. This was a well-known children's programme and some of the players lining up for a place in the new Celtic side were not all that far removed in age from having been *Jackanory* viewers themselves.

The team was in a definite stage of transition, and as the swing doors let out the old favourites, they let in some new faces: goalkeeper and Celtic supporter Denis Connaghan, who had been a Celtic provisional in 1963, and centre-forward John 'Dixie' Deans, who was something of a character and was suspended at the time by Motherwell. When in the mood, Dixie could score goals, and would for Celtic. Results went their way throughout the season, including the League double over Rangers for the first time in 58 years. Celtic coasted to their seventh championship flag in succession. They had beaten the six-in-a-row record of their own club. Could they now create a new tradition of their own?

I saw quite a lot of them in this season, because, as my home was now in Scotland, I preferred to work 'about the doors'. That meant the Lyceum in Edinburgh for theatre or with BBC television in Glasgow, which was ideal for me as long as it didn't involve too much location work. My green Range Rover and I were all set for a new season. Like most supporters at that time, I expected the high tide of good results to keep on coming in. It was good to be a Celtic supporter in 1972. In fact, given the new talent available, I saw no reason why it should not go on for ever.

There were now young boys growing up in Glasgow who thought Celtic won everything. That's all they had known, the 'greenwash' years, victory after victory, in competitions of all kinds, season after season; they thought other teams had no right to beat Celtic. Celtic meant winning, didn't it? It was wonderful to see the fervour in these young faces. By now, I was in my 40s, but, looking at them, I could remember that same feeling; except that I was usually disappointed – I used to celebrate the team getting a corner. How would these young ones, bred on total success, deal with defeat? They would have to one day. Anyone can be an enthusiastic supporter when the going's good, but when it gets tough is when the real supporter is found, for he is fired in the furnace of the future and can take anything. Once you have loyalty, you have it for life. Football has its own fateful ways, as Celtic were soon to find out.

During that 1971–72 season, young Danny McGrain, a find at right-back, fractured his skull at Falkirk. It was as serious as the injury to Delaney all those years before and there were real doubts about whether McGrain's career could be saved. Then there was Dixie Deans' penalty miss in the second-leg shoot-out against Inter Milan at Celtic Park, which lost Celtic the chance of their third European Cup final, one that many, like the boy supporters, were convinced they would have won. The chief recollection of the game for me was the intensity of the silence in the 75,000 crowd before Dixie ballooned the ball over the bar and the noise the Italian players made on the centre line as they saw it. It was a long car trip home to Pittenweem that night.

Some comfort was gained, however, by the manner in which the side won the Scottish Cup against Hibs. The team sent out here was minus McGrain and Hay, but the new-look side gave some indication of the Celtic team to come in the seasons ahead. It was: Williams; Craig and Brogan; Murdoch, McNeill and Connelly; Johnstone, Deans, Macari, Dalglish and Callaghan. Celtic won by a remarkable 6–1, which included a Dixie Deans hat-trick. This more than made up for his penalty miss against Inter Milan. It was also Jim Craig's last match, and he took himself and his winner's medal off to South Africa.

I decided to celebrate afterwards with some old Glasgow friends with a late-night meal at the Duke of Touraine, Tony Matteo's restaurant at Parkhead Cross. My mother was a little surprised to see me beaming broadly at her Dennistoun door so late at night. I had to walk back to the corner of Whitby Street and Springfield Road the next morning to get my car. It was still there. I had a sudden recollection of 'Watch your car, mister?', for I had left it in the one half of Williamson Street still standing. I felt quite nostalgic driving back along the London Road again. Except this time I branched off at Mount Vernon to head for the Kingdom of Fife.

The first cracks had started to appear not in the new young team Stein was creating but in the manager himself. A sudden attack of breathlessness in the car caused him to pull over and when he reported this to the club doctor he discovered he had an irregular heartbeat, which landed him in intensive care in a Glasgow hospital over Christmas and the New Year of 1973. While he was ill, the impish Lou Macari, at the suggestion of Pat Crerand, was transferred to Manchester United instead of going to Liverpool, as Stein had arranged with his old mate Bill Shankly. Macari, it would appear, wasn't a 'jersey player'. That was the difference between his generation and the Lions, who were jersey players to a man. It is not that the youngsters were greedy; they had a more realistic sense of their own monetary worth, as Celtic were later to find out. Macari's defection, as we thought it, was the first hint that the Stein reins might by slackening slightly, not by his dropping them but by others pulling in a different direction. It was a warning, but would he take it? As if in fright, some of the players went down with influenza all at the same time.

I must have come out in sympathy, for not long afterwards I was doing a private Burns show in a Perth hotel and I felt extremely hot in my dinner jacket towards the end of the performance. When I changed afterwards in my room, I found my trousers were soaked in blood. I was shocked, as you might well imagine. I hadn't been ill or anything, although I had attacks of colic fever from time to time. It's the actor's disease, caused by tension, nerves and stress, which is why many of us are good whisky drinkers. I wasn't. Wine was my tipple but only after a show, with lots of spaghetti bolognese if possible.

That night, however, I didn't eat. I wrapped myself up in hotel towels and somehow made my way home to Kellie Lodging, where next morning the local doctor pronounced me 'very ill'. I had given a full evening show the night before and never noticed anything, but that I was sweating more than usual. 'That was a sign of your illness,' said Dr Kennedy. I saw a specialist at the Western General in Edinburgh the next day. His diagnosis was acute ulcerative colitis and his remedy was immediate total rest.

I spent the next two weeks in the Drumsheugh Nursing Home, where my room had radio and TV, so I was able to keep up with the other world. For some reason, I kept getting flowers from people. It wasn't until I overheard a conversation at my door between two newspapermen who had been there most of the day that I understood. One had said to the other, 'Ach, there's nae story here.'

'Right enough,' said the other, a photographer, 'he's gonnae make it.' They must have thought I was dying, for goodness' sake. I was discharged soon afterwards, much to my relief. I went to my mother's to recuperate. After all, she was less than a half-hour walk from Celtic Park, and I had been told to take more exercise.

Celtic, meantime, weren't exactly motoring through the League fixtures. There was just enough experience in the side to make it count and youthful energy, coupled with some skill, ought to have allowed them to play with carefree abandon, but it was hit and miss much of the way. In one match against East Fife at Methil, which I didn't see because I was in Glasgow, they missed three penalties and only snatched a draw because of a Dixie Deans 'steal' near the end. However, their foot eventually went onto the accelerator and they sped in over the line by beating Hibs 3–0 at Easter Road on the last day of the League season.

Championship number eight was in the record books, but significantly there was not one piece of silverware recorded for the League Cup, Scottish Cup or European Cup. For Celtic, historically famed as cup fighters, this amounted to a poorish season, and took a little shine off the Championship trophy. This was unfair, as it is the long haul of the League that finds out the overall quality of any team, as opposed to the lucky break or individual flash that might win a cup match. Cup games are sprints, whereas the Championship is a marathon.

The League Cup jinx had continued and they lost their third final in a row (1–2) to Hibernian, who gained their first major trophy in 70 years. It was Pat Stanton, later to come to Celtic, who scored the opening goal. Second place was shaming to this Celtic generation, who always strove for first. Nobody ever remembers the runner-up. Our luck wasn't any better in the European Cup, going out to a clever Hungarian side, Ujpest Dozsa. However, the Old Firm was still in business and they were scheduled to meet once again to discuss the matter of the 1973 Scottish Cup, the final to be played on 5 May. A win here would restore morale and I was determined to be there to cheer them on.

As bad luck would have it, I was under the Clyde in a submarine with Maria Aitken, escaping to Moscow in a TV serial called *Scotch on the Rocks* for BBC Scotland. The dreaded location jinx had struck again and there was I underwater with a shapely actress wondering what the score was at Hampden. I resurfaced at Faslane and asked the score from the driver taking me back to the Queen Margaret Drive studios in Glasgow.

'3–2 for the Gers,' he replied gleefully. 'Forsyth wi' a scuff-in. I wis listenin' tae the commentary.'

I tried to hide my disappointment as we drove into the city.

'Celtic hid a goal disallowed, mind,' he added.

'Oh?'

'Aye, wee Johnstone it wis, jist efter hauf-time. The referee wis–'

'Was that Davidson?' I asked. He thought for a minute.

'No, I don't think it wis. I didnae get his name,' he said as we pulled in at the gates.

I read later that the referee was Mr Gordon of Tayport. The fact remained that, even though Celtic had snared the Championship yet again, Rangers had won the Cup.

Dixie Deans was to remain on form, netting six against Partick Thistle at Parkhead in November 1973. He also scored a hat-trick in the first-ever Sunday game in Scotland, when they beat Clydebank in a Scottish Cup tie on a Sunday in January 1974. The reason for breaking the Sabbath was that floodlights were temporarily banned to save electricity, which had been rationed nationally because of the miners' head-on collision with Edward Heath. Celtic had their troubles, too.

Dundee, now under the captaincy of ex-Celt Tommy Gemmell, beat them by a single goal in the League Cup final on a ridiculously water-logged Hampden. Of course, it was the same wintry conditions for both teams, but Dundee took full advantage of a Celtic team splashing about in the puddles. Gemmell realised Dundee had been given a gift, but he wasn't for giving it back. He enjoyed his little win over his old boss, who was the first to congratulate the player, but Stein made no attempt to congratulate his bête noire, Mr Davidson. Referees, like goalkeepers, brought out the worst in Jock Stein.

I got back from London to see that game. I arrived late in the pouring rain and was let in free by a man at the stand entrance who recognised me as a Celtic supporter. When I took my seat, I saw I was among the smallest attendance I had ever seen at a League Cup final, only 27,974 I learned later, resulting from the atrocious weather in addition to the lunchtime kick-off necessitated by the aforementioned power restrictions. I sat there watching, wet and miserable, and left at the end, cold and dejected. For the first time in my life, I was fed up with Celtic, as I think they were with themselves. A thin tide of staleness appeared to have crept under the door of the Celtic dressing-room. The team was in danger of sitting back on its laurels.

Nonetheless, Championship number nine in a row seemed to be in the bag. The incentive to strive further might have dulled for the team, but Stein wouldn't see it that way. Winning the League flag was becoming a habit, and it was generally achieved away from home, with

Falkirk being the town where the ninth successive title was achieved, with three matches to spare.

Playing away from home was becoming the usual for me too professionally. I was working in London again. This time it was something called *Special Branch*, a television episode for Euston Films. I was certainly keeping in work, but I was seriously missing the fix I'd had each Saturday when I was based in Scotland.

McNeill, Johnstone and Lennox were now the only Lisbon Lions remaining in the Celtic pool, an indication of the change that was happening at Parkhead. I gathered from friends in high places I had at Celtic Park in those days that there was a growing feeling of discontent among the players. It really had more to do with mental attitude than financial matters. For some, there was obviously more to life than chasing a running ball and kicking it. Unrest was growing in the Celtic camp. Jinky Johnstone was fretting and becoming disenchanted with the game and Davie Hay was involved in a bitter dispute over terms. Even having achieved the world-record-equalling nine championships didn't help lighten the atmosphere. Celtic's obvious domination of the football scene caused the Scottish League to consider the reorganisation of the fixture list for the following season, in order to break the Celtic monopoly. In the eyes of the Celtic support at least, this was an extraordinary compliment to the team's consistency. All Celtic wanted was further competition at the highest level. They needed a stronger challenge.

Their Iberian encounter with Atlético Madrid provided that and more, and it proved to be yet another pitched battle masquerading as a football match. This Spanish policy of outright war against Celtic would suggest that they ought to have hired Goya's firing squad and done the job properly. In the European Cup semi-final first leg on 10 April 1974 at Celtic Park, their main strategy was apparently to cripple Jimmy Johnstone and they wasted no time about it. They put three men on this job and as a result three men were sent off, and seven booked, by the Turkish referee, but the Celtic forwards could not pierce the barricade of flailing arms, kicking boots and thrusting heads offered by the Madrid side in lieu of football skills. They ultimately went down to the savages by two late goals.

Coincidentally, Atlético were managed by Juan Carlos Lorenzo, the same man who managed the infamous Argentina team at Wembley in the 1966 World Cup, a side then described by England manager Alf

Ramsey as 'animals'. On this occasion, Lorenzo was trying to provoke the Celtic crowd into rioting, as had happened to the Rangers fans at Barcelona in 1972. However, he underestimated the discipline of the supporters on the terracing, well schooled by Stein through the pages of the *Celtic View*. I heard about this shameful episode in Newcastle, where I was playing Cyrano in Rostand's *Cyrano de Bergerac* for a season at the Theatre Royal, but my long nose was not at all put out of joint. The fact that the fans kept their heads in the face of such provocation was a kind of victory to me and made up for the shabby 'triumph' that the visitors had achieved, allowing them to reach the final. I felt I wanted to take up my rapier and run it through Señor Lorenzo, whose arrogant irresponsibility caused such an appalling travesty of a football game.

The best comment made was in John Motson and John Rowlinson's *The European Cup 1955–1980*: 'Their persistent disregard for the laws mocked the spirit of international competition. In the city where Real Madrid lit a torch for the European Cup, Atlético did their best to extinguish it.' As Archie Macpherson said, 'The whole saga had been a blot on the sport.' However, Stein didn't let it go further than an impassioned diatribe against the Spanish coach. In his own way, he worked off his disgruntlement by agreeing to go to Germany with the BBC as their official match pundit for the 1974 World Cup. Typically, and quite unofficially, he landed up as unpaid coach to the Scottish team via Billy Bremner. Was he just keeping his hand in or was he sowing seeds? Whatever it was, it seemed to work, as Scotland were unbeaten, one win and two draws, including Brazil, and only went out on goal average. The Stein touch was still sure, no matter the tactics employed against him.

Having created a new record of nine in a row, expectations were high that Celtic could make it ten successive titles, but was this really possible? The squad seemed jaded. They were to ricochet from game to game in 1974–75 in a seemingly haphazard, up-and-down, untypically inconsistent way that was a worry to Stein and a matter of concern for the supporters. The team was playing much in the way that I was playing my own career at the time, going from job to job with no real plan, no long-term aim, just happy to take up the work as it came, do it and get on to the next. This was 'careering' more than fulfilling a career, but it was professionally rewarding, which stilled my conscience.

Celtic started well in the League, but at the turn of the year they began to falter seriously, with defeats to Rangers and Motherwell, two teams that were in a habit of spiking Celtic's guns at vital moments. Three successive defeats in March 1975 left Celtic reeling and their ambitions as Championship contenders were considerably dented. A third place behind Rangers and Hibs looked more likely.

I was almost glad at this moment that I was a supporter *in absentia*. Despite my despondency, I could not help but fall back into that sense of optimism that the last decade of their play had given me and all Celtic supporters. Yet nothing on this earth lasts for ever, and it was beginning to dawn on us that the Stein song might soon become a threnody, that the beautiful serenade he'd created to fluid attacking football over nine whole seasons might be lost in a dirge of negativity and anticlimax. Celtic's majestic, imperious form seemed to have disappeared along with Lord Lucan. We all crossed our fingers, hoping for the best, and prayed to avoid the worst.

Our prayers appeared to be answered in the smooth path they had through the Scottish Cup and, to our relief, they reached the final against Airdrieonians. This was very unlikely opposition, but that is always the kind that can trip Celtic up, as we have seen, so I made every effort to see this game. More importantly, I wanted to be there because it would be Billy McNeill's last game for the team, as he was retiring after what could arguably be called the greatest career in Scottish professional football up to that time. In addition, since *Quizball*, he had become a friend. I wanted to see him go out in glory.

I was then filming in West Lothian in *The Great Road Race* with Russell Hunter. In the picture, I had to drive a very fast sports car at high speed down various country lanes, frightening not only the cows and sheep behind the hedges but the crew behind the camera as I headed straight for them. I was tempted to turn the steering wheel towards Glasgow, but apparently I was only allowed to drive the expensive vehicle while the camera was turning because of insurance. I asked the director, Robin Crichton, if he would like to film the Celtic match and he said, 'The what?', so I knew there was no joy there. Robin was very 'county' and had been educated in Paris, so I couldn't blame him. Luckily, I was able to talk my way into a local house and saw on television Billy's last 90 minutes of playing football.

The team fielded by Stein for this occasion was: Latchford; McGrain and Lynch; Murray, McNeill and McCluskey; Hood, Glavin, Dalglish,

Lennox and Wilson. McNeill and Lennox were still big names and the new arrivals like McGrain and Dalglish had already established themselves, while Hood and Wilson were also making their mark. Wilson was top scorer at the club and his brace of goals settled the issue, with McCluskey's penalty making victory sure. It was moving to see Billy being carried off the field shoulder high by his teammates and hear the roars of the crowd at the Celtic end. The Airdrie supporters added the weight of a few generous hands and Billy left the playing side of his game in appropriate style.

Like the great McGrory, he was a one-club man, and how club and man had benefited. From joining Celtic as a gangly young Willie McNeill from Our Lady's High, Motherwell, in 1957, he had become 'Billy' as soon as he signed. From the start, he rose as high and steadily as one of his own Hampden headers and worthily earned a place as one of the Celtic immortals. As a soldier's son, he was born to take command, and he did so with authority and calm. Over the seasons, he won many vital games for the team he supported by a skill at corners that any forward might have envied.

The Celtic jersey he gave me as a memento of our memorable *Quizball* sessions in Manchester I passed on years later to Joe Brady, when that actor became fatally ill in London. I know he prized it. I similarly treasure the fact that I saw a Celtic great at the top of his game and at the height of his fame. Bravo, Cesar!

Jim Brogan was afterwards sent to Coventry and was followed by the shattering departure of Jimmy Johnstone to San Jose in the United States. This was a reluctant move on everybody's part, but Jimmy's drinking had got the better of the lovely wee fella and Stein's patience was tried that inch too far. In June 1975, Johnstone was called in and told he was being released. Jinky was shocked. He did not want to go. America was the furthest place Stein could send him; he had no wish to be reminded of what a talent was wasted. Johnstone wept bitterly as he went. Why is genius so often self-destructive?

The same question applies to the calm departure of George Connelly a few months later. Connelly was one of the best-known examples of not being able to cope with football's many pressures. He was, along with Johnstone, one of Stein's favourite sons on the playing staff, but Connelly became increasingly prodigal with his talents and with his life. One day after training, he just dressed and without a word to anyone walked away from football for good. It was a tragic loss to the game as well as the club, and Stein tried everything he knew to win him back. 'I was more in the Connelly house than in my own,' he remembered ruefully.

Celtic had won the League Cup and the Scottish Cup in 1974–75, and yet the feeling of failure hung over all of us like a pall. The title towel was thrown in. This was not normal and it took a bit of getting used to. I had seen the club I loved climb to world level in a decade, and in a few weeks it appeared to have slumped all the way back to mediocrity. This wasn't true, of course – they had too many good players for that to happen – but that's how it seemed, how it felt. We had been too near heaven too long, so that even the slightest descent from that felt like hell. Ian Archer in the *Glasgow Herald* on 24 February 1975 struck a chord with me as an actor when he wrote, following the League defeat by Hibernian: 'So when the lights were turned up and the part finished, when it was seen that under the make-up was a tired face, when all that happened on Saturday, it was difficult not to cry a little . . .'

I know that feeling so well: the drained emptiness of the performance given, when the sweat has caked hard on your brow, when the voice is raw, when the shirt is wet and the knees are weak. You rub the make-up from your eyes and stare into the mirror and see nothing except a face that is ashen away from the spotlight and you wonder how you managed to get through the night. You're tired, but the thrill of the show is still tight in your chest. You remember the good moments, the ready laughs, the silences, the generosity of that applause. They actually stood up, what about that? You can't help grinning into the mirror. It was great, but you're glad it's over – at least until tomorrow night. Now you'd better wash your face and get dressed. God, you could do with a drink. It'll soon be time for the dressing-room visitors – and to start acting again . . .

That's how the actor feels after a show and it's little different to how the supporter feels after the match. Especially when you've been beaten and lost the chance of ten in a row, a chance of going ahead of teams like MTK Budapest and CSKA Sofia, who had also won nine championships of their countries in successive seasons. We could have literally been top of the world; now we'd have to start all over again. The thought itself was tiring. So near and yet so very far.

That was my mood as I drove down the M77 one morning towards Ayr. I was heading for Rozelle House in Alloway to inaugurate the first Burns Festival in the courtyard there, in association with the Scottish Tourist Board. My head was full of decisions about casting, music, publicity, ticket prices, dates and budgets, all the things that are involved in a production, but my heavy heart was still carrying Celtic around in it.

That was still how I was feeling as I stood in front of the bathroom mirror shaving one morning, the radio on beside me. I didn't see my frowning, stubbly face; I saw wee Jinky in a meandering dribble, trailing three men behind him down the right wing; I saw Bobby Lennox doing his lancer's run down the left; there was Dixie Deans in the penalty area, daring the goalkeeper to save this one; there was aerial Billy rising again into the sun; young Dalglish, that old head on such young shoulders, the fearless Auld, the fearful Gemmell going for goal, so many images, so many wonderful moments, swirling in a kaleidoscope of all the greens. Then, suddenly, the announcer's voice interrupted my reverie:

In the early hours of this morning, the Mercedes car driven by Mr Jock Stein on the M74 crashed head-on with a Peugeot coming towards them on the wrong side of the road. It was thought at first Mr Stein had died, but after taking a breathalyser test he was hurried by ambulance to the new Dumfries and Galloway Hospital, which was formally opened only yesterday . . .

Screams and confusion, the splintering of glass, and then an awful silence except for the whirring of wheels. I stood looking into the mirror with my mouth wide open as the radio played on in the background.

CHAPTER NINE

Supporting Ever More

Henrik Larsson – Centre-Forward
This daring, dashing, dreadlocked Swede
Answered Celtic's urgent need
And despite a broken leg and jaw
He was crowned king o' them a'.

Being the man he was, Stein recovered, and so did his friend Tony
Queen, who was in the passenger seat. The other driver, a John
Ballantyne of Dumfries, was hardly mentioned in the news reports.
The accident, however, left Celtic rudderless for the whole of the next
season, and bosun Sean Fallon moved up to take care of the ship in the
absence of the captain. Stein was sorely missed and for the first time
since 1964 Celtic won nothing. He came back in season 1976–77, a
little frailer, but with the help of Dave McParland, ex-Partick Thistle,
as coach on the pitch, he steered Celtic to a League and Scottish Cup
double. One man does not a football club make, yet Stein's contribution,
and the lack of it in the Fallon caretaker season, was now seen in a clear
light, further underlining the importance of the manager figure in any
football club.

In my Celtic life, I lived in the valley of hope between the high peaks
of Maley and Stein, with a long green plain stretching behind Maley to
that first open space by the cemetery wall, and behind Stein and Lisbon
a rocky outcrop that included high hills like McNeill and Martin
O'Neill. It was a mixed terrain, but there was enough flowering to
encourage optimism. That's all the supporter needs: a flicker of hope.

The path from the boys' gate to the centre stand was a long
pilgrimage, but it was one I had to make if I was going to enjoy the

mecca of nine in a row. I walked the walk and enjoyed the talk because I spoke the language. I was in familiar country and I felt I knew where I was going. 'Home' is the only word to describe it; to be at the place where all the parts of the self came together and could be at peace. There was no need to travel further; a boy's odyssey had reached its goal. This is the family part of the trinity that embraces faith and football.

It is a religion for many and they express it by attendance at the cathedral they call Celtic Park. In lay terms, it was a safe harbour, one from which you could set out to experience the thrill of the unexpected and one to which you could come home and know again the reassurance of the familiar. This is what a club means, a place where people of like mind gather to enjoy the pleasure of the moment. I entitled my poem on the subject 'The Feast of Football'.

> On rectangle altars of grass
> Between the perimeter white lines
> Set like commandments on the green field,
> The champions parade
> Like hirsute high priests in gladiatorial motley
> In temple playgrounds
> Under a canopy of lights
> Or in the glare of the sun at the peak of day.
>
> In a vast cathedral open to the sky
> The initiated hordes
> Banked on the throbbing terraces,
> A hive of heartbeats,
> Meet to give worship upon the appointed day
> In this, their most accessible shrine,
> Making a multi-coloured congregation
> At the mass of their own making.
>
> Who gaze, as with one eye,
> On the carpet of ever-changing patterns
> Where the chosen acolytes pursue their rites
> In camera
> And for every supporter's notice.
> Playing the game, the selected few,

To whom is due
The homage that men once gave to gods,
Now freely give of themselves
As they relive for others
The pain, the fear, the excitement
That primitive players felt in ancient days
On levelled ground by the graveyard wall.

Now
See how
The new tribes gather
Spectators
Participators
A nameless laity chanting its disjointed hymns
To raise young godlike men
In their own image, as man-like gods,
To praise and give blessing
To the solemnity of men at play,
So that all who see might wonder
And, in a moment, know a lifetime's dream.

It is no accident that Sir Alex Ferguson's workplace is called 'the
Theatre of Dreams', because that's what his players offer the supporters,
a place to dream. For a time, they can give themselves to the moment,
no matter what is happening in the big outside world. I knew this
almost from the beginning at Celtic Park. I surrendered to the spell of
the play, I marvelled at the skill and courage of the warriors who were
fighting my battle for me in green-and-white colours. I was mesmerised
by the patterns of play as they unfolded and never lost hope that we
would win until that final whistle sounded. So many times this
confidence was totally unfounded, but I didn't care. I wasn't into the
science of probability, I didn't bring a rational logic to bear, I felt a swell
of the heart and a beating at the temples, and it made me feel alive.
That's why I follow football, or, rather, that's why I follow Celtic and
Celtic, to me, means being of the people.

By the side of the road in Abercromby Street, in the East End of my
great city and not a hundred yards from St Mary's Pro-Cathedral and
the site of the hall in Forbes Street where Celtic were founded, a pole
by the side of the pavement bears a printed placard that states simply

'God Bless Tommy Burns'. That's all it says, in plain letters, with no ornamentation, just those four plain words. Yet no gilded monument or decorated plinth, no cenotaph or plaque could say more about this man of the people than this plain memorial.

Tommy Burns was perhaps not the greatest player in Celtic's history, he wasn't the most astute manager they ever had, but he was a good player, a good manager and, what is more important, a good man and a great supporter. He was the embodiment of all that Celtic means, the personification of its ethos, which is why this book is dedicated to him. That unpretentious placard was erected in an unpretentious street by ordinary people as a mark of gratitude and respect to one of their own for his dedication to their cause, his upholding of their ideals as they might be seen in the deeds achieved by a football team. No statesman, or celebrity so-called, in our day, has been so spontaneously honoured.

Tommy was, in his own words, 'an ordinary supporter who got lucky'. Joining Celtic as a 15-year-old, he remained to become an accomplished gentleman-player, and in time their manager, but, at all times, he remained at heart a common-or-garden 'fella fae the Galla'gate', except that he was by no means common and he wasn't known for his gardening. Essentially, he was someone who kept the faith, raised a family and made a living out of the sport he loved. After his last game at Celtic Park, he threw his boots into the Jungle, where he had once stood as a boy. He made a point of shaking hands with all the occupants of all the wheelchairs after a match, just to reassure them that they were still part of things at the ground.

I saw him play often, but I never met him. Through an actor friend of his, Martin McCardie, I was invited to attend his Tommy Burns Supper one year. I would have loved to have done, but there was a clash of dates. I would have told him then how often I used his name in my own shows to lighten things up. It was all such a whirl of touring dates for me at times that some evenings I wasn't sure which Burns I was playing – Robert, George or Tommy.

However, I did see him at various off-the-field Celtic occasions and noticed that there was one thing he enjoyed as much as anything to do with the club and that was just saying its name. Tommy said it all as one word, 'Celticfootballclub'. That didn't prevent anyone's seeing the joy in his face as he said it, rolling the syllables lovingly around his tongue – 'Celtic Football Club'. I get something of the same frisson even as I type the words because I understand exactly what Tommy meant by amalgamating the words into one. To him, and to me, and countless thousands since 1887, the club is just that, all of a oneness, the one thing we all share.

From what I've read and heard of the man, it occurs to me that, ideally, Tommy Burns should have been a married Roman Catholic priest with a family, a man who worked enthusiastically for Celtic after saying Mass in the morning and before Benediction at night. This reminds me of a real Catholic priest I know today, who also admires Tommy Burns. When this priest was a young boy in the Garngad, he was taken by his father to all Celtic's away matches and enjoyed the trips to the different grounds, hearing the variety of Scottish accents. The return trip home was another matter. His father, having enjoyed a few beers before, during and after the match, was very much the worse for wear as they ascended the stairs to their tenement door. The priest dreaded the look on his mother's face as she opened the door, and wondered some Saturdays if he should just post his dad through the letter box.

This example underlines the visceral attachment all supporters of the Celtic, as we like to call it, have to the club. As long as there has been a Celtic, there have been supporters. The original followers made the club by contributing their pennies and their labour. As these men and women settled into their corner of Glasgow before spreading into Lanarkshire and their surrounds, so did the Celtic loyalty expand. Families married into families, taking their club with them almost as a dowry and passing on the fervour to new generations.

In the early days of the club, when football games were 'friendlies', the menfolk trudged in their Irish boots from game to game, then, as distances increased, they went by horse and cart in brake clubs, organised as local social societies. When conditions improved for the working class in the twentieth century, they transferred to buses and trains for cross-country trips. After this, they went their own way, by private, crowded car, until, in our day, some even travelled by jet in the same plane carrying the Celtic team.

Celtic supporters will travel by any means, foul or fair, to reach that vital match destination – witness the heroic treks to Lisbon and Seville, about both of which anecdotes still abound. The point is clear. Where Celtic are, the supporter will always be. That is one of the reasons for the club's distinctiveness among clubs: the size and calibre of this extraordinary supporting army, of which I am proud to be but a humble private in the line. I am happy to take my place among the battalions because I know we are all marching to the same tune. As long as that sound arises and the drums beat, then Glasgow Celtic will be there.

However, my happy involvement was severely threatened by a personal event in 1977 that was my equivalent to Jock Stein's terrible car accident. It was a turning point in my life and it all began at London Airport.

My manager, Colin Wright, and I were returning to Britain from a Burns tour in New Zealand. Coming into the arrivals hall at Heathrow, I noticed a letter addressed to me on the message pillar, which was the method in those days of contacting incoming passengers. I thought at first it was from Alannah O'Sullivan, a talented young actress I had met in Auckland. Colin and I had invited her to join us for a show we were planning on the Irish tenor John McCormack. But it wasn't from Alannah. It was a single sheet of notepaper from my wife, Sheila, in Fife.

All it said in effect was 'Dear John, I am no longer in love with you ... I want a divorce.'

'Dear John', right enough. I was stunned. I was aware that my nomadic life around the world with Robert Burns had posed marital problems because of the long absences, but, after more than twenty-four years and five beautiful children, this had come right out of the blue. I was shattered and showed the note to Colin. He read it and handed it back without a word.

My world was suddenly in cloud and misery, but I pulled myself together and tried to do the right thing. Since I was away from home touring most of the time anyway, I thought it would be simpler for Sheila and the children if I stayed away. So I did. I felt awful. I still loved my wife and especially my children, but it appeared I was no longer wanted on the matrimonial voyage. I wasn't hit by a Peugeot but by a ten-ton truck. I just wanted to hide my wounds.

Colin took me in while I plucked up courage to find the right moment to tell my mother in Glasgow. I think she guessed something was up when I kept putting some of my shirts in the wardrobe at her Dennistoun home. Meantime, I told Colin that I would take all the offers he could get that would take me out of Scotland. I was unashamedly running away from my marriage failure, but certainly not from my children. I saw them at every opportunity. Our lawyer,

James Farrell, my one-time *Quizball* companion and Celtic director, saw the inevitable divorce through. When the papers finally arrived, they were dated 29 May 1980 – my silver wedding anniversary.

If the big love affair in my life had now run its course, the other one was just as seriously threatened. Since I was so much on the road, I hadn't seen much of Celtic in the blank season of big Jock's illness and on his return my mind was on other things. My body was also elsewhere, engaged in Burns performances in every country where two or more Scotsmen, or sons and grandsons of Scotsmen, foregathered. I still had a football interest, although it had dwindled from being fervid to being merely curious. Like my marriage, the passion was spent, although an underlying respect remained for both partners, one as the mother of my children, the other as the mainstay of my boyhood enthusiasm.

It was as if I had divorced myself from Celtic as well, but unlike me it was contesting the action. I was delighted to hear they had won another championship under Stein on his return but sad to hear of their slow decline into ordinariness and dismayed by the loss of Dalglish to Liverpool. He was the last rock on which Stein could have built his third great team. Instead, King Kenny went on to build a whole new realm for himself in English football with Liverpool and Nottingham Forest. One has to wonder if big Jock ever really recovered from his horrific accident. Then, just as suddenly, it seemed, he left the club himself after a sour behind-the-scenes exchange with the Celtic board. He had expected a directorship and instead had been offered the handling of sweepstakes and raffles. He made it very clear that was not his strong point and left, handing over at the end of the 1977–78 season to Billy McNeill, whom he himself had persuaded to leave Aberdeen. I thought it was too soon for both of them. Billy was happy as Aberdeen manager and Jock had at least ten years left in him yet as Celtic's boss, although he often said he would retire at fifty-five. What nobody knew then was that Jock didn't have ten years left in him as Jock Stein. Billy justified the appointment immediately with the famous ten-man victory over Rangers to win the League title.

I think my gradual divorce from Celtic came through when they allowed Stein to go. He was never paid his worth at the club, and on the directors' orders, he was as hard financially on his players, which was often to the detriment of his own long-term team plans. Somehow, however, he got the money and the permission to sign Alfie Conn, ex-

Ranger, from Tottenham Hotspur. This was the last, large act of the magnificent Stein tenure. It was like leaving his card, and he couldn't have done it with better flourish. Yet he was still nudged out of the side door in a shameful manner. In 1970, the Queen had given him the CBE for his services to football, and in 1978 Celtic, or perhaps the more diehard of the directors, gave him the push.

Instead of having a red face at Celtic's steep decline, in my estimation at least, I was developing a good tan as I chased the sun around the world in the name of Robert Burns and Robert Louis Stevenson. I often thought I might meet the Celtic team on one of their foreign tours, but as they went west I went east. It wasn't deliberate. However, I did give a performance at the Celtic Club in Kearny, New Jersey, and it was one of the few times my mother, who was on holiday in the States at the time, saw me on the stage. She had actually to step up onstage herself to receive a bouquet from the club. I was revived for a time in my Celtic loyalty by this gesture and by their obvious love for the club and its traditions. I was to meet this kind of devotion by proxy all around the world. By this time, though, I was developing a sense of distance in my own thoughts about the then Parkhead regime.

Despite what I heard about continued inefficiencies from the boardroom and the pitiful procession of managers coming and going like penny candles after the huge blaze given Celtic by Stein, the club still mattered to me. A tower had been toppled and mini-minds were scurrying to replace it with prefabs. It was hard to persist in the all-consuming, nearly mindless support of them that I had known for more than 40 years. Being out of sight, however, they were never quite out of mind. I couldn't get rid of the feeling of guilt I had. It was when they were in similar need that I first offered them my seven pennies at the boys' gate.

Imagine my mortification in the early 1990s when I was led to believe, through various sources, that they were nearly bankrupt and that before long the Bank of Scotland would take steps to foreclose on them. Serve those addle-headed skinflints right, I thought ungenerously. Since I never attended board meetings, I didn't ever know what really went on, but that was how it looked to an outsider. They would need a mercantile Stein now, someone with the money and the will. Fortunately for us all, they were to find him in a canny expatriate Scot in Canada, Fergus McCann.

Meantime, I could only read about events in newspaper reports at various airports and, occasionally, hear all about it on the BBC World Service. On one occasion while I was abroad, I rang Glasgow to check up on my mother. During our catch-up chat, I thought I could hear a radio commentary on a football match in the background. I interrupted our conversation to ask her what the game was. She said she had no idea. I asked her to listen. She sighed and came back in a moment telling me it was Celtic and somebody. I couldn't believe my luck and asked her to hold the telephone receiver down by the radio so I could listen. She did so, reluctantly, and I could just about hear what was going on, but couldn't get the score. After a few minutes, her voice came on again, saying, 'I've mair to do wi' my time than stand here haudin' the phone to a fitba' match.' I protested strongly, but she'd already turned the radio off.

On my visits back home from touring dates abroad, I divided my time between her flat in Glasgow and Colin's house in Edinburgh, and moved by car between the two as the occasion demanded. This was how I had come to meet Willie Woodburn at his Colinton garage and he would always bring me up to date on Celtic – from a Rangers point-of-view. Friends in Glasgow were still good for tickets at short notice and that was how I got to see the 1980 Old Firm Scottish Cup final, or should I call it the umpteenth Battle of Hampden?

The Celtic team by now read: Latchford; Sneddon and McGrain; Aitken, Conroy and MacLeod; Provan, Doyle, McCluskey, Burns and McGarvey. There were new faces I had to get used to, like Latchford, Conroy and McGarvey. Latchford made a marvellous save minutes from the end to send the scoreless match into extra time, during which the tireless McGrain sent a ball into the penalty area that McCluskey managed to divert into the net, and Billy McNeill's men had won the Cup.

The Celtic team properly decided to show off the trophy to their supporters, and in a posse made as if to move to the Celtic end of the stadium. This was a signal for hostilities to begin. I was standing ready to leave, but I had to sit again as I saw a spearhead of young boys heading from the Rangers end like the vanguard of an invading army. They were heading for the Celtic party and with no intention of patting them on the back. I sat transfixed as the players beat them off and made a strategic retreat to the tunnel. Meanwhile, the Celtic fans on the field to greet their team turned on the Rangers assailants and a pitched battle ensued.

The image I still have in my mind is of a blond teenager holding a

Rangers scarf high in his upstretched hands, his eyes staring down at a young Celtic boy lying on the grass, a boy he had just kicked, now with both hands covering his head, as a steward pulled the Rangers fan away. What was this to do with football? I know his team was beaten, but that was poor excuse for attempted murder. I had seen a few skirmishes in Harlem and Hollywood in my time, but this was far more frightening. It was daylight in a moment of celebration, which was suddenly turned to anguish for many by the malevolent actions of a few indoctrinated to accept defeat with venom. I drove back to Edinburgh, sobered by what I'd witnessed. During the trip, these lines of mine kept going through my head.

> I speak Anguish,
> The world's most-spoken language.
> I don't remember learning it,
> I just picked it up as I went along.
> Everybody has a smattering of it
> But I became an expert.
> I was misery-literate
> A sad-face *cum laude* . . .

I almost forgot that Celtic had won.

Celtic were runners-up in the League Championship that year. It was an honourable position, but to me it felt like a defeat. However, I was delighted when Billy, in his managerial reign, went on to win three League titles and a League Cup.

Meantime, I had more commitments abroad, one of which was to return to New Zealand and marry Alannah O'Sullivan. On the first night I met her, in Auckland nearly three years before, standing beside her big motorbike outside an Auckland theatre stage door, I had a startling vision above her head of our being married in front of a rhododendron bush. It was a sudden precognition, a kind of fey premonition. My mother was prone to these occasions, and so was I. It's not a comfortable gift, I assure you. It often tells you things you don't want to know, but in this instance, I had only just met the girl and she was not at all impressed when I told her. She was an up-and-coming actress, very attractive, and nearly half my age, after all.

When she later came to Britain, I invited her to perform at the Edinburgh Festival. This developed into her working in our Shanter

Productions office while Colin and I were travelling. This soon grew into her being an indispensable part of our production team. When Colin moved on to a new career as a computer consultant, Alannah travelled the world with me, performing on the luxury cruise ships and in arts venues around the world as Two for a Theatre, so that finally, by degrees, she 'dwindled into a wife'. The only thing I couldn't do was convert her to Celtic. She preferred the All Blacks. When we had organised our wedding date with Alannah's family, it was for 20 September, which was the Jewish Day of Atonement. Once again, I had a premonition, this time an uneasy one. Sadly, it proved right. On that day, I wasn't marrying Alannah in New Zealand but burying my mother in Glasgow. She had died unexpectedly from a stroke.

When Alannah and I did marry, on 27 September 1980, it was at her mother's country home outside Christchurch – in the garden in front of a large bank of rhododendron bushes. I remember the end of my verse written in the car on the road to Edinburgh:

> But then somebody said something
> One day.
> There was a smile,
> Or was it a look in the eyes?
> It took me by surprise
> Like summer thunder
> And no wonder.
> No words from me, just a sigh,
> And I
> Felt a lift of the heart
> And the start
> Of a long, contented silence.

Due to the change of wedding date, we only had a one-night honeymoon, in Waikiki, Honolulu, before embarking on an American tour, beginning in Chicago, where Alannah played her solo Dorothy Parker before joining me for the life of Mr and Mrs Robert Louis Stevenson. On our eventual return to Scotland, I decided to move Shanter Productions to Glasgow and things went on much as before. The only difference was that I was able to get to Celtic Park more easily.

In 1981, Celtic were champions again. Billy was having a good run, with Tommy Burns hitting the winning goal in the League decider against Dundee United at Tannadice. However, they had lost in the League Cup to the same team at Parkhead, in one of the many matches now featuring the chirpy Charlie Nicholas at centre-forward. Dundee United went on to win the League Cup and also to beat Celtic again in the Scottish Cup. They were one half of the 'New Firm', the other being Aberdeen under Alex Ferguson, who had come to the fore while I was away.

If I was preoccupied with my own merry-go-round around the theatres and clubhouses on the American and Antipodean lecture circuits, with all the intervening sea trips and connecting flights, Celtic, by all accounts, were on their own fairground roller-coaster, with ups and downs in Cup and League. The ups were high indeed and there were exhilarating victories against clubs like Ajax in Amsterdam and a win over Rangers that gave them their first League Cup since 1974. To counter these highs, however, there were just too many draws and losses against much less formidable opposition, allowing, for example, Dundee United to win their first Championship in 1983, even though Celtic had beaten Rangers 4–2 on the final day. Despite their disappointment, the Celtic support at Ibrox Park sang their team all the way to the tunnel. It was typical of their unswerving loyalty.

Billy McNeill took his players to play a friendly against Finn Harp in Ireland, not realising it was to be his last match in charge. He had made the mistake of thinking that the Celtic board of directors would recognise his exceptional career-long contribution to the club. Even as a player, he had made more appearances in the jersey than anyone, living or dead. He also assumed that the success he had made of management would be acknowledged in his being given funds to strengthen the squad, having lost the invaluable Nicholas to Arsenal. He had signed Brian McClair from Motherwell and managed to persuade the popular and dynamic midfielder Murdo MacLeod to re-sign despite interest from Rangers, but when Billy, at a time when he was far from being the highest-paid manager in Scotland, asked for a contract for himself, he was turned down flat. Their excuse was that two championships (1980 and 1983) had been lost in the final run-in.

This was in the face of all the other evidence pointing to his success in the job – his articulate presence as the public image of Celtic, his work rate, administratively and technically, his standing in the game and with the players, his results as a whole – all this thrown aside like so much chaff because of a reluctance to guarantee a long-term wage. Such short-sightedness is little short of blindness and has been too often the identifying element in successive Celtic minds upstairs. Their view was that no manager had had a contract before, why should he? McNeill was a young man with family responsibilities. Not unreasonably, like his players, he felt he should have a degree of security. It was not to be, his request was rejected unanimously, so Billy left to become manager of Manchester City.

It was like a son walking out of the family. He had had his lapses, a black eye here and there, a bit of shouting from the dugout, but what young man doesn't let his emotions have their outlet? Celtic certainly did not behave paternally. Loyalty in any situation should be mutual. No one benefited from this turn of events, neither the club as a whole, the board, Billy, the players nor, most of all, the supporters. They are always the last considered in these situations. Yet, in the end, it is they who pay everyone's money, whether in wages or dividends. There ought to be a supporters' representative on every football club's board. The voice of the people needs to be heard, real people who don't need to protect their shares at all costs. Democracy is long overdue in the boardroom.

As if to emphasise the sorry nature of this kind of recurring dispute over money, the ground itself stood as an unhappy witness to such self-serving frugality. Untidy, peeling, broken, chipped and discoloured, it mimicked exactly the cheese-paring attitude of the owners. When I was attending Parkhead regularly, I had never noticed the gradual running down of the park. I had eyes only for the turf and the events on it, but now that my visits were rarer and I was coming from the world of business class and luxury hotels, I could hardly fail to notice the dereliction all around me. It was like going to your gran's and noticing the tear on the leather chair, the mark of the hot coal on the kitchen carpet. You didn't like to see these things, especially if you loved your old gran. Celtic was beginning to look poor, and in my trade, if you look it, you are it.

It was more of a shovel than a baton that David Hay took over when in 1983 he became Celtic's sixth manager. He had to dig deep. He had been a success at Motherwell, but was not over-eager to enlist as he knew the conditions at the club, but he was persuaded, and, after all, once a Celt ...

Alannah and I were home again from our last round-the-world P&O cruise. We were now touring *Blackout*, our show about my

173

Second World War experiences, all round Scotland, starting from the Mitchell Theatre in Glasgow, so I was right at hand to see Davie make Hay in the sunshine then bathing Celtic Park. Alas, it was not to be. He got off to a good start, winning half a dozen games or so in a row, but then came up against Dundee United, one half of Celtic's new nemesis, and went down 1–2 at Tannadice. His team on that day was: Bonnar; McGrain and Whittaker; Aitken, McAdam and Sinclair; McStay, Melrose, McGarvey, MacLeod and Burns. This was a shake-up side, with new faces but no new ideas. Aberdeen, poised to become champions, underlined this two weeks later with a 3–1 home victory over their Glasgow visitors.

There was an irony in that I was playing every night in a show that evoked wartime memories with wartime songs for audiences and this Celtic team was playing in a manner which brought back memories of those wartime teams that so distressed wartime supporters. 'We'll Meet Again' was sung with a whole new meaning as Celtic embarked on a season that saw them runners-up in every domestic competition they entered, always a galling position for any side, and supporters did not take kindly to this bridesmaid Celtic, even though they tanned Sporting Lisbon 5–0 and narrowly lost to Nottingham Forest, both at Celtic Park in the UEFA Cup. 'Wish me luck as you wave me goodbye . . .'

Old thoughts came back of the Five Sorrowful Mysteries and the tyranny of Rangers' wartime supremacy. I remembered once having to ask my mother if she had any spare clothing coupons to give to Celtic for jerseys. 'Whit a cheek' was her immediate reply. 'Surely they heid yins there can lay their hauns on anythin' they want. Ye can only wear wan fur coat at a time.'

My mother had not been too impressed by Celtic's plea of poverty – even in the matter of clothing coupons being needed to renew playing strips. Looking back, it seems ridiculous that a club of its standing should make such an appeal to its fans. Yet the support obliged. Some of them would have had their wives, aunties and daughters knit 11 jerseys if need be.

Celtic don't know how lucky they are in their support. These are the same men who, in the beginning, brought their shovels to create the first playing pitch, and during the Depression walked across the country to follow their team, and, when there was a war on, did hand over their clothing coupons. However, even they became restive at the way the club was being allowed to amble along in the mid-'80s without any attempt to tackle the feeling of second-best that was creeping in. The country, too, had its problems.

The national coalminers' strike was now obsessing the country and this was a timely reminder that there were social concerns outside football that affected the greater part of Celtic's largely working-class support. Everybody was on the miners' side, but they were on a hiding to nothing from the stony-faced, plummy-voiced Thatcher, who did not recognise such a thing as society and, at a stroke, swept away whole pit communities, as coal was regarded as dirty and old-fashioned, and the miners the same. City money did all the talking at Westminster and the pits closed. I felt for them. It was a national disgrace that a national strike didn't happen in 1984–5, but the other unions were too busy minding their own shops and the poor old miners were left stranded.

In a previous nadir during the Second World War, the Celtic Supporters Association was formed in 1944 by a young supporter, Willie Fanning, who was in despair at what he was seeing on the field and wanted to tell the club he wasn't the only one. He sent a letter to Waverley at the *Daily Record* and as a result 14 people turned up for the inaugural meeting in a Shettleston hall. When a further meeting was called a few weeks later, the crowd was so large they had to adjourn to an open space and conduct the meeting from the top of an air-raid shelter.

The ordinary supporters at last had a forum, a voice to make themselves heard in an organised way rather than standing outside the pavilion after yet another defeat and howling deprecation at the management. The average supporter only wanted a result and he didn't really care how they got it. Quite rightly, he thought he deserved better than he was getting in 1985.

They had survived losing the Scottish Cup to Aberdeen in 1984 through the sending-off of Roy Aitken by referee Valentine. They had to forfeit a deservedly won European tie against Rapid Vienna in the aftermath of a bottle being thrown onto the pitch. I was at that home game and actually saw it land up near the corner flag, a good hop, skip and jump from anyone, and yet the Viennese player went down as if shot. In the melee afterwards, he walked off. A good job, or he would have been dealt with appropriately by the Celtic players. Of course, UEFA ordered the Cup-Winners' Cup match to be replayed in a neutral ground, Old Trafford, and, of course, Celtic lost. They had really been defeated not on the field but in the power game played in Continental corridors. Hooligan behaviour by English Celtic supporters during the match in Manchester only added to the Scottish misery and frustration. Then Celtic returned home to later confound themselves and everyone else by winning the 1985 Scottish Cup.

The miracle men were: Bonnar; W. McStay and McGrain; Aitken, McAdam and McLeod; Provan, P. McStay, Johnstone, Burns and McGarvey. On the bench, O'Leary and McClair. Their opponents were once again Dundee United, who had eliminated Rangers and were keen to make it an Old Firm double. By now, Celtic were sharing the same sponsor's name as Rangers on their strips, the double-glazing firm C. R. Smith of Dunfermline. What you might call a transparent publicity coup but valuable perhaps as a gesture towards a kind of togetherness.

I was at The Byre, St Andrews, playing Oscar Wilde, and could only listen on a transistor radio as I sat on a bench overlooking the Old Course. 'Old Tom' Morris would have thought that a crime, but Oscar famously said, 'Football is all very well as a game for rough girls but it is hardly suitable for delicate boys.' Few would have called Roy Aitken a delicate boy and Davie Provan, for all his generosity of hair, could never have been mistaken for a girl. It wasn't so good for this grown man when I heard Dundee United score ten minutes into the second half, but it was a different Celtic after the interval. Roy became a power in midfield and it was Davie who equalised with a free kick with quarter of an hour left to play. I startled the golfers with my shout of joy. McGarvey scored another five minutes from time and my joy was unconfined. When the broadcast finished, I switched off and just sat there. A golfer passed, his bag over his shoulder. 'Fine day,' he said. I nodded, speechless, but I couldn't have agreed more. The 100th Scottish Cup final and who wins it? Celtic, of course. I sat there until my body clock told me it was time to get back to the theatre.

Chairman Desmond White died five weeks later and took his austere fiscal efficiency with him. He was succeeded by Tom Devlin, who was altogether more approachable, but was not likely to last too long. He had his own health problems. He assured the supporters via the *Daily Record* that 'the board was the team behind the team'. That's what worried them. What was also of concern to that most loyal of football followings was that the Hay–Connor tandem appeared to be riding on one buckled wheel. For some reason, assistant manager Frank Connor, it was rumoured, tried to motivate the players by provoking them. In contrast, Hay, the quiet man, liked to soothe them. It couldn't work both ways, so Hay called his assistant to Celtic Park one Sunday afternoon in February 1986 and sacked him. Decisive action indeed. David Hay had told *The Scotsman* on 11 November 1985, 'Everyone at Parkhead, and I mean everyone associated with the club, has to take a long hard look at themselves . . . and none more so than myself.'

The Lone Ranger had Tonto, but this lone Celt had no one but himself, the new chairman being at a remove even as a leaning shoulder. It seemed a shame that such a likeable young man, intelligent and able as Hay was, should be on the bridge of such a big ship on his own, especially as it seemed to be heading into troubled waters again after that lovely cup triumph and a decent start in the League. There had already been one awful shock earlier in the season. In September 1985, when Celtic were getting ready to face Aberdeen, the defending champions, news came that Jock Stein had suddenly died of a heart attack at Cardiff.

He had been at Cardiff City's ground as Scotland's manager, trying to guide them through to the World Cup finals in Mexico – a win or draw against Wales would earn them a play-off place. A substitute, Davie Cooper, scored with a penalty against Wales, and Scotland were through to a two-leg qualifier against Australia. In the excitement, Stein had a brush with a trackside photographer. It appeared to be a trivial incident, but together with the excitement of pulling off the needed draw it must have been too much for big Jock and, despite his assurance to Ernie Walker, the SFA secretary, that it was 'just the cough' and that he was 'all right and feeling a bit better', he died on the dressing-room treatment table. He was 62 years of age.

Like everyone else in Scotland, I saw the incident on television, in the flat Alannah and I had in St Vincent Crescent in Finnieston. My new domestic luxury was of no comfort at all as I watched the scramble with the photographer. Here was Scotland's greatest-ever manager being reduced to the level of a Sauchiehall Street bouncer as he tried to see the final moments of one of his greatest triumphs. He had taken Scotland to a World Cup play-off. Thus are the gods brought down. Which reminds me of the time a player was asked, 'How do you spell Stein?' He replied, 'G-O-D.'

A minute's silence was observed by the 40,000 crowd at Celtic Park before the Aberdeen game, one they did not dare lose. They duly won 2–1. I would love to have been there standing in that silence, but instead I was on a plane with Alannah, heading off for New York and the office of the Keedick Lecture Bureau for another one-night-stand recital tour of the United States.

I came home again to play one of Glasgow's most famous sons, Charles Rennie Mackintosh. This show had originally been commissioned by R.W. Adams, managing director of Mackintosh Furniture in Kirkcaldy. He was a charming man, brought up in Glasgow's South Side and a committed Rangers fan since boyhood, but this never, ever got in the way of a long and fruitful association and a genuine personal friendship. The Mackintosh show went on to be a great success with architects and the general public alike.

The League Championship of 1985–86 would come down to the last game of the season and, against all the odds, Celtic were still in contention. They needed to win by at least three goals in their final game against St Mirren at Paisley, while Hearts, the League leaders, needed to lose against Dundee at Dens Park for the Parkhead men to win the title on goal difference. Celtic turned the screw on Hearts in impressive fashion by running up a 5–0 lead by the interval (the final score, as it turned out), then – joy of joys – the terracing at Paisley erupted seven minutes from time with the news that Dundee had taken the lead through Albert Kidd, the roars being repeated a few minutes later when the same player added a second. Celtic were champions. Who would have believed it? Soon afterwards, Albert Kidd was elected an honorary Celtic supporter in recognition of his outstanding contribution to the Celtic story.

Another little anecdote illustrates how vital this match was to all Celtic supporters. A friend of mine, Gerard McDade, a good Celtic man and a Celtic author, was being married in Greenock. It had to be that very Saturday afternoon at four o'clock and he could do nothing about it. His closest friend, the late John Dougan, the man who had first introduced him to Celtic when Gerry was a young boy, was also invited and couldn't refuse. Since he was also the linchpin of the local Greenock Celtic Supporters Club, this was a severe test of their friendship, but John was there with the rest of them, sitting in his place in St Andrew's Church. The ceremony completed, the happy bride, Irene, and her compliant groom were coming down the aisle when suddenly John popped out of his pew and came towards them holding a camera.

'Smile, please,' he said. The bride smiled happily, but the groom's smile could only be described as fixed. Make no mistake, the groom loved his wife deeply, but he was naturally, as a Celtic supporter on that day, a little preoccupied. So was his pal with the camera, who then leaned forward and in a church whisper said, 'We've won the League.'

'True?'

'True.'

The bridegroom beamed ecstatically and embraced his friend, while his new wife looked on smiling. She understood – she was a Celtic supporter, too.

Jack McGinn became the Celtic chairman after dear old Tom Devlin passed away shortly after that triumph. Jack was of a new breed, direct and visible, with no ostensible links to auld Ireland or the licensing trade. He had founded the *Celtic View* in 1965, the oldest supporters' magazine in football, and edited it so efficiently that he won a seat on the board, and now he was the chairman. He would apply the same efficiency from this chair. It did not take him long to act.

The summer of 1987 was the 20th anniversary of the Lisbon Lions, and Billy McNeill was in Glasgow to celebrate with his former teammates. Jack McGinn took the chance to make his first move. He asked Billy how he'd feel about coming back. He couldn't have picked a better moment. McNeill had just left Aston Villa and was under the spell of Lisbon euphoria. He was also back home. He could only agree.

The handover was not pleasant, but then neither is any major surgery. The only trouble was, it was all done behind closed doors, and Davie Hay deserved better than that, having won the Scottish Cup and the League titles in difficult times for the club. But the big-money Rangers revival, led by chairman Murray, was impacting badly on Celtic. Hay might not have been the most flamboyant of managers, but his heart was in the right place and he had a good head on him – but he had no contract. Did Billy, I wonder? Or did he rely on the reception being given him as the prodigal son to ensure the promise of better things this time round? That was Billy's business, not ours, but at least he had Jack McGinn.

The new pairing didn't get off to a great start, beaten 5–1 by Arsenal in a friendly. The irony was that Charlie Nicholas, who had done great things for Celtic, was playing for Arsenal that day. Meanwhile, the Celtic players themselves weren't downhearted. They had the feeling that with Billy back they couldn't fail. This was the club's centenary season.

Jersey players like Burns and McStay were already fired up, and new bhoys like Mark McGhee and Andy Walker were of the same breed. Andy was the son of my then accountant, Frank Walker, so I had a vested interest. I was delighted to see him score in the opening League match, a 4–0 win at Cappielow, the same ground where I'd got Stanley Matthews' autograph.

In that first return season under McNeill, Celtic started well and finished brilliantly. They finished ten points clear of Hearts in the League and lost a mere handful of games in the whole year. The previous season had started for me playing Becket, the Archbishop of Canterbury, in St Giles' Cathedral at the 1986 Edinburgh Festival. Becket was killed and so was our season. However, by the next Festival, I was Lord Burleigh in *Mary Stuart*, playing opposite Hannah Gordon at the Assembly Hall. I was flying high and so was our season. I left soon afterwards for another tour of Canada and missed a lot of Billy's continued champagne trail through Scottish football with his team of talents. I was in the United States for most of the next season and I could feel my grip on the club loosening. Like many others, I was astonished by Mo Johnston's transfer, complete with sign of the cross, across the city to Rangers in July 1989. The erosion from Parkhead had begun.

I remember I was invited to Celtic Park around that time and was so saddened by the feeling of depression at the ground. Only a couple of years earlier they had been up among the stars. The McNeill meteor had begun its gradual descent and as the '90s approached it was only a question of when it would crash to earth.

Alannah and I had decided to base ourselves in New Zealand. I had enjoyed a full career, seen the world, made my little mark and, what was even better, I had watched Celtic come into its glorious 100th year in style. Celtic would go on, it would always go on, and I knew I would follow them even to the ends of the earth.

CHAPTER TEN

Looking Back

Charlie Tully, Inside-Left
With a king in the line
A clown prince is fine.
He is proudly part of a regal procession
He scored from a corner, twice in succession.

In the beginning, there was a patch of ground by a graveyard in the East End of Glasgow and in this unlikely soil a seed was sown that developed over more than a century into a social phenomenon called the Celtic. To many, it is much more than a football club; it represents a way of life, epitomises a belief. It was once a faith held only by a minority, holding out hope for better days, and begun by them in the name of charity. Today it flourishes, still adjacent to the cemetery, as a football team that stands as a hub and a reassurance to countless thousands around the world who have never seen them play.

In open spaces within derelict townships, on high plains and in jungle clearings, wherever there is room in the world to kick and chase a ball, there are young men of every shade of skin dressed in the Celtic green and white playing football. They are replicating exactly what those first 'white negroes', as the Establishment termed them, found in the East End of Glasgow in the last decades of the nineteenth century. This was a hope for a better future for themselves, a defiance of their underprivileged status and a confidence born of a new skill learned with a leather ball at their feet. It is a lot to ask of any sport or pastime. It was only a game, but for the ghettos today, just as for that Irish enclave long ago, it is a way out, a passport to a better world.

It dawns on me that the entire fabric of my emotional and cultural life as a schoolboy was conditioned not by the spurious folk traditions fabricated by both sides of the Old Firm but by the simple fact of following a football club. Nor was my future make-up as an adult laid in by my kind of church or school. It was the club I lived for. I existed only for Saturday, whose sole purpose was to give me the chance of watching a game. A simple scenario was worked out in the match to be played. Both teams couldn't lose, so one had to win, or else they could draw. In other words, the team that scored the most goals won. It was the very simplest of dramatic situations but, within it, carried the most complex of emotions. One team tried to score a goal and the other team tried to stop them.

For those of us looking on from the terracing, it could excite tears of joy just as easily as of rage; it could provide an exhibition of wonder and follow it at once with a display of sublime idiocy. It caused thousands to gather as if to worship at a rite, which, in a sense, we were doing. In the open-air cathedral of the football ground, or, if you prefer, the dream theatre of the great unwashed, where vast crowds met to praise their gods, whom they saw before them in shirts, shorts and football boots, I slowly assimilated the faith that was to maintain my first two decades. I was inspired by strutting deities, who for 90 minutes transported my pals and me from whatever hell we had escaped from to another kind if we lost. It was a consolable purgatory if we drew but if we won, an indescribable heaven.

From a boy's point of view, this is not at all absurd. He sees different colours in the beautiful game. It is not a penny-black matter of rules and conditions played out merely to obtain a score, a result. No, it is a thing of gasps and squeals, shouts and gestures, shivers, snorts, chokes of the throat, thuds of the heart and smarting of the eyes.

Football, for the true devotee, is a living act to be experienced, not just passively watched. The secret is that in the course of a match's two halves we become our favourite players and play each touch of the ball with them. True spectating has more to do with the heart than the eyes. It is entirely within, a visceral, totally subjective matter. The actual spectacle offered is only the start. In these material and secular times in which we live, there is little room for the spiritual. It could be that football, and the passion found and aroused by it, is the last resort of the diminishing religious instinct. In the coming-together of great numbers that football creates might be the vestiges of a final holiness, the last chance at a kind of oneness or 'wholeness' that is at the basis of all society.

This underlying intention to make a game support the larger social and economic programme outwith its playing field is evident in ongoing discussions between Celtic and the Glasgow City Council to upgrade the present stadium and its immediate surroundings in time for the Commonwealth Games of 2014 and for the decades thereafter. Celtic Park will become the hub of a far-sighted master plan that will see the regeneration of the entire East End and its consequent elevation to an urban area of architectural significance and environmental worth. It will be an almost unbelievable transformation.

It could be said that Celtic FC is as significant an employer in the Parkhead area as ever was Beardmore's Forge in Duke Street, Barr's lemonade factory in the Gallowgate or Mavor & Coulson's wire works in Springfield Road. Its annual wage bill from chairman to the most remote of scouts must be astronomical – and still growing. A far cry from the church collections that started it all.

When I attended my first Celtic match in 1939–40, it is possible that on that Parkhead terracing that day there would have been old men in the crowd who would have been boys attending with their fathers at the very first Celtic Park. They could never have dreamed that in less than 130 years a new Parkhead and a new East End would stretch out from a 'Celtic Triangle' enclosing a refurbished stadium that will become a showpiece of the new Glasgow.

There are reports of a Celtic Plaza, a whole new environment, which will feature the park at the centre of the completed scheme and see the ground take its place among the master stadia of Europe. London Road School, which I always hoped would one day become a smart hotel called 'The Celtic View', will no doubt be utilised and restyled by the planners within the overall scheme, thus completing the Celtic identity of the immediate area and affording it a very pleasing external unity.

All this change is on the periphery of football; the playing arena is still at its centre and what happens there will still matter most. Nonetheless, it is good to see some thought being given to the overall football environment, which is not always the first concern of the game's decision-makers. In the long term, this extensive renewal of what has been termed 'a moribund district' can only be of benefit in raising the whole Glasgow image worldwide. What a monument this will be to that previous, implanted generation of proletarian side whiskers and cloth caps who brought out their pails, barrows, picks and shovels to clear a space among the tenements.

Celtic, for all this new architectural eminence, is not, at this time, in the first tier of world football. In playing terms, it doesn't rank with the Real Madrids and Barcelonas, with the two Milan titans, nor with Manchester United, Chelsea or Arsenal, or even some of the German clubs in the general calibre of its team. It may have beaten most of these sides, but in terms of playing consistency and quality of contemporary management, it is not on a par. The only real difference between these sides and the Old Firm is that they are rich. However, Celtic also has its wealth – in tradition and in its support. Like Rangers, Celtic should rightly aspire to the top grade.

Football success is not gained by boardroom acuity; it's won on the pitch. And, who knows, a great Celtic team may yet rise again, like certain Lions once did, and restore the club to its rightful place among the elite. An interesting point to remember about Stein's great side of the '60s is that they all belonged to Glasgow and the surrounding area, except for Bobby Lennox on the left wing, who came from Saltcoats in Ayrshire, 30 miles to the south. Contrast that with the ad hoc collection of nomadic professionals currently assembled at Lennoxtown. Some are there on recognised ability, of course, but how many can be said to have that Celtic stamp, that indefinable quality of belonging, that marks them out to Celtic supporters?

For the most part, the contemporary squad is largely made up of strangers in a strange land, given temporary asylum as refugees from the cattle-market conditions of international player exchanges that tie assorted players only to clubs that can afford their extravagant personal terms. It is hoped that by mixing them in and shaking them about they will justify their huge costs, but that's how you make cocktails, not football teams. The irony is that in the first decade of its existence Celtic could boast one of the finest teams in Britain, and in those football days that meant the world.

It had a first-rate board and a strong group of mainly Irish shareholders, so that by the First World War it was one of the richest clubs in the United Kingdom. From the start, it could rely on its committed spectator base, and even now it still has one of the largest and most loyal support of any football club playing anywhere, and certainly the greatest number of female season-ticket holders in Britain. The total world fanbase of the club is estimated at nine million people, including one million in North America. It is also a following much praised for its sporting good behaviour.

This was amply illustrated when around 80,000 Celtic supporters travelled to Seville for the final of the UEFA Cup when Celtic played F.C. Porto in May 2003. As with Lisbon in 1967, many travelled without tickets but with total optimism. Their team lost, but the supporters had the distinction of receiving awards from both UEFA and FIFA for their good sportsmanship and humour before, throughout and after the game. This reflected almost as much credit and prestige on the club as any victory might have done. Not quite, but almost.

Unfortunately, the supporters of all clubs in the modern game are seen now only as a cash cow, as a source of revenue for club merchandise. Witness the constant change of playing strips in order to exploit the incessant demand from Hong Kong to Kathmandu for club colours. These are manufactured on the 'made for a penny and sold for a pound' principle, so it could be said to be sound business. Football is high fashion in some countries. Club shirts are worn by all nationalities, less for playing in, more as badges of status or marks of caste. In many ways, football has lost touch with its primal roots, the ordinary supporters. They are much more than a commodity to be exploited, a mass to fill in the background of a camera shot. They still represent the passion that made the game a spectator sport in the first place.

A football crowd is not just there to be quantified or to be assessed statistically. It is not to be hoodwinked by journalistic jargon or misled by pundit views. The real supporter knows the game because he feels it in every fibre of his being. He is football wise by habit and experience, and his voice ought to be listened to. He is not there to strip to the waist and wave a flag or a can of beer, he is there to watch and wonder, to cheer the good and berate the bad as both unfold before him. More importantly, he is there to remember and take away the memory with him, to stick it into the scrapbook of the mind that every football supporter has been jealously guarding since he was a boy.

The new supporter, however, is too often the corporate hanger-on with glass in hand who sees his football through it. More often than not, he or she is a B-list celebrity who is there to be seen, not to see. To my mind, every honest supporter belongs to the A-list. He should be celebrated for being there at all, given the manner in which he is patronised by those in charge. World football could well descend into nothing more than an artificial medium of television advertising if the ordinary supporter, who is still the lifeblood of the sport, is driven away to the golf course or to help push a trolley in a supermarket.

Modern football has lost touch with this level of support. It works at a corporate and financial level more in keeping with the City than the dugout, where the various managerial assistants are more likely to be holding an iPhone in their hands than a sponge or a towel.

It must never be forgotten that, in an ideal world, the players on the field are the spectators' representation of themselves. They stand in proxy for the dreams of millions every week, and this is a responsibility no player should shrug off lightly. They owe it to the terracings to lift them out of their lives for 90 minutes and, if possible, send them home happy. Yet I wonder how often this is discussed in the dressing-room.

Jock Stein had the prescience to mention the place of the support, especially the away support, as part of the overall Celtic team. He was the kind of manager who would recognise the value in motivation lent to the side by being aware of its powerful demographic basis. His famous 1976 remark confirms this: 'Celtic jerseys are not for second-bests . . . and it's not going to shrink to fit inferior players.' The club itself was the product of community action at the lowest level and, if it is to find its real identity again, it must reassert this link to its roots.

This is not Real Madrid at work in the world but Real Celtic, a vast horde of anonymous people from all levels of society linked by the same dynamic that made the club what it was in the first place. The move to new training facilities at Lennoxtown might have been good business, but it went some way towards loosening the vital environmental connection between supporter and club. Celtic is Glasgow East End in essence and essential ethos. Moving halfway to Stirling and closeting the players behind locked security gates has lost the club its local focus and severed the obvious ties with its origins. Other considerations must have applied and obviously carried more weight than historical support. According to my friend, Jim 'Cairney' Craig, the main demographic of today's Celtic supporter is that he or she is in his or her mid-30s, buys all that he or she can from the Celtic shops and considers that the Celtic story really began with the arrival of Henrik Larsson.

The continual buttress that the support represented over the 12 decades of Celtic is its real strength. Whatever happens, it must not be lost. The very roots of the club are with its own, and these roots go deep. If they are allowed to rot, the club will die. However improbable that may be, it is still a possibility. If the present trends continue, the world's greatest sport will become no more than a parlour game for television. One can't blame that medium for seizing on football as a hugely profitable commodity. Physically, like snooker, the green rectangle of the playing space lends itself to the making of pictures, but more than that the passion that the game provokes, and which informs every aspect of its professional display, allows an all-action platform to which the simplest and the finest minds can relate. It's news, it's documentary, it's drama, it's feature, it's entertainment, it's everything. No wonder the moguls off-screen are drooling at its commercial value and the further profit-making potential it offers. Money matters as much as it ever did and, being human, we learn only too late how little it really counts.

The hallmark of our present age is that there is no longer a class system as we knew it. The new wealth has divided the world into two recognised categories, the very, very rich and the very, very poor. There appears to be a diminishing middle ground. As a consequence, the mega-rich now own the football clubs and the ultra-poor struggle to watch them play. This is already evident in the two types of football spectator emerging in the contemporary scene. One is the traditional stalwart who still attends every home game and travels away whenever he can afford to. The other is the sedentary version who never moves from his or her couch and watches every move of the game at home. There are no away games for them, no ticket worries, no travel anxieties. They buy their season ticket from IKEA and settle back in cushioned comfort, with feet up from kick-off until extra time. He or she is just as enthusiastic as the stalwart, but they see a different game, in my view.

They might be able to lip-read player exchanges in close-up, but however close the camera gets it can't really convey the bigger picture. It can't reproduce the reality of being in the open air, that most primitive element of the football experience. The viewer is denied the wider picture, which means he loses the essential perspective of seeing the game as a whole and is the passive receiver of some unseen director's choice of angle or close-up at any given moment. No matter the evident expertise, the camera can't transmit the living and breathing atmosphere of the match. You have to be there.

The football television viewer is a member of an audience at a recorded performance; the football spectator is an active participant at an event that is happening there and then. The football onlooker knows that what he is seeing and hearing is real and is happening before his very eyes. He is living and breathing the primitive action as it happens. He is feeling every kick, suffering every bruise; a sympathetic sweat runs down his brow. This is football in its totality. This is its physical thrill, and no camera, of whatever dimension, is capable of replacing the genuine article.

However comfortable the couch, or available the can of beer, is it really the same now that non-stop football is available on the box? Between games, the player-pundits will pontificate in the familiar, unintelligible monotone, sharing out the ubiquitous adjective 'massive' between them, monitored by articulate studio presenters, prompted by autocue, who talk the reclining couch spectators through every move of the game. While this kind of coverage makes the match available to billions worldwide, the danger is that the beautiful game will expire not of starvation but of excess, and the spectator will suffer from soccer obesity as it declines into television fodder.

The power of FIFA is virtually that of a self-governing state. It has prestige and status only because it has access to immense television revenue. Our own SFA has shown how much it is in thrall to television's treasure by the draconian manner in which it is attempting to reconstruct the present league system. The money involved is astronomical and this carries more weight in football circles now than any sporting performance. TV is the ringmaster in the modern soccer circus and the clubs, for the most part, run around the periphery gasping for inclusion. Certainly, they should regroup in terms of modern demands, but not cave in utterly to become the tools of a mechanical medium.

Even the players are caught up in this need to satisfy the media. Too many live on the edge of hysteria, confused by media hype, dazed by the sheer amount of money they earn and gradually coming to believe what is written about them rather than realising who they actually are. We are a long way now from the paltry win-or-draw bonus system, but we are light years away from any sane or sensible system of financial reward for footballers. Many present-day players live in a false world of their agents' making, where a quite obscene and unnatural wealth removes them entirely from any contact with reality. Not all the twittering and tweeting on their websites can hide the fact that footballers now live in a gilded world of their own, far removed from their mainstay, the ordinary man and woman.

Players are undeniably worth their temporary hire. After all, a footballer's career is brief and the sun does not shine long into their manhood. Hay has to be made, but they don't need to take over the whole cornfield or immure themselves behind high walls and security gates like medieval barons. The relationship between them and their supporters, once the very kernel of the game, is deteriorating. What was once a love affair is now a matter of business; the great romance is now no more than a transaction.

Despite their several homes, their designer suits, their seemingly uniform blonde wives, their state-of-the-art cars, and other trappings of the good life, these are, in the main, ordinary young men who have not the capacity or training to handle great wealth, and this is evident in how they react to their sudden change in station. Before long, it shows itself in drink problems, excessive social behaviour or psychological aberrations. Not every player can face this Jekyll to Hyde transformation, a metamorphosis that would challenge the most balanced of minds, especially when young. Every football follower knows such instances; these were evident even in the past.

Dan Doyle was the first lovable rascal on Celtic's books, signing for them in 1891, while at the same time receiving wages under the counter from both Everton and Bolton Wanderers. His view was that they were breaking the rules by paying him at all, so he took it all with a clear conscience. He even received his Celtic wages a season in advance, but gave it back on the pitch with a series of fearless displays at left-back. He made enough to start a distillery business in Bellshill when he left. Perhaps he over-sampled its wares a bit. Eventually, he lost everything and ended up as a general labourer. He died aged 54 in the Glasgow Cancer Hospital. Willie Maley visited him and was shocked at the sight of Doyle's emaciated legs. 'Ah, well,' said Ned, as Doyle was nicknamed, 'in their time they made a little bit of Celtic history.'

Tommy 'Snally' McInally, a forward in the 1920s, was a comedian in the literal sense of the word. He was also a talented and speedy centre-forward, when he bothered. The trouble was he rarely bothered. Despite all his skill, he neglected to train and preferred to hone his skills as the dressing-room joker, getting fatter all the time. When Celtic finally lost patience, he signed for Sunderland, who made him their captain. The Celtic supporters were sorry to see him go. For all his faults, they loved him. A comedian was a word they kept for a clown on the park, a poor player, but in Tommy McInally, they saw a real player. Even in his faults, they recognised one of their own.

It was the same with Jimmy Johnstone. He was voted Celtic's all-time great by his generation's supporters, and, as evidence of this honour, his figure in bronze stands outside the doors of the present ground, with those of Brother Walfrid and Jock Stein. For a small man, his shadow looms large on Celtic's wide stage, but offstage, as it were, his antics were eccentric to say the least. One can only say that his business acumen was not on a par with his dribbling skills and latterly, before he succumbed to motor neuron disease in 2006, he was forced to sell his large store of medals to shore up his latest commercial scheme. Fortunately, the buyer, successful business tycoon Willie Haughey, a former Celtic director, valued Jinky's deserved high football reputation and very kindly refused to take them, giving them to the Celtic museum at Parkhead, no doubt adding a suitable cheque to help the wee man out in the latest crisis. Somehow, Johnstone's latter-day monetary manoeuvres were never really tragic; his situation always seemed more humorous than sad. Such was the man.

Another tale of waste that is just melancholy is that of a Fifer, a Celtic utility player and a recognised football genius, George Connelly. George made his name initially as a 14-year-old boy when he played keepie-uppie in front of the main stand at Celtic Park as a half-time entertainment at the suggestion of Jock Stein. Incredibly, George continued to play it all around the track to the astonishment of the appluading crowd. The manager was a great admirer of the player's natural skills and expected great things from him as a putative successor to Billy McNeill. Stein was not to be disappointed and very soon young George was playing in the first team as that rare thing, a ball-playing centre-half who could also score goals. Inevitably, he was capped for Scotland with great success and when he was named Scottish Footballer of 1973 by the Scottish sportswriters, his future seemed assured.

However, cracks were already beginning to appear. His easy-going, almost languid manner hid an interior panic, which first showed itself when he refused to board the plane at Glasgow Airport carrying the Scotland team and officials to Berne in Switzerland. Then his pal at Celtic Park, Davie Hay, was transferred to Chelsea and George seemed to go right off the rails. 'I hate the pressure of all the football publicity,' he said. 'I just want to be unknown.'

In 1975, he walked away from Celtic. He was just 26. He took to drink, experienced marital problems and possibly the finest all-round footballer Celtic had had since the incomparable Malky MacDonald was lost to his private world. Then again, George Connelly never did the expected thing; that was what made him an exceptional footballer. However, he paid for it in turmoil of mind and a career cut off before it reached the heights his huge talents deserved.

Brian McLaughlin, who spent six years at Celtic Park in the 1970s, was another who showed extraordinary precocity when very young. Unfortunately, a serious injury cut short his highly promising Celtic career, but he made a reasonable fist of it later at Ayr United. Andy Ritchie, a contemporary, was a gentle giant who, when on the ball, could move as lightly as a ballet dancer, yet for reasons that are not quite clear, he was not allowed to fulfil that natural promise at Celtic Park. These young players were all naturals and were revered by supporters as such. They knew how rare this breed of player is and recognised a natural when they saw one. The species is becoming rarer as the modern footballer is increasingly regimented and his play becomes the tool of tactics instead of the joyful manifestation of his own spontaneous creativity. He is required to patrol channels and is given areas of the playing field, being restricted to them instead of being allowed to roam freely as his playing instincts suggest. If these were allowed free rein, and his playing talents were less inhibited, he would, in the natural course of things, end up in the right place at the right time. He would go with the flow and be more relaxed in his attitude to the game. His body would be less tense and consequently less prone to injury. In short, he would play like a boy again.

Modern players are runners and passers of the ball. They show an extraordinary reluctance to hold the ball and beat a man. They are confined to their tight triangles and rely on geometry and pace rather than trying to beat opposing players by basic ball skills. Where have all the dribblers gone? Is Paddy McCourt the only one left to fly the flag? The true footballer should treat the ball as if he owns it.

There is no doubt that the present-day footballer is a superb athlete. Why, then, are there so many injuries in the course of 90 minutes? It is because the mental attitude towards the game on the part of the players has changed. They see themselves as part of show business now, instead of as jobbing sportsmen. They know the camera is on them and respond accordingly, hence the extravagant gestures and theatrical posturing after scoring a goal. Not to mention the rehearsed dives in the penalty area, all of which would earn many of them an Equity card. They are paid as professional footballers, not professional actors.

Since football's Victorian beginnings as a game to be played by rules, the players have always been the flowers and they have continued to blossom by the decade, but the stem has now grown out of all proportion to the plant. The spectators, their former companions on the Saturday march, have been made to stand at a distance, at a remove, and, as a result, are now too much in awe of the media-made stars they watch.

In its virgin state, the game itself remains the same simple affair that I knew, but recently there have been many changes in the elements surrounding it, some good, some not. As well as the demands of television, the sport has to cope with the phenomenon of the peripatetic manager, the whims of the billionaire owner and, most deadly of all, the unassuageable greed of football's latest scourge, the footballers' agent, who is paid in millions for what appears to be tuppence-worth of real effort. This aberration arrived with the Bosman ruling of 1995 and has been gnawing away like a canker at the very innards of the game ever since.

Many professional football agents are decent, honourable men who perform a fine professional service for their clients, but as a lifelong lover of football, I deplore the effect such a service has had on the game. Certainly, before Bosman, the conditions of the average professional player at a club were more akin to those of a medieval serf than of a labourer worthy of his hire, but the dominance of the agent in the acquisition and transfer of talent has reduced the making of a football team to the buying and selling of livestock on the market to the highest bidder. More than ever, financial considerations carry a completely unproportionate weight in any discussion about the merits of a footballer.

Of course, money was always a factor when star players were involved. Golden guinea coins were found in boots, and pubs and shops surprisingly found new owners, but even allowing for the change in currency values, the moneys involved were not astronomical and were within the means of the directors involved. Nowadays, even the most successful teams carry an inbuilt deficit, which is not only incongruous but also an insult to the supporter, who struggles to pay the ever-increasing entry fee while some players receive obscene financial rewards for their efforts thanks to the machinations of the ubiquitous agent.

Now everyone has one. Even the 11-year-olds at the football academies, or their parents, have caught the money disease. What a shame professional football should come to a young boy in this way.

Some would argue that the single most obvious fault in the football structure in Scotland is the disappearance of the casual street game as a result of the advent of the car and football's absence from the school curriculum. The counter-argument is for the greater development of the football academy structure, as in the parallel development of the five-a-side enclosures. Young footballers need to get to know the game on their own terms and be not intimidated by the skills shown by seasoned professionals on TV but inspired by them. Training is essential. Football has not yet thrown up a Mozart who had it all at seven. It is a muscle matter; it has to keep pace with the body. It's a man's game played by boys who think they are men, and if they don't catch up with themselves in their careers they will never reach their full playing potential.

The only aim of the professional in any field should be excellence. If this is attained by the necessary hard work, study or experience, then it is accepted easily and the consequent fame that success brings is dealt with as part of the job. Unfortunately, some players think fame is the only end, and spur their efforts accordingly. They can only be disappointed, for fame doesn't last, and its after-effects can be damaging as well as disillusioning. There is no sadder sight than an ex-player who resents it.

There are a lot of disgruntled old men still in their 40s who retired from football not knowing what to do with their lives. This is a real tragedy, all this wasted man-power occasionally used in football commentaries as the 'general labourers' of the media arena, when once they were knights of the lists, the weekly heroes of every boy's imagination. Others are crippled by the echoes of ancient injuries and limp towards the old-age pension. A single tackle can cost a career, as in the case of John Kennedy, a left-back and grandson of the inimitable Jimmy Delaney, another case of how the Celtic playing line goes down through families. However unfortunate such stories are, the game continues to grow and will adapt itself to its own generation as they evolve.

In 1982, Celtic won a national five-a-side football competition at Wembley, the first Scottish club ever to do so. It made me smile to think that the sport I chased around in those wartime summers should find its way onto the big stage at Wembley, and that Celtic should win. It was a throwback to a more innocent time and quite unexpected. Looking back on my lifelong Celtic obsession, I have come to the conclusion that it's not I who have supported them season after season, but they who have supported me. Whatever I was doing in my professional life, wherever in the world the work took me, the result of a match was always sought for, no matter the time differences.

As a boy, I moved in a man's world at the football match. As a man, I treasure the memory of great Celtic games seen, great players watched, great moments enjoyed in the green-and-white odyssey that my Celtic journey still is. It is only a game, but for me it is much more. At its centre, it is still a matter of the heart. It encapsulates an attitude to life. In my growing years, it was my sole adventure, my wonderland, my treasury of emotions. There was a time when my whole world was related to the prospect of a match, the business of being there and of reliving it all over again that night, the next day, in the coming week, for years afterwards and for the rest of my life – and I don't regret any of it.

We must let childhood things go with childhood toys and childhood games. But something will not go away from these nursery times. Something remains that colours the years to come and, for me, it has been Celtic. The colours are still fused in the blood and will not wash themselves away, no matter the trafficking I've known in my life since I paid my own way in at the sevenpenny gate.

Why is this? What is in the allegiance to a football club that lingers despite all the counter-attractions and other legitimate priorities that come the way of everyone in life? It is because the football obsession, for me at least, was planted early and took firm root before the rest of the world's concerns sought for room in the garden of the soul that is the centre of every being. There is a deep part of all of us that defies definition but demands attention. This is where our enthusiasm for whatever finds a home. It is where love is and, in the end, this is where we all find our true self. The hobby often tells us more about the person than the job he or she does, or whatever school they went to, because the hobby belongs where the passion is, and it is this passion that is part of our lifeblood, pumped out continuously from the heart.

As Burns said:

> Nae treasures nor pleasures
> Could make us happy lang;
> The heart ay's the part ay
> That makes us right or wrang.

CHAPTER ELEVEN

The Ultimate Trial

Bertie Auld, Outside-Left
Another Celtic joker in the pack,
He put opposing full-backs on the rack,
He'd a football brain, courage, power and drive
Watching Bertie play made you feel alive.

William Faulkner, the American writer, said, 'The past is never dead. It's not even past.' I feel my own past in me at all times; it is the made-to-fit garment encasing the history of my life right up to this point. Celtic is part of that fabric intricately woven through every part of me. It is more than just another football team.

This final chapter is pure fancy, a wrapping-up of incidents and personnel that is entirely imaginary. Its sole purpose is to create my picture of a Celtic totality down the years that is fact-based, but is also a fiction of my imagination. Let's call it faction and enjoy it as a bit of fun. The idea is that I choose the 22 best players Celtic have produced since 1888 until the present day and play them against one another in an idealised public trial game at Parkhead, somewhat akin to the old pre-season trial matches that were a feature of the Scottish game up to the mid-1960s. Who the best are is, of course, only my opinion, just as you will have yours. The formula is traditional, Greens v. Whites, Greens being the first team and Whites the reserves.

I have selected my teams from the football learning gained from a lifetime's scrutiny of club records, knowledge of Celtic playing greats and the hearsay evidence of comments heard from fellow supporters around me at games and those I have met on my travels. I have also made use of recall, games witnessed or read about or described to me by my elders. What does it matter if these events owe more to romance or wishful thinking than stark truth? They are all part of our Celtic heritage, something that we can retain and enjoy at leisure. It is more than nostalgia, it is the respect we show to our origins and the honour we accord to great players and their deeds. The crowd will be huge, for there are a lot of us, dreamers of dreams, hopers for better days, wishers for the impossible. This is an in-house mind-play of my Celtic all-time greats.

If there is not a precise Celtic way of doing things, there is certainly a Celtic way of playing football, even if this wasn't immediately evident in the first side fielded on that May day in 1888 against a Rangers XI, that team being an ad hoc collection of assorted individuals hurriedly gathered together for the purpose of initiating a football club.

The following pages may be regarded as the programme notes for the dream game to come. The quality and calibre of these names are already signalled in the person of Celtic's first star player and captain, **James Kelly**. As pivot and central controller of play in midfield, he set the template for all other Celtic pivots up to and including the modern era.

Kelly was very much a player of his time and was unquestionably Celtic's first star. A Renton boy, he became a household name in early football following Renton's success against West Bromwich Albion in the first Champions of the World match in 1888. A few days later, he was playing for Celtic and doing his famous triple-cartwheel somersault on scoring against the Rangers Swifts in that inaugural match. He was to remain with Celtic all the rest of his playing days, retiring to become chairman from 1909 until 1914. However, it is as a player he was most influential and is best remembered.

There was no nonsense about him; his style was thorough and commanding. 'Get there first and then diddle about' was his dictum. It well illustrated his distaste for fancy footwork and his reliance on straightforward football that was intent on scoring goals or saving them. He captained the first Celtic side to win the Scottish Cup in 1892 and the Scottish League in the following year. He won the Glasgow Cup final of 1895 almost on his own after Celtic were down by two at the interval and was capped by Scotland when internationals were few. Celtic were fortunate to have such a man in the team during their formative years and he set the standard that all Celtic teams have tried to follow ever since. As one boardroom member remarked, 'No

Kelly, no Keltic!' Kelly would captain the Greens, but who would lead the Whites? There is only one answer to that and it is from our own day – **Billy McNeill**.

He was nicknamed 'Cesar' by his teammates after Cesar Romero, that old-time film star with the smooth, imperturbable manner, reflecting Billy's style both on and off the field. However, 'Caesar' would have been more appropriate, as Billy played his way into legendary status as the all-conquering leader of the Celtic legions and emperor of the football world. His football status was as high as he ever jumped for one of his many famous headed goals, and he trumped his own career by becoming Celtic manager twice: 1978–83 and 1987–91. There can be no better candidate for captain of the eternal Whites.

There are more than a score of good goalkeepers to choose from in the Celtic catalogue of players since 1888. Pat 'Packie' Bonner played the most games, 642, and had the most shut-outs, to use that ugly but correct word. L.R. Roose, an amateur and Welsh international, played only once, in a 1910 Scottish Cup tie against Clyde, and lost 3–1, but he is remembered for running up half the field to give gentlemanly congratulations to the Clyde player who had just scored a good goal against him. They don't make goalkeepers like that any more. Tom Sinclair is unique in that he was borrowed from Rangers for the start of the 1906–07 season because of an injury to Davy Adams, yet another sterling custodian.

There is no doubt that the most famous of all Celtic goalkeepers is John Thomson, due to his tragic and untimely death at Ibrox in 1931, but whether John was the very best is open to question as his career was so brief. Romantically and sentimentally, he deserves the highest ranking, and there is no doubt that the promise he showed both for Celtic and Scotland indicated he might have attained that pinnacle, but to my mind that belongs to only one name: **Willie Miller**.

For his valiant wartime efforts in goal on Celtic's behalf and for the sheer bravery in action he showed, Willie Miller ought to have been offered the football equivalent of the George Cross. He was the hero in Celtic's darkest hour, but he was also a very good goalkeeper technically. That's why he is my selection to keep goal for the Greens. It is just reward for a Celtic career that was a miracle of defiance against constant odds, often fighting a lone battle against what seemed the whole of the opposing team, such was the pressure on him in game after game.

He was more than a great goalie; he was a symbol of sanity for the supporters in a mad, unhappy time. On one occasion, after a 1–4 defeat by Third Lanark in 1946 (I was there), he was cheered by Celtic supporters gathered around the pavilion to voice their anger at yet another inept display by their team, but they exempted Willie from their fury and allowed him to speak. He calmly told them that their action would do no good, that the team would have to play themselves back into form, and asked them to be patient. On his request, they dispersed quietly. This was real player power, applied effectively.

For the Whites in goal, the choice must be between Thomson and Shaw, who was guardian of the net for Celtic from 1913 to 1925, an incredible span by any standards, and for that very durability **Charlie Shaw** must win. His was the first name in an XI drawn from that period, a litany that every Celtic boy learned to quote almost like a mantra: Shaw; McNair and Dodds: Young, Loney and Hay; Bennet, McMenemy, Quinn, Somers and Hamilton. It was one of the great Celtic teams and Shaw was its mainstay. Having started off with Baillieston Thistle, he was picked up by Queens Park Rangers in London in 1907 and it was from there he came to Celtic four years later.

A small, slim figure, he had a good spring, a vice-like grip on high crosses and, from the outset, helped by the two backs in front of him, Celtic stopped losing goals. He was an immense favourite with the crowds and was a popular barker at the Parkhead Cross Fair. When he took over as captain from Sunny Jim Young, his strong voice could be heard all over the park, bellowing advice and encouragement. He was the first Celtic player to have his name chanted by supporters before a game. He used that name and voice to speak for his teammates in their protest over low wages at Parkhead and was often at odds with the directors. They wanted to transfer him just to get him out of their top hats, but they knew it would cause a revolt among the support. He was still on top of his game when he was eventually replaced by Peter Shevlin, and he played out his career in the United States, where he died of pneumonia in 1938.

The full-back pairing for the dream teams may be drawn from the following: **Alec McNair** (who played with Shaw), Dan Doyle, Barney Battles and Danny McGrain. In his day, McNair held the record for appearances by a Celtic player, more than 600 in the first quarter of the twentieth century, during a long, successful career. Because of his cool, calm temperament (he was known as 'the Icicle'), and having brains as well as brawn, he could out-position a speedy winger rather than outrun him. A most versatile player, he filled in any position in the team as required, having all the skills necessary to defend or dribble forward. His last full-back partner was Hugh Hilley, who was five years of age when Alec signed for Celtic. McNair is a must for the Greens.

Dan Doyle was one of the many eminent Celtic Victorians. A colourful figure, his many eccentricities often hid a great football talent that attracted many clubs, north and south of the border, but he was a Celtic man at heart and gave his best for them. He also captained Scotland, the first Celt to do so after James Kelly, but he was too much his own man to be a reliable team man. He was often missing, but he was always badly missed.

Barney Battles lived up to his name both on and off the field, but he could play. In his two spells with Celtic, he was loved by the crowd for his fighting spirit and inspirational effect on the team. He was sacked by Celtic for leading a dressing-room revolt against pay conditions and joined Liverpool but was later brought back to the club by popular demand. When he died of influenza in Bridgeton in 1905, 40,000 people lined the route from his home to Dalbeth Cemetery. Barney would make a strong pairing at the back for the Whites with **Dan Doyle**.

Danny McGrain was born in 1950 in Glasgow. Like Jock Stein and Kenny Dalglish, he was a non-Catholic and a Rangers supporter when Sean Fallon signed him for Celtic after seeing him play for Scottish Schools at Ibrox in 1967. He was to remain at Parkhead for the next 20 years and become a master footballer and a genuine world-class player. He attracted a lot of attention from other clubs but chose to stay and grow his famous 'Barabas' beard. He was nominated Scottish Player of the Year in 1977 and captained Celtic on a tour of Australia where he was called 'The Best Footballer Ever Seen'. His autobiography, entitled *Celtic: My Team*, was published in 1978. That says it all, and fits Danny to link with Alec McNair as full-backs for the Greens.

At wing-half, I have no hesitation at all in naming **Malcolm** or **Calum MacDonald** as my choice for the Greens. I know we have Sunny Jim Young and Pat Crerand in contention. Fine as these players are, neither has the all-round class of 'Malky', who, like most greats, could play anywhere and often did, from his 1936 debut until his 1945 departure. A born footballer with all the ball skills, he was a lovely passer of the ball. What more could you ask? There was also his coolness in the roughest of going. He and the Icicle (McNair) behind him would prove a formidable refrigerator barrier down the right side. Sunny **Jim Young** would perform for the Whites beside Billy McNeill.

Peter Wilson is a good candidate for left-half, despite the claims of Paul McStay and Shunsuke Nakamura of Japan, a most unlikely but worthy Celtic legend, if only for that wonder free kick at Kilmarnock that won a League championship. Yet my choice is the enigmatic midfielder **George Connelly**, who had a God-given talent and played the very devil with it. He has to be in the team of all the Celtic greats because he is all Celtic, and if he wilfully shed most of his own lustre, there was enough of it left to allow him his place among the all-Green immortals.

Peter Wilson would play for the Whites, since this quiet Beith boy was virtually a mirror image of Malky MacDonald. The very opposite of Bobby Evans, this shy, diffident country boy was a deft performer where it mattered – on the field. He caressed the ball in the manner of MacDonald and Fernie, made it work for him, the sign of a natural. It would be no bad game with two such 'carpet artists' gracing the field of play. Peter frequently got lost in the big city of Glasgow, getting on and off trams and buses, and once couldn't find his way out of a department store, but he was never lost on a pitch in the 1920s and 1930s, as his unerring passing skill showed.

My man for the Greens at outside-right can only be the third of my personal Celtic heroes, **Jimmy Delaney**, despite the presence of wee Jimmy Johnstone, already nominated as the greatest-ever Celtic player. For me, Delaney is the quintessential winger, fast, brave and a wonderful crosser of a ball, yet at the same time capable of cutting inside and going for goal himself. He also has the extra benefit of being able to move to centre-forward at any stage of the game. **Jinky Johnstone** can shine for the Whites.

The other wing is less quickly decided. Jimmy Quinn, Johnny Campbell, David Hamilton, Bertie Auld, Willie Fernie and, of course, Bobby Lennox all starred in this role, but my Greens first choice would be **Charlie Tully**, if only for his nuisance value. He was liable to do anything in a game as long as it was unorthodox. Often these were the very things that would turn a match, as witness his two corner kicks at Falkirk. All this plus a quick football brain, and he could dribble with the ball like a street player. He may not have had the greatest work rate in the world, but what did that matter when he could do what he did? Besides, even a game between immortals needs an entertainer.

I would put **Jimmy Quinn**, despite his making his name as a centre-forward, on the Whites left wing because of his fearlessness and his driving force, which were enough to allow him to win a game on his own. It's hard to leave out Johnny Campbell from the early days, a man who once scored 12 goals in a reserve game. Nevertheless, Quinn was capable of exploding into effectiveness at any moment in the game, a one-club man with a total commitment to it and all it stood for. A giant of his time, he was synonymous with Scottish football in the early twentieth century.

Patsy Gallacher must go in at inside-right for the Greens, if only for his acrobatic ability and sheer effrontery in front of goal. He was Tully with industry but with the same Irish whimsy, which cloaked a deadly menace if there was a goal opportunity. His slight, Chaplinesque physique was misleading, as he was able to take on the heavyweights clustered around him in most games with a quick pair of feet and good pace. His most famous goal was scored against Dundee in the Scottish Cup final of 1925. There were 20 minutes to go and Celtic were down by a goal when little Patsy got the ball on the halfway line. A contemporary newspaper account best describes what happened next:

> He jinked, jouked, hurdled, swerved, dribbled, jumped, fell, got up, ran on, jinked again, stumbled, jouked once more, went over his wilkies with the ball still grasped between his feet, and suddenly he was over the line, him and the ball, past an astonished Jock Britton, and Hampden, to the last 75,000th man, was rising in starry-eyed tribute to a genius in bootlaces.

That goal has passed, with so many others, into Celtic history, as has already been related in these pages, but it bears repeating and loses nothing in the retelling in the words of his own day. Patsy is still the man.

Who could follow him but 'King' **Kenny Dalglish**, almost a folk-hero now at Liverpool as well as in Glasgow, but it was at Parkhead that it all started for this most reticent of great Celtic stars. He will let his football speak for him at inside-right for the Whites.

At inside-left, we start with 'Napoleon', aka **James McMenemy**, from Rutherglen Young Celtic. He played a trial for Everton before 'signing up a close in Union Street' for Willie Maley and Celtic in 1902, and he became a fixture at inside-left until 1920. He returned to Celtic as coach and trainer in 1934 before being abruptly replaced in the Celtic manner by Alex Dowdalls in 1940. This minor postscript does still not detract from an illustrious playing career with the club, which makes him a walk-in at inside-left for the Greens. 'Nap' was the general of the attack in the six-in-a-row side of 1905–10 and the four-in-a-row team of 1914–17, as well as the champions' XI of 1919.

He won a drawerful of medals and badges, as well as international caps, but, like Patsy Gallacher, he was freed by Celtic at his peak to save on the wage bill. The McMenemy and Gallacher legends are something better than tidy book-keeping and that's what puts them among the immortals. **Willie Fernie**, of 'Hampden in the Sun' fame, takes the Whites inside-left slot, and deservedly so, as in his prime he was genuine Celtic class.

Last position to fill is centre-forward, the matinee idol of any football team, as he is the showpiece player, the spearhead, the forward lance, the cynosure of all eyes, the one the public loves to adore, for he is the one who is supposed to score the goals. **Jimmy McGrory** did just that in a career that comprised a short loan spell with Clydebank after joining Celtic in 1921 and included 13 representative games; his grand goal total is 550 goals from 547 appearances – a phenomenal statistic in anyone's book. It is difficult for me to write just a paragraph about Jimmy, because I wrote a whole book about him (*Heroes Are Forever*) and, in doing so, grew to love the man.

It is hard to reconcile the affable public-relations officer he became and the shadow Celtic manager he was for so long under the Kelly thumb with the dashing, fearless centre-forward he was at his peak, but that was his life, one totally devoted to Celtic. He had a short stay at Kilmarnock as their manager after his playing days were over, but it was almost incidental. He was Celtic through and through, and to the end thought it an honour to pull their jersey over his head. In 1928, he refused to join Arsenal for a huge fee, as he wanted only to play for Celtic. At the time, he was earning £8 a week and thought he was being well paid.

He is acknowledged as the instigator of the Hampden roar when he scored his second goal for Scotland against England in 1933 before a crowd of 134,170. An apocryphal story relates a conversation he had in the dressing-room with his young teammate John Thomson, who was upset that Rangers supporters behind his goal were calling him a Fenian bastard. 'Don't worry, John boy,' said McGrory. 'I get called that every game I play.'

'That's all right for you, Jimmy,' replied Thomson. 'You are one.'

If not the greatest footballer, Jimmy McGrory was certainly, in my eyes, the greatest Celt of them all. Therefore, I nominate him wholeheartedly as the Greens' centre-forward.

For the Whites, hail another king, the 'King of Kings' himself, **Henrik Larsson.** Between 1997 and 2004, the gentle Swede won over the Celtic support to such an extent that they willingly became subject to him every time he ran onto the field, dreadlocks flowing, or later fashionably shaven-headed. Coming to Celtic from the Dutch club Feyenoord at the suggestion of new manager Wim Jansen, he took time to settle. Once rooted, he flowered to such an extent that supporters were constantly singing adulatory song parodies about him during matches. There can be no greater praise and, though I saw him rarely, Henrik rightly belongs among the canon of Celtic gods.

On the Greens' bench are:

John Thomson (goal)
His is a mythical name among the support, not only because of his fateful end but for the impression made in his playing days, so sadly cut short. A very fine talent, whose promise indicated greatness.

Paul McStay (left-half)
Had almost a family permit to play for Celtic, his blood ties with the club were so strong, but his natural, poised ability would have earned him that right in any case. He was Celtic's most-capped Scottish player, starting as a schoolboy and playing 72 times for Scotland.

Pat Crerand (right-half)
A Gorbals boy whose heart was given to Celtic but whose aggressive instincts, despite his sophisticated football skills, didn't endear him to the Kelly regime and led to his unwilling departure in 1963 to Matt Busby at Manchester United, where he was more appreciated.

Bobby Evans (centre-half)
'Mr Energy' himself, Bobby didn't have red hair for nothing. He was determined to the point of pugnacity and that applied in the dressing-

room as well as the pitch, as Charlie Tully could testify. But Evans never stopped running for Celtic.

Paddy McCourt (inside-forward)

The Londonderry Pelé, as he is often called, is a player of the twenty-first century, but he is also a throwback to the most skilful players of the twentieth and even the late nineteenth centuries. He has quick feet, and can pass a ball, is not afraid to beat a man and has the extra gift of being able to surprise. In short, he represents the best of Celtic from its beginnings.

Bobby Templeton (outside-right)

Templeton was normally on the right wing, but he wouldn't lose much by moving to the left, I'm sure. I just couldn't leave him out of the Greens squad, even though he is out of position. A class footballer can play anywhere.

Manager – Jock Stein

There is nothing more I need say about Mr Stein. The name speaks for itself.

On the Whites' bench:

Pat Bonner (goal)

'Packie' Bonner is the longest-serving Celtic custodian, 642 games between 1978 and 1993, when he was unexpectedly freed (once again to save on the wage bill). Tommy Burns brought him back to Parkhead for season 1994–95. He was Celtic's most-capped international player, playing 78 times for Eire, including World Cup appearances in Italy and the USA.

Tommy Gemmell (full-back)

Tommy was a defender with the goal-scoring propensity of a forward. Possessed of a ferocious shot, he was never afraid to unleash that deadly right foot, although he played at left-back. Fast and with a strong tackle, he was voted the best full-back in the world at one time.

Sandy McMahon (inside-left)

A Selkirk man, 'the Duke' was a class act. He was well read, articulate and could play the piano, so he was as sought after for the socials as for the games. He absconded to Nottingham Forest in 1892, but Celtic went after him and brought him back to partner Johnny Campbell. When Celtic beat Rangers 4–0 in a 1900 Scottish Cup tie, Sandy is reported to have said, 'We have taken Kruger's advice! We have staggered humanity.'

Bertie Auld (outside-left)

Bertie is the type of player needed on every team – joker, singer of songs and completely imperturbable, he sometime kids to such an extent that one can easily forget what a good professional footballer he is. Speed, ball control, distribution, he had it all, according to his manager, Jock Stein. Bertie, or 'Ten-Thirty' as he was called, was simply irrepressible.

Shunsuke Nakamura (midfielder)

There couldn't have been a bigger contrast to Auld than this sleek, velvety midfielder from Japan. There was an element of mystery about him that only added to the affection shown to him by supporters. He kept himself to himself and slipped off at the end of each game to get himself fully fit and ready for the next one. In his time at Parkhead, five seasons from 2005, he achieved almost iconic status, hence his inclusion here.

Johnny Campbell (outside-left)

Just too good to leave out of the Whites' pool, Johnny could play anywhere in the forward line and often did, both for Celtic and Scotland. Although a right-footer, he generally played on the wide left. He was transferred for a season to Aston Villa and helped them win the FA Cup but came back to Celtic before joining Third Lanark to help them win the Scottish League (in 1904). Yet he was always a Celt, as befits a boy from Saracen Street.

Manager – Willie Maley

For half a century, until his 1940 departure, he *was* Celtic, first as a player in the early teams, then taking charge as manager for 50 full years of triumphs and recessions, but, in the main, it was a case of rise and rise from the makeshift days until the arrival of the Celtic way. Along that way, he also became owner of the Bank Restaurant in

Queen Street, which became the alternative dressing-room or treatment room for many Celtic players past and present. Mr Maley, as he liked to be called, cannot be denied his place as a vital Celtic force in his own way.

The teams are now selected, the crowd is ready and waiting. To a mighty roar, the Greens and the Whites emerge from the tunnel and run onto the pitch, led by their two managers. They line up to be introduced by their respective captains, Kelly of the Greens and McNeill of the Whites, to the guest of honour, Brother Walfrid. To shouts of encouragement all round, both teams then move to take up their positions. The players look bigger than we remember them because they loom largely as memory figures and in the slight mist that descends, again due to the given conditions of this match, they stand waiting for the starting whistle from the referee, Conscience, who has taken on the generous frame of Tom Wharton from Silverdale Street. A murmur of anticipation runs all round the ground as the voice of the commentator is heard . . .

'This game that never happened is now waiting to get under way and we must adjust our respective imaginations to take everything in as Mr Wharton tosses the coin at centre. Billy McNeill wins. Billy was always lucky with the coin, as some of the spectators might remember. To remind you, the teams today in the battle of the All-Time Celtic Greats with their dates of signing are:

Greens: Miller (1942); McGrain (1967) and McNair (1904); MacDonald (1932), Kelly (1888) and Connelly (1964); Delaney (1933), Gallacher (1911), McGrory (1922), McMenemey (1902) and Tully (1948).

Whites: Shaw (1913); Battles (1893) and Doyle (1891); Young (1903), McNeill (1957) and Wilson (1923); Johnstone (1961), Dalglish (1967), Larsson (1997), Fernie (1948) and Quinn (1900).

Two incomparable sides, and they promise an intriguing game. This is a once-in-a-lifetime experience and is unlikely ever to be repeated, but the best of these players here today will win a place in the greatest-ever Celtic team, which will make them immortal-plus. The whistle sounds and Larsson touches it to Fernie, who immediately releases it to Tully, who lifts his leg and the ball passes under his feet for a shy. First laugh of the evening to Mr Tully, who is already laughing his head off on the touchline. Connelly has thrown the ball infield to Gallacher, who meets it with an overhead kick to McGrory, running to the edge of the penalty area, who connects with his head, and the ball flies to the corner of the Greens' net – and it's a GOAL! No, it's not! Shaw somehow springs right, reaches the ball with the tips of his fingers and it's a corner for the Greens. What a start! Perhaps we should have expected this from such a field of players. Tully goes to take the corner and the crowd's anticipation is heard in a huge, collective intake of breath on the packed terracing. He takes his time in setting the ball within the diamond. Still crouching, he kicks it hard along the ground towards the goal. The players around the goal are so surprised they let it bounce off them and Charlie, running forward, coolly flights it into the top corner for the first goal for the Greens. Applause and laughter.

It is a typical case of Tully mischief and the crowd love it. But Jimmy Quinn doesn't and, as soon as he gets the ball from the White's kick-off, he heads for Willie Miller with chin down, throwing off Green defenders, Kelly and all, as if they were flies. It is a case of an unstoppable force not even noticing the wall, and while the echoes of the Tully celebrations are still sounding, Quinn puts a thunderbolt past the advancing Willie Miller to level the scores. This is indeed dream stuff from the immortals, but we aren't finished yet.

The trouble is the two teams are so evenly matched that it would need a flash of individual brilliance to create any chances at all. This is shown when George Connelly, 30 yards out, catches the ball chest high, flips it onto his shoulder and, still running forward, knocks it up to his forehead, and playing 'wee heidies' with himself, advances into the penalty area with the White defenders uncertain how to tackle him. In that moment of hesitation, Connelly heads it forward to Gallacher, who ducks and the ball and flies straight into the path of the onrushing Delaney, who puts it in the net with a volley to the far post. Yet another impudent goal. There is too much quality on the field for goals to be scored any other way. The speed of play is incredible, almost unreal, but it is all happening in this metaphorical twilight time at Celtic Park.

Jinky Johnstone gets so tired waiting for the ball to come to him that he goes in search of it among his own defence and Billy McNeill can be seen telling the wee bugger to get back into position, but Jinky pays no attention. Eventually, he gets in the way of one of Dan Doyle's more swashbuckling clearances and immediately ties the ball to his bootlaces. He twists and turns, turns and twists, beating man after man until he inadvertently runs it over the Greens' byline. When he realises this, he is so annoyed with himself, he kicks the ball into the crowd behind the goal. They give him a great cheer, in no sense derisory. It is more an acknowledgement of a wonderful feat of old-fashioned dribbling. However, Billy McNeill is having another word with Jinky and, from his expression, it isn't congratulatory.

The next excitement is a wonderful save by Willie Miller from a snap shot from Dalglish. This is followed by an overlap from McGrain that needs all of Doyle's athleticism to push over for a corner. Delaney takes it quickly and McGrory throws himself at the ball about two feet from the ground and gets it past Shaw at the near post. A typical McGrory effort and it elicits another roar. The supporters know they are being served up a feast and they are greedy for more. The noise is astonishing and the sheer volume lifts all these great players to even greater heights as the interval approaches. It can't go on at this pace. To everyone's relief, the large Mr Wharton blows for the interval and everyone in the ground is glad to draw breath. Loud cheers rise from all round the ground in appreciation of what they have seen in the last 45 minutes. The score doesn't matter.

There is nothing at stake here but reputation, rather supra-reputation, because every player on the field is already held in high regard by all Celtic supporters, indeed has legendary status. Players like Kelly, Gallacher, McGrory, Delaney have no need to add further to this, but here they are, as they were in their glory days, playing again like boys, just for the joy of it. What a joy it has been to watch. What adds to the pleasure of this one-off occasion is that the players stay on the field at half-time and for the first time you can see that they were all teammates, they were all Celts. The players on the bench join them and everyone mixes freely, with lots of obvious banter and back-slapping. The two managers and both trainers come on with trays of orange juice. It is like a carpet of Celtic history laid out for all to see and be glad in. Only Connelly stands apart, but then George always does. Peter Wilson and Dan Doyle join him after a moment. They can't let a fellow Celt stand alone.

Now what's this? The gangling figure of the comedian Glen Daly emerges from the tunnel, singing his original version of 'Hail, Hail, the Celts Are Here'. No one is at all surprised; it is that kind of day. It is certainly a change of mood, and the crowd respond by joining in. So do the players, who stand like a choir behind him. Listen.

> Hail, hail, the Celts are here
> What the hell do we care,
> What the hell do we care,
> Hail, Hail, the Celts are here
> What the hell do we care now . . .
> For it's a grand old team to play for,
> For it's a grand old team bedad,
> When you know the history
> It's enough to make your heart go sad.
> God bless them.
> We don't care if we win, lose or draw,
> Darn the hair do we care
> For we only know
> That there's going to be a show,
> And the Glasgow Celtic will be there.

As Daly sings the last chorus, he begins to fade gradually and his voice slowly dies away in the huddle the players make around him. In the golden twilight, memory takes him back where he belongs, and, on the last note, he disappears among the flurry of all-green and all-white jerseys. Am I imagining it or is it getting darker? The crowd settles back for the second half. Henrik Larsson causes a sensation at the restart by darting through the middle from the return from Dalglish. Outpacing Kelly, he rounds the diving Miller and taps it into the empty net. All square. 'Pure dead brilliant' was one comment heard.

From here on, the game takes a strange turn. The players appear to diminish in size, imperceptibly at first, but definitely getting smaller. The pace slackens, or rather it changes. It takes on an exhibition feeling, until it is almost like a play, deliberate and considered, the moves precise like a dance, and the ball, glowing white in the green haze, does its own dance around the feet of these shadowy figures. It is mesmerising to watch, like an elegant ballet, as the light continues to fade.

Suddenly, in the gloom, a female voice starts to sing 'The Fields of

Athenry'. It is immediately picked up by the crowd and the melody swells and echoes as it rises up like an anthem, a heart-breaking threnody for a long-ago Irishness.

> By a lonely prison wall, I heard a young girl calling
> 'Michael, they are taking you away
> For you stole Trevelyan's corn
> So the young might see the morn.
> Now a prison ship lies waiting in the bay.
> Low lie the fields of Athenry
> Where once we watched the small birds fly.
> Our love was on the wing,
> We had dreams and songs to sing.
> It's so lonely round the fields of Athenry.'

The players on the field now cluster at the centre circle again, gradually fading into a speckled green-and-white mist as the impact of the song begins to make its effect. An emotional wave, like a great tide of feeling, is threatening to engulf everyone and everything. It is a massed choir of pent-up love, nothing less, rising up in one ghostly voice as the light slowly goes down.

> By a lonely prison wall
> I heard a young man calling,
> 'Nothing matters, Mary, when you're free,
> Against the Famine and the Crown.
> I rebelled, they ran me down.
> Now you must raise our child with dignity.'

By now, it is almost dark and the song recedes until there is only silence. Nothing. Only the blackness. The game is over and everyone knows it, but the feeling it leaves is good. In the end, we know we are still one big family and still care, that, despite the troughs encountered, we have also scaled the heights and in our Celtic time we have been privileged to have watched some great players in their pomp. Now they have gone and it is time, too, for us to leave the scene.

> By a lonely harbour wall
> She watched the last star falling

As the prison ship sailed out against the sky
Sure she'll wait and hope and pray
For her love in Botany Bay,
It's so lonely round the fields of Athenry.

I like to think that my adventure with Celtic, from that innocent boy at ten to the old sinner I now am, parallels in a way my progress in the world as a professional actor. I was in constant pursuit of a goal; so were Celtic. We wanted the same thing – applause for a good job well done and to get paid for it – but there was more to it than the mere superficial. I realised as time passed that mine, like everyone else's, was also a cosmic chase. There are apparent trivialities in life that embrace the whole self, although they don't add a jot to health, status or income. Some trivialities matter in ways you can never see at the time. The true importance of things is only realised retrospectively. It takes a lifetime to learn that. Your values change as you age, but the verities remain constant. Honour your parents, love your children, treat everybody as a mirror of yourself, etc. But one thing is rarely mentioned: the importance of enthusiasm. Enthusiasm – for anything – is the best-kept secret of a full life.

Celtic has been my lifelong enthusiasm. It matters to me in the way that my religion does, that Mahler does or Caravaggio or Burns. I was born into the first affiliation and the other enthusiasms grew as I grew. A love for Celtic set in early and it stays a part of the self as long as you are enthused. You tend it, nourish it, cherish it, to all intents and purposes you marry it, and divorce is no option. It is not a question of names and games and trophies. It's something deeper, an ethos, a spirit, a conviction. That is the real end of everybody's goal, I suppose, to find something to believe in, better still to love. I shall continue to pursue both goals until the final whistle.

The great timekeeper in the sky is noted for his unpredictability and doesn't always allow extra time, but I shall play on as long as there is a game to be played. In my wife's phrase, 'longevity has its own currency', and I have dipped into that purse. In life's tighter situations, I've fallen back on nothing but sheer experience, sure in the knowledge that I've been there, done that, got by. Everything's survivable if you believe you will. In the end, you realise that nothing is ever entirely new. It's all happened before, one way or another. This is a fact of life, and it's so very reassuring. Change is endemic in the very act of living itself, and the basic process of being human requires that we acknowledge this in every generation. Progress of any kind is always circular, every action generates its own reaction and so we go on, round and round, twisting our mortal coil to suit ourselves in our own tiny, ego-driven bit of crowded time. I tried to say this once in a verse:

Like Goya's old man on the swing
I feel myself blown on the wind,
Caught in the upsurge of my winter years
As giddy as the flying boy
I thought I'd left behind.
Isn't it good to let yourself go,
Fall back,
Safely held.
Impelled
By your own inertia,
Knowing the force that pulls you back
Will also push you up
As high as you can go.
You know
This is Nature's power.
Free for all,
No better fuel
Nothing to do but hold on
Trusting in God's breath
To blow where it will.

Extra Time

Paddy McCourt, Inside Forward

I've got to play Paddy, he's my ideal
Of a Celtic player, however you feel.
He'll make you laugh, he'll make you cry
But his natural talent will make you sigh.

Alannah and I came back to live in Scotland in 2008. My coming home was almost as casual as my going away had been in 1991. After nearly 20 years away, I had returned for no other reason than it had 'come up my back', as my mother might have said, but I did find that when the sun sets in New Zealand it rises in Scotland. I needed to feel again that pale imitation of solar heat after the splendid warmth of 'the Shaky Isles', that 'Land of the Long White Cloud'.

We live in a lovely flat that is only a loud shout from Hampden and a reasonable taxi ride from Celtic Park. While I'd been living in New Zealand, I'd kept up with Celtic affairs via the Celtic Supporters Club in Auckland and through continued monitoring of the sports results on the Internet. I also watched every game shown on Sky television. It was through a connection with Celtic TV that I was invited to attend a game in Celtic Park soon after my return. Despite having seen the development of the ground over the years on occasional return trips, I was startled by its finished appearance. It resembled more the Museum of Modern Art in New York than the old Celtic Park.

I remember walking down from where we left the car, somewhere near Parkhead Cross. We entered the ground at Janefield Street. I used to roller-skate on its smooth, tarmacadam surface, but it is now virtually covered with stalls selling everything from flags to fanzines, plus a van selling second-hand Celtic books. I looked in vain for my own McGrory story but the man in the hat only said, 'Aye, we had wan wance.' Instead, I bought Graham McColl's official history of Celtic, with a foreword by Paul McStay. 'Have you a bag?' I asked the hat. 'Nae bags,' he said with a grin. I had to lug the book around with me all afternoon.

We walked towards the stadium. I felt I was approaching a forbidden city. The great concrete edifice soared above my head. I was overawed. This was a far cry from my old wooden sevenpenny gate, but the excitement was just the same. I could feel my heart pounding in the same old way as I took in the banter again, and the pleasure of being part of that big, grinning swirl once more. I must admit, though, I was a little taken aback when I was handed a leather strap and told to put it round my neck. It looked like a baggage label, but this was my ticket. It had been bought by my host, a young executive from Gourock, that town that's 'aw tae wan side' on the Clyde.

'Shouldn't you be supporting Morton?' I said.

'Aye, that'll be right,' he answered.

He led us through corridors lined with Celtic photos, up staircases with walls decorated with murals depicting Celtic scenes, into large reception rooms, served by slim young men dressed in black who all looked like undertakers, except that they wore large Celtic badges and smiled all the time. Television sets talked at us from every corner and well-dressed young ladies tried to sell us tickets for the half-time sweepstake. I felt we had walked into one huge, overheated emporium where you could buy anything, including fish and chips with Guinness. The young couple with us in our party of four were completely at ease in the environment. They had grown up with it as supporters and revelled in its vast celebration of their favourite club.

For me, it was the face of modernity with full make-up on and hair done, and I didn't trust that constant, commercial smile. Hands were offered everywhere to give assistance but also to take your money. Then it was another corridor, more stairs and suddenly we were in the open air. I felt giddy, as if I had just stepped out of an airship. The noise hit me like a blast. Multi-amplified music, blaring announcements of someone's birthday, laughter and singing and all the fun of the fair. The decibel weight of it all pushed me back, stunned, into my seat. I had to lip-read what my new friends were saying, but I could feel their unashamed exhilaration in just being there, which transferred itself to me after the first few vertiginous minutes. We were so high up you could get dizzy just looking around. It was a good five minutes before I was calm enough to take it all in.

I was in a giant metal box, sealing me in that cauldron of noise with the minimum glimpse of sky. I had a slight but unnerving feeling of claustrophobia. It was all at once magnificent and daunting, marvellous and intimidating, glorious and captivating in the literal sense. I was trapped in this towering artificiality, a monumental cage enclosing a green space that almost apologised for its naturalness. It was as if steel fingers were holding 50,000 people in their grasp. Yet I could see at the same time that I was the only one ill at ease. Mine was very much a minority reaction. Everyone around me was having a whale of a time and the game hadn't even started. I was out of my depth here and I rapidly tried to adjust, as any good guest should.

The teams came out and bedlam broke out. Here was I, a self-proclaimed, lifelong Celtic supporter, eager to see them play again after such a long separation, but now feeling out of it. I didn't recognise this Celtic Park. It looked like what you might call an outsize McCann-o set, very transatlantic. It was more like Soldier Field in Chicago, except they had pretty cheerleaders. The cheerleaders here were the Green Brigade, I was told, and their songs and constant drumming only added to the mayhem. There was no way to beat it, this powerful environment, so I had to join it. I tried, but I didn't know a word of any song everyone was singing. Aesthetically, this was no loss, but I dearly wanted to show that I belonged here too. Yet I felt apart and sat back. Let the people sing.

These were not chants but singable songs, which reminded me that it was indeed a grand old team we played for. There was such an intense feeling of anticipation that the match itself could only be an anticlimax. It was. This was the first time I'd seen these particular players live. They had seemed larger and more effective on television. I did not recognise their style of play. The game was played more side to side than end to end. The Celtic players were as alien as I felt, all tall and lithe, and showing a ready propensity to pass the ball rather than keep it at their feet and beat a man, and there was an awful lot of aimless heading of the ball in midfield. Was this Celtic or a machine-made assembly of athletes rehearsed meticulously not to lose rather than being free to play and win with flair and style? There was no scoring at half-time. At the interval, I asked if I could just sit on my own and read my glossy programme. I wanted to make contact with this new world of football, but I didn't feel confident somehow.

Then I saw him. A young boy, no more than nine or ten, coming up the stairs towards me, carefully balancing a small bottle of Irn-Bru in one hand and a chocolate bar in the other. It wasn't these things that caught my eye but the sheer pleasure in his face and the blush that showed his excitement at being there. I was so glad to see him. This was exactly what I needed – a reminder that young boys still came to matches with their dads. I immediately cheered up, in time for my friends' return for the start of the second half.

I don't know if it was my change of mood or whether there was a dressing-room discussion, but it seemed a different Celtic on the restart. A game of two halves indeed. Significantly, they scored as a result of one player's flash of solo brilliance, which set up a teammate to hit the back of the net with a volley from the edge of the box. I was up on my feet at once, with arms held high and embracing my friends on either side of me. So what had changed? After nearly two decades away, I was back within *me* again, and at one with 50,000 others of the same mind. For the first time that day, I felt at home.

I have deliberately not mentioned the players, nor the scorer's name, nor even the name of the opposing side, because in this instance it didn't really matter. What did was the importance of the return to my field of dreams, my personal Paradise, re-dressed in twenty-first-century clothing yet still holding all the associations the park has had for me since 1940. I use the word 'park' advisedly because that slab of green is the only memorial for me of my boyhood in the place. That young boy was leagues away from all this razzmatazz, this show-biz blazer that football wears today. Then I remembered the little boy I'd seen at the game and I knew that Celtic was still in good hands. I had seen the future and it was safe in hands that carried a bottle of Irn-Bru and a chocolate bar.

After the game, we sat in one of the many bars available and talked while we waited for the crowds to clear. I told my hosts tales of the past and the fact that my early boyhood years of supporting Celtic didn't really exist, for they took place in wartime, and as far as the record books are concerned those games never happened. As they began to tell me their own stories, I realised I was passing on the baton I had got from my dad and uncle Phil just as they had got it from the relation, near-relation or close friend who took them to their first Celtic game.

Like me, they could remember the details of their Celtic baptism. It's like being rubber-stamped, except that it's more like a tattoo, hard to get rid of.

My period of total adherence had lasted until the second exit of Billy McNeill in 1991, but they took me on a conducted tour of the minor procession since. These included former Celtic players Lou Macari, the beloved Tommy Burns and Kenny Dalglish, who, despite their obvious playing merits, did not quite echo that skill as managers, even though Dalglish in his brief spell won the League Cup. My companions then glowed in reminiscence of Wim Jansen, the darling Dutchman, who saved Celtic's pride by preventing Rangers going ten in a row. He is still venerated to this day for the additional fact that he brought Henrik Larsson to Celtic. Then followed Dr Jozef Venglos in 1998, of whom they had nothing to say. It mattered little, as he stayed only a season. The dream team followed, John Barnes and Kenny Dalglish, but in less than a year John Barnes had returned south, leaving King Kenny on his own. Nonetheless, he managed almost regally to win a League Cup in just four months. At this point, all knees bowed as they remembered blessed Martin O'Neill, who had five glorious years until 2005 and brought back more than pride, restoring real belief in the club again. If Jansen was venerated in their eyes, Martin O'Neill was canonised. He left for personal reasons, to everyone at Celtic's regret, and eventually found a niche at Aston Villa.

He was followed by Gordon Strachan, who, much to his own surprise, did not succeed at all at first, but, to his credit, he stuck in there and brought a fine level of attainment, including three championships in a row, the first since Jock Stein, and only the third manager to achieve this. In their opinion, the next manager, Tony Mowbray, meant well but tried too hard, and when it came to Neil Lennon all three agreed it was too early to judge. 'We'll wait and see what happens,' said one.

The debate continued as to who was really responsible for the success of any club, its players or its manager. A player could be coaxed or bribed to play well, but a good manager, like Stein, was never missed until he was gone. The same had applied to Billy McNeill when he left for Manchester or when Dalglish moved to Liverpool. Sometimes the chance had come and gone before they knew it. As Pat Woods says, 'This fitba's a rough game.'

My own favourite quatrain of managers, the first two of whom I knew historically and the last two personally, were Willie Maley,

Jimmy McGrory, Jock Stein and Billy McNeill. I mentioned that they were Celtic through and through, a vital quality in my mind. Two of them, Maley and Stein, stood like giant pines in contrast to the managerial saplings named above. We agreed on this eventually, and all returned to the car in a happy Celtic amity.

It is important that we know where we stand in the face of our enthusiasms, to confirm that we are still in control, or else they will run away from us and trail us helplessly behind them. I no longer shed tears for every Celtic defeat; I don't feel the same degree of anguish when I watch them play. Is maturity a gradual drawing away from childish things or is it a very gradual descent into a second childishness and forgetfulness? The world's affairs do not hang on a football result, however important the match. Why then do we invest this supposedly superficial phenomenon with universal status? Because, as I have tried to show, it is not trivial. It acts on the individual psyche of the average football follower as if armies had been pounding at his consciousness. He feels the weight of this siege and cannot easily throw it off.

Non-football people may find it easy to discount this as so much overblown nonsense, attributing to a football passion a power beyond its capability. Yet each person's hobby may be his neighbour's bête noire; no two persons can agree on absolutely everything, so *vive la différence*. Life is thrilling in its infinite variety and will never stale to the curious mind.

The old artists used to say that if you have vocation, a true vocation, you will never be out of work, for the vocationist is his own work. He is able to make a vacation of it, enjoy the doing of it, the working at it, as long as his limbs are able and his mind alert. Jimmy McGrory, Stanley Matthews, Jimmy Delaney were footballers who knew this secret, and Ryan Giggs of Manchester United still is. These men are the end product that began as the pastime of muddied oafs fighting for the possession of a pigskin, and it is now a highly sophisticated institution with worldwide ramifications.

My concern is that I see a valuable product, the game of football, a traditional resource available at all levels at little cost, now being threatened by its own success, its long-term future jeopardised by greed and compromised by the need to appease demands that are outside football. My dread is that those who only want to continue to love their club are being held to ransom each season by ever-increasing entry costs and commercial blandishments.

More and more, I see parallels between my job as an actor and the modern player's role as performer. When I meet people offstage who have seen me onstage, they can't help but see me via the performance I've just given. In a sense, I'm still wearing the costume I've just taken off. The actor understands this and assists the offstage encounter as much as he can by being himself, so that the member of the audience is not misled by the patina of the performance. I was aware of this when I met my football heroes off the field. I have already told you about working with Jim Craig and Billy McNeill in *Quizball*. Even though I met them in my world, it was theirs I was aware of when we were away from the cameras. I was just as impressed meeting Jim Baxter of the Rangers after one show. Even though he looked a little uneasy in the studio atmosphere, all I could see was the player who had the poise to play keepie-uppie with the ball during an England–Scotland international at Wembley. That was his performance patina showing. I noticed, too, how eager footballers were to talk about football. This is a good sign. Actors are less eager to talk about their craft; they would rather talk about other actors.

While on the subject of theatre, there was a wonderful moment in the play *The Celtic Story*, performed some years ago by the Wildcat Theatre Company in the Pavilion Theatre, Glasgow, when the coffin, supposedly carrying goalkeeper John Thomson's body, was brought in silently from the back and moved slowly down the centre aisle towards the stage. As soon as it became visible, the whole audience rose unbidden and stood silent with heads bowed as it was carried onstage. This was not in the script; it was a completely spontaneous reaction by a theatre full of unsophisticated, ordinary Celtic supporters who well knew the John Thomson story and even at this long remove wished to express not their admiration for a piece of *mis en scene* but their sympathy for and love of a true Celtic hero.

That's what it is all about in the end: love. That's what sits in the frame as the biggest picture of all, the pursuit of, the need of, and the value of love in all things under the sun. Celtic Football Club is only one of these things, but it was enough to inspire me to write this valentine to a lifelong love affair.

Postscript: On Wednesday, 27 April 2011, I was the guest of Richard McBrearty, director of the Scottish Football Hall of Fame, at Hampden Park, where the year's SFA Youth Cup final was being played between the Under-19 players of Rangers and Celtic. What a pleasant occasion the whole thing might have been. Here was a chance to see the Old Firm in its future guise. I was seated in comfort after receiving pre-match hospitality in the Arran Room. It was a beautiful, still, windless early-spring evening, with the last of the sun just touching the crossbar of the goal at the Celtic end. The playing surface was pitch-perfect and the game was flowing easily in front of me. Yet from either side of me came the Rangers and Celtic fans wearing the old rags of sectarianism and bigotry, two separate swathes soiling the splendid atmosphere by senseless jumping up and down and mindless chanting. It was nearly unbearable and the only thing to do was to deliberately switch off. In the end, Celtic won 2–1 in the second half of extra time.

The score did not really matter. It was the spirit of the game that pleased me. I had braced myself against feeling the hackneyed tensions of an Old Firm encounter and gained the benefit of a football spectacle per se, which was exciting and encouraging. Here was a free, fluid match between 22 young thoroughbreds who showed off their putative skills before a crowd of more than 9,000 packed into one side of the national stadium. Many of them, like me, had endured the miseries of Celtic past and now have to tolerate the extremities of Celtic present – world-beaters one week, world-weary the next. Here, however, was a match that was a pleasure to watch for both sides' sake. On the pitch, this was what a Rangers–Celtic match ought to be like: no sly fouls, no histrionic injuries, no blood spilled. This was Rangers and Celtic to come, prancing and dancing at times, constantly menacing even if they only managed three goals between them. There was such an evident enjoyment in their play that it excused the occasional adolescent lapses. These apprentices are still learning their trade and, from what I saw, many of them will make proficient journeymen. Who knows, another Old Firm legend may emerge from the pack.

On the Rangers side, their captain, Kane Hemmings, led from the number 9 spot and did well. Gary Inglis looked good in goal and wingers Fotheringham and Naismith gave a good account of themselves. Rhys McCabe's equalising goal for Rangers sent the game into extra time, which was needed to separate these two fine attacking teams.

For Celtic, goal-scorer Greig Spence impressed, as did inside-forward Patrik Twardzik, and full-back Kieran Brennan caught my eye with some opportune overlapping, which on another day might have yielded several goals. Liam Gormley came off the bench just in time to score the winning goal and spark off the scenes of jubilation at the end following their 2–1 win. The youthful Celts had also won their equivalent of the League Championship the week before, so they had much to celebrate.

Their delighted cavorting at the end reminded me of so many boys let out of school early. I'm sure young Thomas Doherty, who wrote the foreword to this book, would have been quite at home among these particular green-and-white jerseys. It is a warming thought, and one on which I'm happy to finish my lifelong Celtic journey.

Epilogue

Overheard in a Gallowgate pub, Glasgow, on a Saturday night in May 2011:

'Well, that's that.'

'Aye.'

'The League Cup loast in extra time and the League itsel' thrown away.'

'Bloody Inverness.'

'Aye. Still, there's always next year.'

'There always is.'

'And we won the Cup.'

'Here, so we did. Are ye fur another?'

'Aye. Why no'?'

'We're still here. I mean, it's no' the end o' the world, is it?'

'Right enough.'

Bibliography

Ball, Peter, and Shaw, Phil, *The Book of Football Quotations*, Stanley Paul, London, 1984

Bradley, Joseph M., *Celtic Minded: Essays on Religion, Politics, Society, Identity . . . and Football*, Argyll Publishing, Glendaruel, 2004

Cairney, John, *A Scottish Football Hall of Fame*, Mainstream Publishing, Edinburgh, 1998

Cairney, John, *Heroes Are Forever*, Mainstream Publishing, Edinburgh, 2005

Campbell, Tom (ed.), *Ten Days That Shook Celtic*, Fort Publishing, Ayr, 2005

Campbell, Tom, and Woods, Pat, *The Glory and the Dream: The History of Celtic F.C. 1887–1986*, Mainstream Publishing, Edinburgh, 1986

Campbell, Tom, and Woods, Pat, *Celtic Football Club 1887–1967*, Tempus Publishing, Gloucestershire, 1988

Campbell, Tom, and Sheridan, George, *Celtic: The Encyclopaedia*, Argyll Publishing, Glendaruel, 2008

Cooke, Gavin, *The Football Pocket Bible*, Crimson Publishing, Surrey, 2010

Crerand, Pat, *On Top with United*, Stanley Paul, London, 1969

Docherty, David, *The Celtic Football Companion*, John Donald Publishing, Edinburgh, 1986

MacBride, Eugene, and O'Connor, Martin, with Sheridan, George, *An Alphabet of the Celts: A Complete Who's Who of Celtic F.C.*, ACL & Polar Publishing, Leicester, 1994

McColl, Graham, *Celtic: The Official Illustrated History 1888–1995*, The Book People, Surrey, 1995

McDade, Gerry, *Celtic: The Supersonic Seventies!*, Black and White

Publishing, Edinburgh, 2009

MacDonald, Hugh, Pattullo, Alan, Robertson, Rob, et al., *Ten Days That Shook Scotland*, Fort Publishing, Ayr, 2010

Macdonald, Kenny, *Scottish Football Quotations*, Mainstream Publishing, Edinburgh, 1994

McGinn, Matt, *McGinn of the Calton: The Life and Works of Matt McGinn, 1928–77*, Glasgow City Libraries, Glasgow, 1987

McNee, Gerald, *The Story of Celtic: An Official History 1888–1978*, Stanley Paul, London, 1978

Macpherson, Archie, *Jock Stein: The Definitive Biography*, Raceform Ltd, Berkshire, 2004

Motson, John, and Rowlinson, John, *The European Cup 1955–80: A History of Europe's Premier Football Club Competition*, Queen Anne Press, 1980

Murray, Bill, *The Old Firm*, John Donald, Edinburgh, 1984

Murray, Bill, *Glasgow's Giants*, Mainstream Publishing, Edinburgh, 1988

Paterson, Bill, *Tales from the Back Green*, Hodder & Stoughton, London, 2008

Potter, David, *Jimmy Delaney: The Stuff of Legend*, Breedon Books, Derby, 2006

Potter, David, *Celtic FC: Cult Heroes*, Pitch Publishing, Durrington, 2008

Potter, David, *Celtic's Greatest Games*, Know the Score Books Ltd, Warwickshire, 2009